The Resource Program
Organization and Implementation

The Resource Program

Organization and Implementation

J. Lee Wiederholt
Donald D. Hammill
Virginia L. Brown

pro·ed
An International Publisher

8700 Shoal Creek Boulevard
Austin, Texas 78757-6897
800/897-3202 Fax 800/397-7633
www.proedinc.com

© 1993 by PRO-ED, Inc.
8700 Shoal Creek Boulevard
Austin, Texas 78757-6897
800/897-3202 Fax 800/397-7633
www.proedinc.com

Library of Congress Cataloging-in-Publication Data

Wiederholt, J. Lee.
   The resource program / J. Lee Wiederholt, Donald D. Hammill, Virginia L. Brown.
      p.   cm.
   Rev. ed. of: The resource teacher. 2nd ed. c1983.
   Includes bibliographical references.
   Contents: v. 1. Organization and implementation.
   ISBN 0-89079-571-1
   1. Resource programs (Education) I. Hammill, Donald D., 1934– . II. Brown, Virginia, 1931–   . III. Wiederholt, J. Lee. Resource teacher. IV. Title.
LB1028.8.W53 1992
371.9—dc20   92-35594
                                CIP

This book is designed in 10/12 Palatino (text); 11/12, 10/12, 10/12, 10/12 Palatino (A, B, C, & D heads respectively); optima for other elements.

Production Manager: Alan Grimes
Production Coordinator: Adrienne Booth
Art Director: Lori Kopp
Reprints Buyer: Alicia Woods
Editor: Amy Root
Editorial Assistant: Claudette Landry

Printed in the United States of America

3   4   5   6   7   8   9   10   09   08   07   06   05   04   03   02

Contents

Preface

The Resource Teacher: A Guide to Effective Practices was published in 1978, with a second edition in 1983. We have been very pleased with its acceptance since that time. However, it is time again for an extensive revision of the text. This revision seems appropriate for two major reasons.

First, many of our colleagues have made excellent suggestions for expanding the text. Most important, they suggested that we break the book into two separate books. This was because of the length of the manuscript as well as the fact that practitioners in many cases needed the information in only one section of the book. Specifically, they felt that the description of the rationale and implementation of the program was particularly helpful to administrators, supervisors, and resource teachers. Conversely, the section concerning the planning of appropriate individual programs was useful in most cases only to resource teachers. Second, we wished to include a growing body of research and literature on resource programs. To incorporate all of this information in one volume would be cumbersome indeed.

Consequently, this volume contains a detailed discussion of the resource program concept, the roles of the resource teacher, and specific directions for implementing and operating resource programs. The second book, which will be published at a later date, contains information relative to planning individual programs. We think school personnel will find the separation of this information particularly helpful.

We recommend the resource program as a viable mechanism for serving most students with learning and behavior difficulties. In addition, we delineate three roles to be performed by resource teachers in the schools and include practical suggestions for organizing and managing these programs in the schools. We hope that readers will find many effective practices in this book and that their use will result in programs that work for students.

PART I

The Resource Program Concept

Part I of the text introduces the resource program concept. In Chapter 1, the rationale underlying these programs, their historical development, and the types of resource models are described. A critical analysis of resource programs including the research-based effectiveness of this approach is presented in Chapter 2. The advantages of the resource model are also listed.

Chapter 1

The Development of
Resource Programs

In the schools today nearly 15% to 20% of the students cannot meet the curriculum's requirements. Many of these students come from backgrounds that do not prepare them to meet the demands of the educational system; as a result, they fall behind from the start, become discouraged early, and drop out as soon as possible. In addition, some students have physical, intellectual, psychological, and/or social disabilities that seriously impede their advancement in the curriculum. Some of these students perform normally (or even excel) in some school subjects, but perform marginally or totally inadequately in others. Other students function below average in almost every area of school performance. Further, there exists a group of students who fail for no readily apparent reason at all.

To cope with the uniqueness, diversity, and range of the educational problems of these students, over the years schools have developed a wide variety of instructional service arrangements, including special classes and schools, evaluation centers, provisions for home-bound instruction, tutoring and remedial programs, consultation programs, vocational education, and alternative schools. Since the late 1960s, the resource program has been one of the most popular of these arrangements. Before that time, resource programs were used almost exclusively for providing remedial reading instruction, speech therapy services, and classes for individuals with visual and hearing impairments. They now exist in one form or another in most schools as a service to other types of students and their teachers.

This chapter will provide readers with (a) the basic rationale underlying the resource program, (b) the historical development of interest in this approach, and (c) the types of resource models.

RATIONALE UNDERLYING THE RESOURCE PROGRAM

Resource programs furnish educationally related support services primarily to students who are failing or at risk for school failure. In a comprehensive resource program, three types of services are provided: (a) assessment of the student's aptitude, interests, achievement, and/or affect; (b) direct instruction through remedial, developmental, or compensatory teaching and/or behavioral management; and (c) consultation services for classroom teachers and parents. These services are conducted in the student's general classroom and in a room designated specifically for resource activities (i.e., the resource room).

Resource rooms are necessary for comprehensive resource programs in that they provide a suitable, stable environment for the resource teacher as well as a consistent setting to which the student reports. Students being served in resource programs often report to the resource room to receive assessment and instruction commensurate with their individual needs. It is important to note, however, that although this time in the resource room is usually an integral part of the student's program, students receive the majority of their education elsewhere (usually in the general classroom). Therefore, resource classes are not part-time special education classes where students with disabilities are integrated with students without disabilities only for lunch, gym, or art. They also are not consultative programs where the students remain full time in a general classroom setting and where modifications are made in instruction. Nor are they study halls, discipline or detention centers, or crisis rooms. These arrangements have legitimate places in the schools, but they are not resource programs.

Unfortunately, many schools confine their resource program to the resource room. In those instances, the resource teacher assesses the student's instructional and skill needs, makes teaching plans, and carries out remedial programs all within the confines of the resource room. Little attention is given to assessing the factors in the school, classroom, home, or curriculum that might be contributing to the student's failure. Furthermore, in this situation, the possible need for understanding and modifying the skills and abilities of the referring teacher is overlooked. In fact, the resource teacher in the schools is neither expected nor encouraged to communicate with other class teachers to any appreciable extent, and the communication that does take place between them usually is restricted to general discussions of students who attend the resource room. In short, the idea that the resource teacher is a support person for faculty and staff as well as for the few students enrolled in the resource program is not considered.

It is obvious, then, that the resource program concept should encompass more than merely "running resource rooms." The resource format is a means by which many services can be provided in a variety of settings, to students, parents, and teachers. Even though a well-equipped resource room is an important component of a comprehensively planned resource program, it should not be the only place in the school where resource teachers perform their duties.

This role of the resource teacher should not be mistaken as an invitation to frustrated teachers to ill-advisedly refer students to the resource program. Although many resource programs are comprehensive in their scope and services, they are not meant to address and serve all problems that arise within a school. Resource programs are only one of several support services that should be provided within a school. For that reason, care should be taken to see that the resource program is not misunderstood, and consequently abused. The teacher or administrator who is responsible for resource programs must be alert to ensure that they do not become tutorial programs, study halls, or dumping grounds.

The resource program is not intended as a tutorial service to help students comprehend and complete their daily lessons. Such a service may be needed, but it is not a primary function of the resource program. Rather than relying on the resource program to fulfill these functions, peer tutoring, cross-age tutoring, or volunteer services should be set up.

Current interest in teaching independent study behaviors has served as a rationale for turning some resource programs into supervised study halls where students can work under adult supervision. This, too, is a misuse of the resource program, for although study behaviors can be taught in the resource program, these behaviors must be implemented and practiced in the classroom and at home doing homework.

Resource programs can become dumping grounds in several ways. First, teachers may send troublesome students to the resource teacher simply to remove the annoyance from their classrooms. If such students are consistently accepted, classroom teachers soon come to understand the resource program as a dumping ground for problem students. The resource program can also be misunderstood to be a small-group remedial program. Resource teachers in these circumstances may soon have so many students that they are unable to provide assessment services and individualized instruction. When this occurs the purposes of the resource program are obscured. The resource program is further in danger of becoming a dumping ground when it is seen as an alternative to special class placement. It may become a semi–self-contained program for students across inappropriate ages and disability. Abuses of the resource program model can be avoided, however, usually through appropriate cooperative planning such as we describe in Part 3.

Occasionally, resource programs have grown too rapidly and are inappropriately large. Consider a school where the curriculum is focused so narrowly that it is inappropriate for a considerable portion of its student body. In such cases, growth of the resource program is not positive, as such growth indicates that resource services may be serving as a safety valve for inappropriate general classes. In fact, in these instances, the presence of the resource program becomes detrimental; it obscures the school's real problem: failure to consider the actual needs and characteristics of students by revising the curriculum. As a rule, where 5% or more of a school's students are being referred for resource help, serious questions might be raised about the school's ability or willingness to meet realistically the educational needs of its students.

HISTORICAL DEVELOPMENT

During the early part of the 20th century, segregated self-contained classes were being rapidly established to serve students with disabilities. This growth of segregated classes was motivated by the prevailing belief that these students would receive a sound education only by placement in special settings where specially trained teachers could appropriately adjust the education curriculum. It was also widely held that children without disabilities would be able to learn more quickly without the disruptive influence of having children with disabilities in their classroom (Wallin, 1924).

However, throughout this time, there was some opposition to this segregation. For example, Samuel Gridly Howe, who had helped establish some of the first residential schools for students with disabilities in the latter part of the 19th century, stressed the need for integration of these students into regular settings. He noted that segregating individuals with disabilities resulted in stamping "deeper certain original peculiarities which the teacher would fain efface" (Howe, 1971, p. 14). Semmel, Gottlieb, and Robinson (1979) pointed out that later, in the early 1900s, segregation of students with disabilities into special classes was again not uniformly accepted. The reasoning at that time was that this separation would deprive these students of the opportunity to learn to deal with their age-mates and possibly create in them a negative self-image. Despite these concerns, however, segregationist practices primarily prevailed in serving students with disabilities until the 1960s.

In 1968, Lloyd Dunn wrote an article that became a catalyst for changing this segregation policy. In the preface to the article he stated, "I have loyally supported and promoted [segregated] special classes for . . . most of the last 20 years, but with growing disaffection. In my view, much of our past and present practices are morally and educationally wrong" (p. 5). He proposed a blueprint of change in which he recommended the use of resource programs.

> Special educators would be available to all children in trouble (except the severely handicapped) regardless of whether they had, in the past, been labeled educable mentally retarded, minimally brain injured, educationally handicapped, or emotionally disturbed. Children would be grouped continually throughout the school day. For specific help these children who had a learning problem might need

> to work with itinerant or resource-room special educator. But, for the remainder
> of the day, the special educator would probably be more effective in develop-
> ing specific exercises which could be taught by others in consultation with her.
> Thus, the special educator would begin to function as a part of, and not apart
> from, general education. (p. 14)

Shortly thereafter, other writers followed Dunn's call for a decreased use of segre-
gated classrooms (cf. Cegelka & Tyler, 1970; Christopolos & Renz, 1969; Garrison
& Hammill, 1971; Hammill & Wiederholt, 1972; Iano, 1972; Ross, DeYoung, &
Cohen, 1971; Semmel et al., 1979).

However, the content of these publications was not accepted without counter-
argument from the supporters of segregated education. For example, Chaffin (1974)
wrote an article with a subtitle of, "Should Dunn Have Done It?" In his discussion of segregation and integration, Chaffin quoted Helen Wooden, who, in a panel
discussion in 1944, had noted that the environment selected for a child's development "must be based on a thorough understanding of the particular child involved
rather than on an administrative expediency of segregation or a blind ideal of non-
segregation" (quoted in Chaffin, 1974, p. 2). MacMillan (1971) also expressed some
concerns about the content of Dunn's article. He noted the flaws in the research
Dunn had used to support increased integration. He questions Dunn's theory and
research on self-fulfilling prophecy (e.g., if one is labeled retarded, he or she will
perceive himself or herself as retarded, act retarded, and be viewed by others as
retarded). Later, after an in-depth review of the literature on self-fulfilling prophecy,
MacMillian (1971) noted:

> A number of variables that may influence what impact labeling has on a child
> have been isolated. They include the child's pre-labeling experiences, whether
> he carries more than one stigmatic label, whether he is informally called names
> like "stupid" by his peers, whether he is formally labeled "retarded" by the
> school, how he and his family react to the labeling, what label is used, and what
> kind of community he lives in. We do not yet know what the impact of each
> variable may be and whether labeling affects the child only in school or in all
> aspects of his life. Without such knowledge we cannot make any blanket gener-
> alizations about labeling that can safely be applied to all who are labeled. (p. 278)

Despite these criticisms of the rationale for increased integration, resource programs became the most popular service delivery systems in special education during the 1970s and 1980s. Interestingly, as noted earlier, the resource concept was
neither a new nor a novel idea. Robert Irwin had operated resource programs for
individuals with visual handicaps as early as 1913, and similar arrangements for
individuals with hearing impairments were developed soon after (Frampton & Gall,
1955; Frampton & Rowell, 1940). Furthermore, during the 1950s and 1960s, many
schools had implemented resource programs specifically to help students without
disabilities overcome difficulties in reading, math, and speech.

In the early 1960s, Maynard Reynolds proposed what has become known as
a "continuation of services" for students in special education services. Figure 1.1

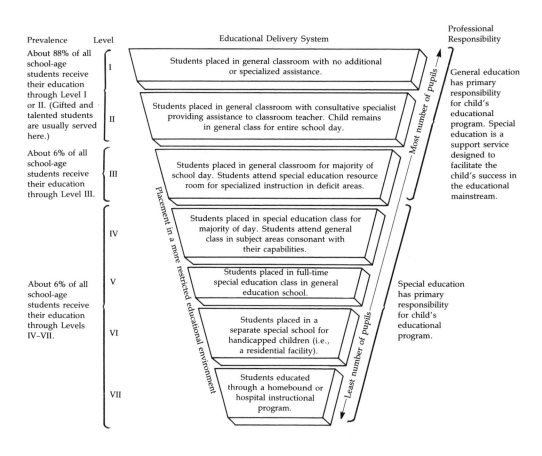

Figure 1.1. Service options for exceptional students. Adapted from *Human Exceptionality* (3rd ed., p. 45) by M. L. Hardman, C. J. Drew, M. W. Egan, and B. Wolf, 1990, Boston: Allyn & Bacon. Adapted with permission.

depicts a recent modification of this continuum of services. At the top of the figure are the general class services, the next level down is the general class with consultation services, next the resource program services, and so on. Of particular importance is the information presented on the sides of the triangle. Students are moved toward more restrictive services only when it is absolutely necessary. In addition, they should be returned to the least restrictive service as soon as possible. The figure also illustrates the fact that fewer students should be found at the bottom service levels than at the top service levels. Most students should be served within the top levels of the continuum.

Recently, Reynolds (1989) reflected on this continuum of services and posited the idea that the American public education system has reached a point where it is in a position to eliminate the bottom two levels of this continuum. He believed that it had been adequately researched and well established that the general public schools can meet the special needs of students through the proper planning and implementation of special services. Furthermore, these services can and should be administered within general school buildings. In this way, the need for day and residential special schools as delivery mechanisms for special education services would be eliminated.

The dismantling of the bottom two levels of the continuum has not met with unequivocal acceptance. Kaufman and Pullen (1989) stressed the need to preserve the entire continuum of services—from fully integrated classrooms to segregated education in separate schools. They viewed such preservation as necessary for achieving and maintaining appropriate education for all students.

Some professionals have analyzed programs in special education, including resource programs, by specifically considering the ethics of segregating students with disabilities from their peers. Some have posited that segregation into special settings is morally right and just; others have stated that such segregation is morally wrong and unjust and that total integration of individuals into the general classes (i.e., mainstream) is consistent with the value of equality and fair treatment (Bicklen, 1985; Bicklen & Zollers, 1986; Gartner, 1986; Gartner & Lipsky, 1987; Hagerty & Abramson, 1987; Lilly, 1987; Pugach, 1987; Sapon-Shevin, 1987; Shepard, 1987; Sleeter, 1986; Stainback & Stainback, 1988; Wang, Reynolds, & Walberg, 1986; Will, 1986). The following quotes vividly describe the positions of those who are opposed to anything less than total integration.

> Our basic societal values should not be subjected to quantitative (or qualitative) investigations or reviews of research to determine their efficiency or popularity. Rather, they should be evaluated according to what is right, just, and desirable. The right to life, privacy, equality, religious choice, marriage, or having a family are value choices that are made based on the type of life we wish to live, not on research indicating their popularity or ease of implementation. For instance, research on the abolition of slavery probably would have indicated negative attitudes toward it by some people and probable economic hardship for many people in the early years. Similarly if the Brown vs. Board of Educa-

tion ruling was based on research findings regarding attitudes among citizens in the 1950's, or on the enormous obstacles that would have to be overcome to achieve it, racial desegregation in our schools and subsequent in our society might never have begun to occur. Instead, it was recognized that slavery and segregation on the basis of race were in conflict with our societal values. The abolition of slavery and racial desegregation was based on the values of equality and fair treatment of all people on which our society is based. These goals were accepted and strategies for achieving the goals were implemented throughout the nation, regardless of reviews of research by some "social scientist" done in the 1950's that these goals might cause difficulties and be hard to achieve. Likewise, it is the same societal values of equality and fair treatment for all individuals that constitute the basic value on which the integration of persons classified as disabled into the mainstream of education and the community is based. (Stainback & Stainback, 1988, pp. 452–453)

Some people would have us wait for science, in this case educational researchers, to prove that integration yields faster, more effective learning than does segregation. But . . . to look to science for an answer to the question, "Is integration a good idea?" is like asking . . . "Is it good and right for people to care for their aging parents?" In other words, the practice of integration . . . is not fundamentally a question that science can answer. From science we can learn some of the effects of such a policy (e.g. . . . types of education possible . . .), or how to make it work better, but science cannot tell us that integration is right. . . . We can answer it only by determining what we believe, what we consider important. (Bicklen, 1985, pp. 183–184)

A certain superficial logic and emotional appeal exists in these arguments for total integration of students with disabilities. For example, it would be difficult, if not impossible, to find educators who support slavery, or who would deny the right to life, privacy, equality, religious choice, marriage, or having a family. We would also be hard-pressed to find colleagues who deny that people should care for their aging parents. In addition, most would support equality of treatment for people of different races, sexes, socioeconomic levels, and so forth. However, total integration of individuals with disabilities is not a similar ethical question.

Following the logic of the previous arguments that we should seek scientific evidence before ending slavery, or caring for aging parents, one could ask: Should nursing homes be available for people who are ill and incapable of caring for themselves? Should we have separate treatment and research centers for the care of cancer patients? Should we have segregated drug and alcohol abuse centers? Should we have residential centers for individuals with the most severe disabilities such as extremely low or unmeasurable intellectual abilities and severe physical and medical disabilities? But these questions are equally spurious if coupled with the question, Should we provide resource programs with specialized services for students with mild to moderate learning and behavior problems? Although outwardly similar, these questions do not have similar qualities. Each question needs to be considered on its own merits with its own set of special circumstances.

Braaten, Kauffman, Braaten, Polsgrove, and Nelson (1988) discussed the set of special circumstances concerning full-time integration of students labeled as behaviorally disordered (BD) into regular classrooms. They stated:

> BD students placed in regular classes present particular problems because their characteristics demand additional instructional resources, including specially trained staff to manage extremely disruptive and dangerous behavior. Other students' right to a safe and supportive learning environment [is] neither minor or moot when the assumptions that *no* student should be segregated forces the integration of BD students. (p. 23)

Broad, sweeping generalizations about the ethics of segregation versus integration are probably fruitless and unnecessary polemics. A more productive and rational approach may be to consider the ethics in placement for each student identified as having disabilities. This can be done, and in fact in many cases is done, in developing individual education programs as mandated by the Individuals with Disabilities Act. In this process, consideration can be given to the individual student's special set of characteristics as well as the characteristics of the alternative programs in which the student can be placed. We believe all of the educational services in Figure 1.1 need to be available at least at this time.

To this point, we have discussed only general education and special education, but a relationship also exists between the resource program and other instructional service arrangements. That relationship, in simplified form, is presented in Figure 1.2. From time to time, students (and teachers, too) need additional help that is obtained from one or more supplemental support persons, such as the school psychologist or guidance counselor. The supplemental services provided vary from one geographic area to another.

TYPES OF RESOURCE MODELS

At least five types of resource programs currently operate in the schools: (a) categorical, (b) cross-categorical, (c) noncategorical, (d) specific skills varieties, and (e) itinerant. The first three of these models are organized to serve gifted populations or specific disability categories such as learning disabilities, speech and language disabilities, or visual impairment. The fourth program is built around specific skills deficiencies, whereas the fifth model is set up around the location of students and teachers.

The Categorical Resource Program

Services provided in the categorical resource program are available only to students who are officially diagnosed as gifted or disabled, including those with mental retardation, learning disabilities, emotional disturbance, sensory impairment,

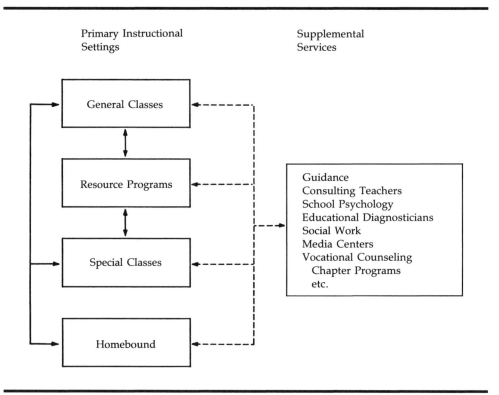

Figure 1.2. The resource program in relation to other school services.

speech disorders, and physical disabilities. In this model, one resource program enrolls only students labeled mentally retarded, another serves only students labeled emotionally disturbed, and so forth.

The rationale for categorical programs, where personnel are trained to work specifically with one type of population, is that teachers will have a better idea of the problems, related services, and recent advances associated with the specific condition. Presumably, they will be able to suggest and/or provide students with the most appropriate educational evaluation and programming available.

The Cross-Categorical Resource Program

As in categorical resource programs, enrollment in cross-categorical programs is reserved for students who have been classified as gifted or disabled. In this model, however, the resource teacher serves students in two or more disability areas (e.g., those with learning disabilities, mild retardation, and/or emotional disturbance).

These programs are currently the most numerous, in part because they are believed to facilitate the grouping of students according to instructional needs rather than by overall diagnostic labels. Also, if the number of students of a particular disability category is too low to justify a teacher for each area, then programs can be combined under one teacher. This teacher is usually certified in at least one of the categorical areas. In many states today, teachers are certified to teach several categories of students; they may receive a certificate such as "generic" special educator.

The Noncategorical Resource Program

The noncategorical resource program is designed to meet the educational needs of students with or without specified disabilities who exhibit mild or moderate learning and/or behavior needs. The advantage to this resource program design is that it may include any student who will benefit from the program. Students may be referred to this program from both general and special education classes, and they may or may not be legally classified as gifted or disabled.

A major strength of this arrangement is that exceptionality labels are not considered in determining eligibility; students do not have to be diagnosed as such to receive appropriate services. The noncategorical approach avoids the administrative necessity of having to classify each student as exceptional so that he or she can qualify for special services.

The Specific Skills Resource Program

Specific skills resource programs are organized around the need for remediation of students in specific skill areas. Most often, these include reading, mathematics, or speech. (In states where speech disabilities are legally defined as a disability, students with speech impediments would be referred to a categorical program.) Specific skills resource teachers work almost exclusively with students not identified as exceptional. Therefore, the availability of specific skills programs is viewed as desirable in schools that use a categorical or cross-categorical resource approach, because these programs meet the needs of only the students designated as exceptional, whereas the specific skills program serves the nonexceptional problem learner as well. Teachers in specific skill programs usually are certified in remedial reading, remedial mathematics, or speech and language pathology, rather than in general special education.

The Itinerant Resource Program

The itinerant resource program, which can be organized as a categorical, cross-categorical, noncategorical, or specific skills resource program, is literally a resource program on wheels. The itinerant resource teacher moves from school to school to work with students individually or in small groups, to provide materials and teaching suggestions for the classroom teacher to carry out, and to consult with the classroom teacher about special problems. The itinerant model often is adopted in areas that have insufficient students to support a full-time special program in each school. Itinerant programs are most often employed with low-incidence handicapping conditions (e.g., hearing and visual impairments) or in sparsely populated rural areas.

Comparison of the Program Types

Today, most resource programs are established either categorically or cross-categorically. That is, a student must be identified as exceptional in a certain manner to be served. Specific skills resource programs, as noted earlier, are reserved for those students who do not fit a special education diagnostic category, but who nonetheless have learning and/or behavior problems.

For some time, professionals have debated the relative merits and drawbacks of the various resource models. A paramount issue in these debates has been the need for the categorization of students for them to receive resource support. At the heart of this debate is the question of the degree of similarity of the abilities, achievement, and behaviors of students with specific types of mild to moderate disabilities or problems. A group of professionals believes that students with different disabilities will follow very similar behavior and achievement patterns. As a result, interventions are seen to be essentially similar for these populations (Becker, 1978; Cullinan, Epstein, & Dembinski, 1979; Epstein & Cullinan, 1983; Gajar, 1979, 1980; Hallahan & Kaufman, 1977; Hammill & Wiederholt, 1972; Hewitt & Forness, 1974; Ysseldyke, Algozzine, Shinn, & McGue, 1982).

For the most part, these debates have been limited to those students who have been identified as having mild to moderate learning disabilities, emotional disturbance, or mental retardation, as well as to students not identified as having disabilities but who qualify for remedial services in specific skills resource programs. It is generally recognized that other special populations, such as individuals with hearing and visual impairments, are indeed unique in their need for specialized classroom interventions. The same is true for those with severe disabilities.

Hallahan and Kaufman (1977) provided what they believed to be justification for considering students with mild disabilities or problems from a noncategorical rather than a categorical framework. They proposed that children traditionally labeled learning disabled, mildly emotionally disturbed, and mildly mentally retarded should instead be considered within a more behavioral framework. They stated that

> historical analysis reveals that the three areas have evolved from highly similar foundations. In addition, no behavioral characteristics can be found that are associated exclusively with any one of the three areas. Children who are usually

identified as learning disabled, mildly disturbed, or mildly mentally retarded reveal more similarities than differences. Consequently, successful teaching techniques do not differ among the three areas. A noncategorical orientation is recommended in which children are grouped for instruction according to their specific learning deficits rather than their assignment to traditional categories. (p. 139)

A few researchers have provided evidence that appears to support Hallahan and Kaufman's (1977) position and in doing so have given support to the idea of the noncategorical resource program as well. For example, Algozzine, Morsink, and Algozzine (1988) examined the overlap in the nature of instruction in categorical self-contained special class programs for students with emotional handicaps, learning disabilities, and educable mental retardation. They concluded from these observations that similar degrees of variability were evident in more than 90% of the instructional activities of teacher communication patterns, learner involvement, and instructional methods when working with these separate categories of students. They further noted that the magnitudes of structural student time, learner feedback, and class directions were also similar. Consequently, they concluded that the teachers in the study were not performing differently relative to the category of student being served.

While Algozzine et al. (1988) provided some support that the instructional activities of teachers may not differ significantly as the teacher moves to instruct students with different handicaps, other studies were being conducted to investigate the activities of students across categories. In a series of three studies, Jenkins, Pious, and Peterson (1988) investigated the relationship between disability and student characteristics. In one study they compared the instructional levels of students being served in learning disabilities classes to those of students being served in remedial programs. They found that although the average student with learning disabilities scored lower than the average remedial student in reading and mathematics, achievement levels for many of the students across the two groups were identical.

In the second study these same researchers (Jenkins et al., 1988) examined the curriculum-based instructional level of students in learning disabilities classes, Chapter 1, bilingual, and remedial programs. Out of 173 such instructional level groupings, 67 included at least one student with learning disabilities, and only 4 were composed of students labeled learning disabled. These researchers concluded that when these students in various programs were grouped for instruction, they were formed across the different categorical programs.

Finally, these researchers (Jenkins et al., 1988) investigated the learning rates of students identified as learning disabled and compared them to the rates of remedial students. Again, they found considerable overlap between the two groups. They concluded that learning rate would not be a serious obstacle to the establishment of noncategorical programs.

Although these particular studies appear to support noncategorization and noncategorical resource programs, other researchers have found conclusions that argue against noncategorization. Becker (1978) compared the learning characteristics of students with learning disabilities and emotional disturbance (educational handicaps) with a group of educable retarded students on five problem-solving tasks. He found that the separate groups differed on four of the five tasks and that the students with retardation approached the tasks in a manner dissimilar from those with educational handicaps.

In another study, Epstein and Cullinan (1983) compared the academic performances of students labeled behaviorally disturbed with those labeled learning disabled. They found significant differences in 10 of 12 comparisons. They concluded that these groups were significantly different and that, as a result, the interventions should probably differ.

Using the studies just cited, it is possible to argue for either categorical or noncategorical resource programs. Although it is frustrating that research has presented conflicting results, it is not surprising when one considers that different populations, different tests, and different analyses were used. For example, in the Jenkins et al. (1988) study, the categories of students were compared in terms of their overlap in achievement. In the Becker (1978) study, however, mean differences were analyzed. This type of analysis would not account for overlap, and therefore would not account for similarities between groups. In addition, no studies that deal with the teaching and learning effectiveness of categorical and noncategorical programs could be located.

We believe that differences exist among individuals with mental retardation, emotional disturbance, slow learning, and so forth. Unfortunately, these differences are not always addressed in instructional programming. We have experienced that, all too often, intervention is based on such factors as teacher training, the curriculum used in a district or school, or the materials available in a resource program, rather than on a thoughtful understanding of the needs of the child or youth being served. Future researchers should strive to account for these variables when addressing the question of the superiority of one resource model over another.

In the meantime, the selection of a model will depend on philosophy, needs, and other administrative concerns of the local school personnel. The possibility of five models merely provides school personnel with a variety of programs from which to choose. Conceivably, a large school district would use all five approaches in response to varying situations existing within the district. For example, low-incidence areas might be best served by itinerant programs. The more severe cases could be transferred to other schools that had special classes and categorical resource programs. It is highly unlikely that a single school will need to implement all five types of resource programs; it is equally unlikely that a school district will have its needs properly met by having only one type of resource program. A proposed model for using all five varieties of resource arrangements in a school district is depicted in Figure 1.3. This model should not imply that students progress in a stepwise fashion between or among the services. Rather, it illustrates that needs may be addressed on a temporary basis in any one of the programs.

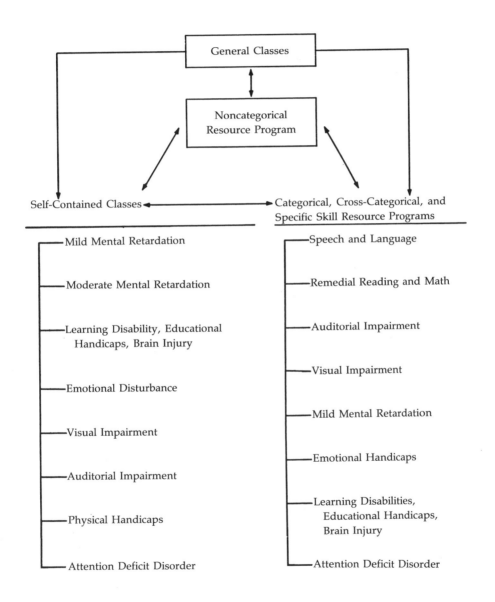

Figure 1.3. A model for delivering daily resource program services to students with learning and/or behavioral problems.

In summary, we believe that the resource program can be an effective instructional arrangement for helping many students who have learning and behavior problems. We recognize, however, that for any model to work successfully, resource teachers must be proficient in performing their duties, notably those duties relating to assessing individual needs, planning and implementing instructional programs, and consulting with principals, teachers, and parents. Resource teachers also must be able to manage daily details, such as scheduling and grading. The rest of this text is devoted to discussion of these topics. However, first a brief overview of the research literature and the advantages of resource programs are presented.

Chapter 2

An Analysis of Resource Programs

Many researchers have studied the effectiveness of resource programs. Their results are discussed in this chapter, after which the resource program's advantages are listed.

THE EFFECTIVENESS OF RESOURCE PROGRAMS

A large body of controlled research that deals with the effectiveness of various types of resource arrangements has accumulated over the years. In these studies, the researchers have compared the academic and/or affective performance of resourced students with the performance of similar students who remained in self-contained classes or who were integrated into general classes. The characteristics of these studies and their results are summarized in Table 2.1. For ease of interpretation, the results of each study have been coded $+$, 0, or $+/0$. Results favoring the resourced students are indicated by $+$. In these instances, the differences between the resourced and nonresourced students were found to be statistically significant at or below the .05 level. A 0 in the table indicates that a significant difference between the two groups was not detected. A $+/0$ means that the researcher performed several tests and that one or more of the analyses significantly favored the resourced students and that one or more of the analyses was not significant.

Table 2.1. Investigations of the Effectiveness of Resource Programs

Researcher	Date	Model	Subject	Approach	Contrast	Academics	Affective
Affleck et al.	1973	Noncategorical	ED, MR, LD	Direct instruction	Regular class	+	
Affleck et al.	1988	Noncategorical	LD	Direct instruction	Regular class	0	
Barksdale & Atkinson	1971	Noncategorical	EMR	Both	General class	+	+
Bersoff et al.	1972	Categorical	LD	Direct instruction	Special class	0	
Bersoff et al.	1972	Categorical	LD	Direct instruction	Regular class	0	
Budoff & Gottlieb	1976	Noncategorical	EMR	Both	Self-contained	0	+/0
Cantrell & Cantrell	1976	Noncategorical	"Low Achievers"	Consultation	Regular class	+	
Carroll	1967		EMR				
Carter	1975	Categorical	EMR	Direct instruction	Special class	0	
Carter	1975	Categorical	EMR	Direct instruction	Regular class	0	
Coleman	1983a	Noncategorical	Mildly handicapped, academically deficit, behavior problems		Regular class		0
Coleman	1983b	Noncategorical	Mildly handicapped, academically deficit, behavior problems		Regular class		+
Cox & Wilson	1981	Noncategorical	LD	Direct instruction	Regular class	0	
Gampel et al.	1974	Noncategorical	EMR	Both	Self-contained	0	+/0
Gerke	1975	Cross-Categorical	EMR/ED	?	Special class	0	0
Glavin	1974	Noncategorical	Behavior Problem	Both	Regular class	0	0
Glavin et al.	1971	Categorical	Behavior Problems	Direct instruction	Special class	+/0	+/0
Gottlieb et al.	1975	Noncategorical	EMR	Both	Self-contained		+
Hammill et al.	1972	Noncategorical	EMR	Direct instruction	?	+	
Iano et al.	1974	Noncategorical	EMR (nonlabeled)	Direct instruction	Self-contained, Regular class		0 0
Ito	1980		LD		Regular class		+

Table 2.1. *Continued*

Researcher	Date	Model	Subject	Approach	Contrast	Academics	Affective
Jenkins & Mayhall	1976	Cross-Categorical	EMR/LD	Direct instruction	Special class	+	
Kerlin & Latham	1977	Noncategorical	"Low Achiever/Problem Students"	Consultation	Regular class		+
Kerlin & Latham	1977	Noncategorical	"Low Achiever/Problem Students"	Direct instruction	Regular class		+
Knight et al.	1981	Noncategorical	"Low Achievers"	Consultation	Regular class	+	
Macy & Carter	1978	Cross-Categorical	EMR, TMR, MBI, ED	Direct instruction	Special class	0	0
Miller & Sabatino	1978	Cross-Categorical	EMR/LD	Direct instruction	Regular class	+	
Morrison	1981	Noncategorical	EMR, LD, BD	Direct instruction	Self-contained	0	0
O'Conner et al.	1979	Noncategorical	"Low Achievers"	Direct instruction	Regular class	+	
Quay et al.	1972	Categorical	Behavior Problem	Both	Regular class	+	+/0
Ritter	1978	Categorical	LD	Direct instruction	Self-contained	+	
Rodee	1971	Categorical	EMR	Direct instruction	Special class	+/0	0
Rodee	1971	Categorical	EMR	Direct instruction	Regular class	0	0
Rust	1978	Noncategorical	"Learning Problems"	Direct instruction	Regular class	0	
Sabatino	1971	Categorical	LD	Direct instruction	Special class	+/0	+/0
Sabatino	1971	Categorical	LD	Direct instruction	Regular class	+	
Sarfaty & Katz	1978	Categorical	Hearing Impaired	Direct instruction	Regular class		+
Schiff et al.	1979	Categorical	LD	Direct instruction	Special class	0	0
Schiff et al.	1979	Categorical	Severe LD	Direct instruction	Self-contained	+	+/0
Sheare	1978	Categorical	LD	Direct instruction	Regular class		
Smith & Kennedy	1967	Noncategorical	EMR	Direct instruction	Regular class	0	0
Tilley	1970	Categorical	EMR	Direct instruction	Special class	0	0
Walker	1974	Noncategorical	EMR	Both	Special class	+/0	+/0

Table 2.1. *Continued*

Researcher	Date	Model	Subject	Approach	Contrast	Academics	Affective
Wang & Birch	1984	Noncategorical	LD, SD, ED, Visually Impaired, Gifted	Both	Adaptive learning environment model		
Weiner	1969	Noncategorical	EMR	Both	General class	+	+

Note. See Glavin (1973) and Ito (1980) for results of follow-up studies. ED = emotional disturbance; EMR = educable mental retardation; LD = learning disabilities; MBI = minimal brain injury; SD = speech disordered; TMR = trainable mental retardation.

Basically, two kinds of students were enrolled in these resource programs: (a) students with disabilities, for whom the resource programs served as a mainstreaming alternative to special class enrollment, and (b) low-achieving students who were not labeled as disabled but who needed remedial or catch-up work. The results of the research for each type of student were different.

For the most part, the collective results of this research indicate that students with disabilities who received resource services did as well as students with disabilities who remained in special segregated classes. Given the general acceptance of the idea that students should be taught in the least segregated school environment possible, it would seem that, in general, resource programs were preferable for these students to special, segregated classes. In cases where those receiving resource help were students without disabilities who needed remedial work, the collective results of the research are quite clear. Such students consistently did better than their peers who stayed in a general class and receive no supplemental help.

The results of the noncontrolled research (i.e. Affleck, Lehning, & Brow, 1973; Hammill, Iano, McGettigan, & Wiederholt, 1972; Ito, 1980) have uniformly and significantly favored the resource program. However, these studies should be viewed as providing only tentative or supplemental support for the resource program. Their results should not be given the same weight as others reported in Table 2.1 because of the absence of control subjects. The table is intended to provide only an overview of the state of the research concerning the resource model. Conclusions and observations should be drawn judiciously, for by combining the results of the studies for group analysis, as we have done, some significant aspects of individual studies may have been lost. A more detailed description of the 37 studies that examined the efficacy of resource programs is given in Appendices A through D. The studies are organized by type of comparison (i.e., students in resource programs compared to those in self-contained classes, students in resource programs compared to those in general education classes, a combination of both of these, or students in resource compared to one another). Each study is reported by author(s) and date of study, type of students participating in the study, duration of the study, students' characteristics, process variables that describe the interventions implemented, and outcomes.

In Appendix A we compare resource placement with placement in a self-contained classroom. In two studies (Carroll, 1967; Walker, 1974) a significant difference in academic achievement was indicated favoring the resource program, in two other studies (Budoff & Gottlieb, 1976; Ritter, 1978) no significant difference between achievement was indicated in the two programs, and in another study (Schiff, Scholom, Swerdlik, & Knight, 1979) a significant difference was found favoring the self-contained classroom. On personal and social adjustment measures, four studies (Carroll, 1967; Budoff & Gottlieb, 1976; Gottlieb, Gampel, & Budoff, 1975; Walker, 1974) showed significant differences favoring the resource program. Morrison (1981) found a significant difference favoring resource placement, but this finding might be accounted for by different sample sizes.

In Appendix B we identify and analyze studies that have compared resource placements to placements in general classroom settings. In four of these studies (Affleck, Madge, Adams, & Lowenbrau, 1988; Glavin, 1974; Rust, Miller, & Wilson, 1978; Smith & Kennedy, 1967) no significant differences were indicated in academic achievement between the two placements. In one longitudinal study (Glavin, Quay, Annesley, & Werry, 1971; Quay, Glavin, Annesley, & Werry, 1972) a significant difference was indicated favoring placement in a resource program. Another study (Wang & Birch, 1984) showed a significant difference favoring placement in a general classroom setting. Miller and Sabatino (1978) compared resource programs to general classrooms that either did or did not receive consultation from a special education teacher. They found a significant difference that favored either resource placement or placement in a general class that received consultation support from a special education teacher. Of the five studies that looked at personal and social adjustment, in three studies (Flynn, 1970; Glavin, 1974; Smith & Kennedy, 1967) no significant difference was reported between programs, whereas in two studies (Glavin et al., 1971; Kerlin & Latham, 1977; Quay et al., 1972) a significant difference was reported favoring resource programs.

In Appendix C we report resource placements that were analyzed in terms of student growth. In four studies (Affleck et al., 1973; Barksdale & Atkinson, 1971; Hammill et al., 1972; Weiner, 1969) significant academic improvements were reported when students who were experiencing academic difficulty were placed in a resource program. Researchers who looked at the effect of resource programs on personal and social adjustment measures found mixed results. Barksdale and Atkinson (1971) found positive results for students in resource programs, but Weiner (1969) and Iano, Ayers, Heller, McGettigan, and Walker (1974) found no significant differences between the resourced and the nonresourced students. Sheare (1978) reported increases on measures of peer acceptance but no increases on measures of self-concept.

Appendix D contains studies in which a variety of comparisons relating to the efficacy of resource programs were proposed and analyzed. Most of the comparisons were of changes in academic achievement. The individual studies themselves, when looked at in relation to one another, indicated mixed results. Sabatino (1971) found a significant difference in favor of resource and self-contained programs over general classroom placements, whereas Miller and Sabatino (1978) reported a significant difference favoring resource and general classroom placement over placement in self-contained classrooms. Conversely, Cox and Wilson (1981) found a significant difference favoring self-contained classrooms.

Obviously, these studies yield conflicting results. On closer examination, however, it is equally obvious that most, if not all, suffer from serious methodological flaws. This statement is supported by other researchers who have also studied the efficacy research in special education (Gottlieb, Alter, & Gottlieb, 1983; Hallahan, Keller, McKinney, Lloyd, & Bryan, 1988; Keogh & Levitt, 1976; Robinson & Robinson, 1976; Tindal, 1985; Wang & Baker, 1985–1986; Wiederholt, 1989). These flaws are: (a) The treatment interventions are inadequately defined; (b) students were not, in many instances, assigned randomly to different treatments; (c) often poor or outdated experimental designs were used; and (d) the tests used to measure growth were often poorly constructed instruments.

Many of these studies contain other factors beyond the technical flaws that necessitate the use of caution in interpretation. As noted earlier, different categories of students were often lumped together and subsequently studied as if they represented a homogeneous grouping. These groupings not only threaten the internal reliability of the studies, but they also make broad comparisons of programs across the studies questionable. In addition, the criteria used for specific disability conditions were not always consistent. Also, programs that, for research purposes, were subsumed under the same category heading often differed greatly in actual practice. For example, in some studies general classroom settings were analyzed with teacher consultation, whereas in others general classroom settings were analyzed without teacher consultation. In both cases, the classrooms received the label of "general classroom."

A further observation in considering efficacy research on resource programs is that longitudinal studies and studies that assessed the progress of students after they had been moved from a resource program into the mainstream are rare. Glavin (1974), who is an exception, reported no significant difference between students who had previously been enrolled in a resource program and students in the mainstream who had no resource supplement. In addition, in only one study were high school programs examined. Sarfaty and Katz (1978) analyzed eighth and ninth graders, whereas all other researchers analyzed elementary or junior high programs. Two further observations are that information on students' previous educational experience was not always inclusive, and no studies explored students' writing abilities.

In several studies variables other than program effect were analyzed. For example, Coleman (1983) looked at mothers' predictions of their children's gains in personal adjustment. Schiff et al. (1979) compared younger students to older students in a particular program, and similarly Budoff and Gottlieb (1976) compared high-ability and low-ability students. In a study that neither compared resource programs to other programs nor analyzed student growth (and was therefore not included in the appendices), Bruininks, Rynders, and Gross (1974) compared peer ratings of students in urban and suburban resource programs to peer ratings of urban and suburban nondisabled students, and at the same time compared peer ratings across genders. Finally, Morrison (1981) compared acceptance-rejection scores of self-contained and resource students in both general and special classroom settings. The educational implications of acceptance-rejection scores may not be how to teach students with disabilities how to be better accepted, but rather how to teach other students to better accept students with disabilities. At any rate, isolating specific variables such as these should provide insights into the effectiveness of service delivery programs, as opposed to making large-group comparisons and then affirming or refuting a program.

As the body of research on resource programs grows, it is important to consider the issue of replication of studies. If we hope to explain the conflicting results throughout the resource program research, then such research must be founded in uniform guidelines for the replication of studies. Hammill, Bryant, Brown, Dunn, and Marten (1989) cited a 1984 article by the Research Committee of the Council for Learning Disabilities (CLD) that established minimum standards for learning disability researchers to follow when describing their subjects. These standards included providing information on the total number of subjects participating in the study reported by gender, age, racial composition, socioeconomic status, intellectual status, and relevant achievement level. Hammill et al. noted:

> Obviously, no research in learning disabilities is replicable unless it adequately accounts for all of the characteristics identified by the CLD Research Committee in their guidelines for subject description. The results of a nonreplicable study cannot be generalized. Without generalizabiity, results cannot be validated and are thereby essentially worthless. When the bulk of a discipline's research is invalid (i.e., nonreplicable), the studies accumulate into a noninterpretable, useless heap; and their findings cannot be related clearly to the results of any other studies. The result of course, is that no body of consistent findings accumulates . . . (p. 178)

Replication of studies requires knowledge of both specific student characteristics and the specific intervention(s) that were employed. The great majority of studies on the efficacy of resource programs lack adequate descriptions of both these areas, and are therefore unreplicable. Future research should focus on effectiveness studies that overcome many of the flaws cited in the current efficacy studies. That is, researchers should describe the interventions in detail, student characteristics should be adequately chronicled, students should be assigned randomly to settings, sound experimental designs should be employed, and tests that are technically adequate should be used. Hallahan, Kaufman, and McKinney (1988) suggested some general guidelines for research on the effectiveness of instructional arrangements. They stated:

> that it might be important to consider how the characteristics that differentiate general education settings affect the delivery of effective instructional practices to handicapped and nonhandicapped students. Settings may interact with certain kinds of instruction to produce differential effects, but if we only examine gross variables, such as setting (e.g., regular class, resource room, self-contained class) without specifically looking at the variables that define setting, we are limited in our understanding of why any effects occurred. Combinations of characteristics of the learning environment—such as number of students in the setting, homogeneity of the students' abilities, severity of learning and/or behavior problems, teacher abilities, and curricular demands—may be responsible for such effects. What is needed is efficacy research that examines the relationship of the characteristics of different learning environments with methods found relatively effective with mildly handicapped students (e.g., direct instruction,

cognitive training, peer tutoring, cooperative learning). This should help to define more specifically the environmental parameters within which these methods are most effective. Also, such research might lead to a better understanding of how general and special education, under particular environmental situations and using certain instructional methods, can best work together. (p. 31)

ADVANTAGES OF THE RESOURCE PROGRAM

Although resource teachers and administrators are faced with several knotty and persistent difficulties in operating resource programs, the advantages associated with these programs far exceed any problems that are likely to be encountered. Nine of the most apparent advantages of using resource programs are listed below.

1. Students can benefit from specific resource support while remaining integrated with their friends and age-mates within the school.
2. The resource teacher has the opportunity to help more students than does a full-time special class teacher. This is especially true when the resource teacher, by consulting extensively with teachers, provides indirect service to nonreferred students.
3. Resource teachers can serve as informal resources to school personnel, to parents, and to students themselves.
4. Because young children with mild, though developing, problems can be accommodated, more severe disorders may be prevented later.
5. Flexible scheduling means that remediation can be applied almost entirely in the classrooms by the general education teacher with some resource support in another room by the resource program personnel when necessary; also, the schedule can be quickly altered to meet the students' changing situations and needs.
6. Because the resource program will absorb most of the students with disabilities in the schools, the self-contained special education classes will increasingly become instructional settings for students with severe handicaps.
7. Because resource teachers have broad experience with many students who exhibit a variety of educational and behavioral problems, they may, in time, become in-house consultants to the school.

8. Resource teachers can serve as ombudsmen for the students they serve.
9. Most students with disabilities can receive help in their neighborhood school; the necessity of busing them across town to a school that houses an appropriate class is reduced.

PART II

The Roles of
Resource Teachers

The roles of resource teachers are described in Part II. Specifically, we believe that resource teachers (a) should conduct the educational assessment of referred children; (b) should instruct some children in a special room and/or in the general classroom; and (c) should consult with teachers, other school staff, and parents about the educational problems of resourced children. In Chapter 3 we discuss the assessment role of the resource teacher; in Chapter 4 the teaching role; and in Chapter 5 the consultation role.

Chapter 3

The Assessment Role

The resource teacher is expected to assess the educational needs of students. In this chapter we (a) address the purpose of assessment; (b) describe the assessment process; and (c) discuss the tools and procedures of assessment.

At least five ideas about assessment are used consistently in this book. First, the assessment procedures we recommend are intended primarily for planning instructional programs for individual students. Second, the assessment will include at least four sets of activities that range from planning the assessment to evaluating it. Third, the resource teacher may need to become competent in the assessment of an extremely wide variety of areas. Fourth, the measurement procedures or tools used in assessment can be interpreted in either a norm-referenced, a non-referenced, or a criterion-referenced manner. And fifth, there are at least eight basic tools or procedures that the teacher can use to collect information that will assist with instructional planning for an individual student. Each of these ideas is discussed in this chapter.

THE PURPOSE OF ASSESSMENT

As used in this book, the term *assessment* refers primarily to all activities that resource teachers use to develop instructional programs for individual students. Assessment can also refer to the entire process by which students are differentially diagnosed and categorically labeled—for example, as mentally retarded or emotionally disturbed. This type of assessment is done usually by psychologists, physicians, and other nonteaching personnel, although often in conjunction with teachers. Some of the information gleaned in the process of differential diagnosis can be helpful in educational programming. However, the topic itself is better considered separately and at length in a categorically based book on assessment. The focus of this book is assessment for instruction.

THE ASSESSMENT PROCESS

We believe that evaluation is a process that includes at least four sets of activities, regardless of the purpose for the assessment. Further, these activities are rarely the responsibility of one person; usually a team of persons is involved, often including both the parent(s) and the student. The responsibility for coordinating the activities of team members does, however, often fall to the resource teacher; it is for this reason that the resource teacher should be well aware of each phase of the process.

The first step in assessment actually occurs before any additional information is collected. The teacher or the team must give thought to the student, the system, and the situation. The purpose of this thinking is to generate appropriate questions, which will be used to organize the assessment. Information should be collected only to answer specific questions about the student and his or her environment, and not as a routine measure to create a fat folder of unused data. When relevant questions have been generated and written down, the instruments and procedures of assessment are selected because they are the ones that are most likely to answer the questions posed during the planning stage. Although the need for this stage seems self-evident, we cannot overstress its importance.

The second step is the administration and interpretation of appropriate tools and procedures used to obtain the information that will be necessary for making informed decisions about the student's educational program. At this stage, responsibilities for the use of specific procedures are assigned to the person(s) who will be best able to administer or interpret them.

After the information is collected, the assessment moves into a third phase where the information obtained is integrated to note consistencies and inconsistencies in the patterns of information, to recommend instructional priorities, and to recommend instructional strategies that have a high probability of success with the student. This integration is best accomplished with a transdisciplinary approach so that any team members involved share their information and skills.

The fourth phase or set of activities is seldom considered in the assessment process: that of designing procedures that will provide data to validate or to invalidate the recommendations made. Any recommendation made should be considered as a hypothesis to be tested and reevaluated in light of data about its effectiveness with the individual student.

These activities may not occur as separately as they have been described; but however they may occur, it is clear that assessment should involve much more than the information-gathering phase usually associated with the term.

Areas Targeted for Assessment

To become competent at assessment, the resource teacher must be prepared to evaluate a wide range of important areas. Academic performance is certainly critical in most cases, but other areas are important, too. Attitudes are closely associated with achievement and behavior. Not only should the perceptions of the students toward themselves, their peers, teachers, families, school programs, and problems be investigated, but also the perceptions of others about those students and their problems. The resource teacher will also want to analyze various aspects of the classes or programs that the students attend, especially the climates of those classes, the instructional programs used there, and the teachers' attitudes and expectations. Further, behaviors such as those of the independent study habits or vocational readiness may need to be checked. Whatever the area, the types of instruments and/or procedures used are basically the same.

Reference Concepts in Assessment

The assessment of individual needs is heavily dependent on information-gathering tools, which we describe in the next section. We need to preface these descriptions by noting that all of the information eventually obtained will be interpreted in one of three ways: either in a norm-referenced, criterion-referenced, or non-referenced manner. These terms have strong historical associations with tests, but the concepts involved are so important that we discuss them broadly.

Norm-referenced applies to any measurement tool, task, or procedure where an individual's relative performance is discussed in comparison with that of a normative group. It does not matter whether the group is the original test standardization population or whether it is a group of young students in a class whose language patterns were observed, recorded, and then indexed to chronological age. If a student is said to be at the 40th percentile on a math test; if a 3-year-old child does not yet demonstrate the language forms shown by most 2-year-olds; if a student is the least-chosen by peers; or if a student's "talk-outs" are above the modal number for the class as a whole, then the student has a relative standing, and a norm-referenced interpretation has been made. Norm-referenced interpretation is especially useful where the goal of assessment is to determine whether there is a problem that needs further assessment and intervention, as for screening and where entire programs are to be evaluated. Both of these uses are possible because norm-referenced measurement or interpretation allows comparison of the performance of individual students both with that of their peers and with their own aptitudes or abilities.

Criterion-referenced applies to any measurement tool, task, or procedure where we describe the student's performance in somewhat absolute terms—whether the student has met a predetermined criterion and where the student's performance is viewed essentially as a pass or a fail. If 80% is needed to pass a math test; if a student must read correctly 75 words per minute; if handwriting is noted on a scale from legible to illegible; or if a student must be in his or her seat 90% of the time—then the student essentially passes or fails a preset criterion. If the description is without reference either to what any other students do or to how much below or above the criterion the student performed, then a criterion-referenced interpretation has been made. Criterion-referenced interpretation is especially useful where the goal of assessment is to inventory the student's conduct, attitudes, abilities, or performance and to find out if the student has sufficient mastery of whatever is being taught to proceed with a course of instruction.

The differences between criterion- and norm-referenced interpretations can be seen in this example that uses a familiar test. On the *Test of Written Spelling–2* (TWS-2) (Larsen & Hammill, 1986), students are asked to spell 60 words from dictation. The number of words they spell correctly is totaled and converted into scaled scores using norm-referenced tables. If Sally were 7-3 years of age and spelled 31 words correctly, her scaled score would be 119. This figure indicates that Sally spells better than 90% of the youngsters her age. Although this is useful information for some purposes, such as reporting to parents, it tells the resource teacher nothing about what words or what kinds of words Sally cannot spell. To get the type of detailed information that can be more relevant for planning specific programs for individual students, a criterion-referenced interpretation is required. At this point, the examiner or teacher may either subject the results of the TWS-2 to an item-by-item criterion analysis or administer another test specifically designed for criterion interpretation, such as Greenbaum's (1987) *The Spellmaster Assessment and Teaching System.*

Because it implies a close relationship to instruction, the term *criterion-referenced* has become a popular adjective in education. The implication is so strong that criterion-referenced testing, mastery learning, and informal assessment have lately become synonymous in the minds of many educators. They are not the same at all, however. A criterion-referenced test is a test that is taken by students. It is subject to the same demands for demonstration or reliability and validity that we ask of any other test, although the nature of the evidence provided will vary with the type of test.

Criterion-referenced tests usually are built around behavioral objectives for a course of study or a content area. One or more items are written for each objective. The items may look like those of any other test, but they are keyed to specific objectives, and they directly reflect the skills of those objectives. As we have noted, a level of mastery is set so that a student who scores, for example, 80% or above, is a pass, and a student who then scores 79% or below is a fail. The purpose of setting such a criterion is the assumption that people who perform at this level have mastered enough of the material that they will be able to do the next unit in the sequence successfully. Although 80% to 90% is often taken as an appropriate level, in most cases the level is chosen arbitrarily, rather than on the basis of empirical evidence.

Most classroom teachers construct, administer, and score many tests with criterion-referenced ideas in mind. For example, a teacher assigns 15 words on Monday for a spelling test on Friday. The criterion for mastery is set at 80%, or 12 words spelled correctly. The students know what the items on the test will be; the criterion for mastery is known; the 15 items are specifically taught; and every student could potentially achieve a mastery level because the range of scores, other students' scores, and the magnitude of a score either above or below 80% are all unimportant. The test is given, and students A, B, C, and D score as follows:

Student A = 100%
Student B = 80%   (missed *percentage, generous,* and *capitol*)
Student C = 60% ⎫
Student D = 60% ⎭   (Each missed the same words, as shown below.)

Expected Word	Student C	Student D
percentage	persentij	percentege
generous	jenerus	genrous
capitol	kapitle	capital
calculate	kalkuelat	calculator
tribute	tribuet	tribut
reliable	relible	reliabel

The relevance of such a test to instructional decision making can be seen in the mastery information it provides. However, it is equally clear that the resource teacher remains in charge of a series of decisions that the test does not address:

- Student A can continue to the next series of words. Did she or he know how to spell the words prior to the introduction of the lesson?
- Student B has passed 12 of 15 words. Are the three misspelled words important?
- Why was 80% set as an appropriate criterion? Who set the criterion?
- Students C and D have both missed the same six words. Will their scores be recorded and the students continued to the next unit?
- How long should instruction continue if the students fail again?
- Will students C and D be expected to learn 15 new words in addition to those they missed this time?

- Will the remedial instruction differ from the regular instruction?
- Does it matter that even though C and D missed the same words, their misspellings were very different from each other?
- Which three words should students C and D learn to spell to attain a mastery level?
- Were the specific words selected for the test actually appropriate to the educational goals for each?
- Is this test the *best* way to determine mastery?
- Will mastery of these words ever be checked again?

We could continue to suggest more questions related to the use of criterion-referenced tests that set mastery levels; however, the purpose of raising these questions here is to emphasize the idea that even informal, criterion-referenced mastery tests merely contribute information that is to be used by instructional decision makers such as the resource teacher.

Educators are particularly interested in the mastery learning aspect of criterion-referenced testing, primarily because it provides accountability for instructional programs. Teachers wish to inventory what the student knows and does not know. Specific items not known are the items targeted for instruction and then for further mastery testing. Where we are interested in mastery of specific items or behaviors, the pass/fail criterion is applied to each item. The items are usually listed in a checklist.

The term *informal evaluation* is often mistakenly used as a synonym for *criterion-referenced assessment.* The resource teacher may read a report about a student that tests and informal assessment were used in evaluating educational needs. Frequently, this means that the teacher observed the "passing" or "failing" of daily tasks. But, one can never be sure just what is meant by a term such as *informal evaluation.* When information about a student is based on informal evaluation, the resource teacher should interview carefully to find out what was actually done. Further, the resource teachers who use assessment techniques other than tests (and we hope and expect that they do so) should describe the actual techniques used. For example, "The analysis of permanent products showed that . . ." is less ambiguous than "Informal evaluation showed that . . ."

We have described the differences among criterion-referenced assessment, mastery learning, and informal assessment so that the resource teacher can both use the terms correctly and be sensitive to the communication problems that can occur when they are used interchangeably.

Nonreferenced interpretation is widely used by school personnel and has many desirable qualities. Like norm- and criterion-referenced interpretations, nonreferenced interpretations also concern what students do. But in this case, the concern is focused on learning what strategies or systems students used to solve problems and reach answers.

Naturally, answers that students give to problems and to teachers' questions, even when incorrect, are not always reached by guessing. Usually, students use what for them seems to be a logical procedure for reaching their answers. Knowledge of these procedures is useful for the examiner, because if the teacher understands how a student has reached an erroneous conclusion or how a student has reached an acceptable conclusion in an inefficient way, it is often an easy matter to provide the student with a new strategy that works better. Consider the example where students have given wrong answers to the following two math problems:

Problem A	Problem B
17	17
+ 5	+ 5
112	85

The teacher is well aware that the answers are incorrect. What he or she desires to learn is *how* the students came to make their errors. Neither norm- nor criterion-referencing will give the teacher this information; a nonreferenced approach is required. To determine how a student reaches a wrong answer is often a simple task: Just ask the student to verbalize the process he or she uses while working out a problem. For example:

While working problem A, Sally verbalizes, "Seven and five are 12. Put 12 below the line and bring down the one up there next to the seven. That makes 112." In this problem, she is using a process to solve the problem that she thinks is correct, a process that she likely applies to all similar problems.

While working Problem B, Bill verbalizes, "Seven times five is 35. Put the five below the line and hold three. Five times one is five. Add three to it and put the eight below the line in front of the five. The answer is 85." He has obviously misread the sign and multiplied instead of adding.

Readers who wish to know more about the applications of nonreferencing to arithmetic are referred to the book by Ashlock (1986) and to Ginsburg and Mathews's (1984) *Diagnostic Test of Arithmetic Strategies*. Several of the currently popular approaches to assessing reading also make use of nonreferencing procedures. Chief among these are the miscue techniques designed by Goodman and Burke (1972), Wiederholt (1985), and Wiederholt and Bryant (1992). In all of these instances, the teacher is as much concerned with the nature of students' answers and how they arrived at their answers as he or she is with the correctness of those answers.

TOOLS AND PROCEDURES OF ASSESSMENT

This section describes eight major tools or procedures that are used systematically by resource teachers and others who gather information for assessing individual needs. We recognize that some specific procedures, such as performance tests, may also be used for assessment. They are not described here, however, because they are more likely to be used with special populations and situations; therefore, they have less applicability to the general role of the resource teacher. The tools or procedures we describe are (a) reviewing and analyzing records; (b) observing and recording behavior(s); (c) administering standardized tests and rating scales; (d) developing and using checklists; (e) conducting interviews; (f) using rigorous educational technology; (g) conducting analytic or diagnostic teaching sessions; and (h) analyzing permanent products made by students.

Reviewing and Analyzing Records

The analysis and review of records of the student is one of the most important assessment activities, and it is also one of the most overlooked sources of information. Review of records is relatively unobtrusive, is inexpensive, and is one of the major sources of information for generating assessment questions.

Records are often in disarray and may be poorly organized because no one has taken or been given the responsibility of records collection and organization. When records are not organized, it is impossible to evaluate the relevance of information gathered. People may continue to collect information superstitiously, believing that it is of value when it is not, or they may understandably complain about collecting information that is never used. People rarely mind collecting information that can be shown to be helpful to a student. Especially where the resources for data or information collection are limited, the resource teacher, usually in conjunction with others in the school, will want to make a careful study of the records system.

The kind of information we can expect from a review and analysis of records is reflected in the following questions:

1. What is the nature of the information provided? The information should be relevant to any presenting problems. It should also be comprehensive enough to describe the problem and/or the student adequately. Both positive and negative information is important. We will also want to know if any information is missing. This is especially true of information that is needed to rule out possible causes of problems or certain instructional methods. Instructional records often lack enough detail to permit a real analysis of the instructional history of the student.
2. How current is the information? There is no need to duplicate information that is already available. On the other hand, if people are making decisions based on old information, there should be an updating to be sure that the information used is currently valid.

3. How reliable and valid is the information? The data base for any statements made about the student must be known. The data base is then evaluated literally as to its goodness. Some statements, such as "John has a central auditory processing disorder, because he mispronounces words such as *chimney* as 'chimley' and *came* as 'come,'" are clearly in need of further interpretation. In addition, statements based on a one-time observation, or on a single setting, may be suspect. Observable fact must be separated from professional fiction.

4. What discrepancies about the student or his or her behavior are apparent from the records? These discrepancies may be between one time and another, between one setting and another, or between an expectation and an actual performance. The sudden onset of social, emotional, or academic problems, as well as gradual declines (as in IQ scores), are signals either of invalid information or a serious adverse change in the student or in his or her environment.

5. What consistent patterns of behaviors, comments about the student, or test scores are noted? Consistencies provide some evidence of reliability in information and evidence for the chronic nature of a problem. On the other hand, we would be concerned about the effectiveness of the instructional program if records showed a consistent pattern of no change during any time of remedial effort.

6. How is the information in the records organized? Although this question is not about the student, it has implications both for the wise use of the resource teacher's time and energy and for public relations with those who will be asked to gather information on behalf of the student. When records are not organized, it becomes impossible to evaluate the relevance of the information recorded, and people continue to collect information that is irrelevant or unused.

In addition to the need for organizing records, the form of the organization is important. Although there is an apparent advantage in having a purely chronological account of a student, eventually the information should also be reorganized around presenting problems as well. The problem-oriented record described in Weed (1971) is often used in settings where more than one person works with a student or is to observe the student or where the problem is persistent across time and settings.

Observing and Recording Behaviors

There are a variety of reasons for observing a student in both classroom and nonclassroom settings. First, observation can confirm or disconfirm statements or hypotheses made about the student. Second, patterns of student participation and interaction with people, with tasks, and with objects (such as trading cards, marbles, or furniture) can be noted and documented. A third purpose for observation is to note consistencies and inconsistencies in patterns of behavior, both over time and from setting to setting. Fourth, factors that appear to influence the student's behavior can be identified. And fifth, any student behaviors of concern may be described more accurately as the observer sees what the student actually does.

When observations are highly standardized, it is necessary to determine the interobserver reliability, to specify the particular skill or behavior to be observed, and to predetermine the method of observation, the notation system, and the allowable interpretations of the data. Techniques for such observations are presented by Hall and Van Houten (1983) and by Sulzer-Azaroff and Mayer (1982).

Observations of ongoing behavior or vignettes of behavior require yet a different kind of framework for observation and recording. A good anecdotal record gives the date, place, and situation in which the action occurred; describes the action(s) of the student and the reactions of other people involved (including the student's reactions to the reactions); quotes what is said by the student and to the student; supplies mood cues; and provides a description that is extensive enough to cover the episode.

Observations traditionally have included only the student's actual behavior and immediate transactions. Observations should also describe the setting in which the behavior(s) occur, sometimes giving diagrams. For example, a floor plan drawn of the classroom may include the seating arrangement and note the target student's seat location in comparison with peers and with that of the teacher.

Bloom and Lahey (1978) noted that the technology of observation is important, but even more important is the knowledge of the observer. Having both an appropriate focus to the observation and a credible interpretation of what was observed depends on the presence of a well-informed observer. Consider an example that is far from education. Two people, a winning jockey and a casual appreciator of horses in general, may view a particular horse. Although both see the same horse, the jockey will bring more relevant information to bear on an observation than will the horse appreciator, because of accumulated knowledge and experience. So, too, can two people observe the same reading lesson. The more knowledgeable and experienced teacher will often provide a more focused description and a more appropriate interpretation of that lesson. The resource teacher will have to become knowledgeable in many areas of assessment and therefore in areas in which observations are to be made.

Administering Standardized Tests and Rating Scales

Tests and rating scales are said to be standardized when they have a common item content administered to those who take the test or make the rating and when they have standard administration and scoring procedures (including standard meanings for the scores). These tests and scales may be interpreted in a norm-referenced or a criterion-referenced manner when there are appropriate statistical data to support the interpretation.

Because the topic of standardized tests is so familiar, this section is organized around two topics that need special comment: interpreting standardization information and guidelines for the appropriate use of tests.

The resource teacher can learn a great deal about a test merely by reading the manual. For example, one popular test manual notes that the test is not to be used with "provincial subpopulations," whatever that means. Caution must be used in choosing, recommending, and/or interpreting these measurement devices. When selecting any standardized test, the teacher should find out and report how the manual treats the following questions:

1. *Are the instructions for administering and scoring the test clearly stated?* If the instructions are ambiguous or subjective, the examiners will have to improvise. The use of this test then becomes idiosyncratic to the individual tester, and the benefits of standardization are lost.

2. *Are the reliability data adequate?* Any test that will be used to measure the abilities of individuals must be highly reliable. Of what value is knowing a student's test score if it varies widely on a day-to-day basis? In norm-referenced measurement, internal consistency and stability are the two most common types of reliability data reported, and estimates of at least one of these should be reported in the test manual. Estimates of reliability are reported as correlation coefficients; they must reach a certain level if the test is to be clinically useful. Generally, a coefficient of 0.80 (Anastasi, 1988) is suggested as the minimally acceptable figure for the diagnostic uses of tests.

For criterion-referenced tests, we need to know how likely it is that students will respond in the same way each time the test is given and whether any observers or scorers will score the test consistently. We will also want to know how likely it is that students who either pass or fail on one administration of the test will fall into the same category of pass or fail on a second administration. If the pass or fail decision is not reversed on a substantial number of cases, then the test is believed to be reliable. Test-retest and interscorer reliability provide evidence for this kind of reliability.

3. *Are any validity studies reported to show that the test measures what its authors say it measures and to show that the test has some practical uses?* A test is valid when it is demonstrated experimentally to measure the skill or trait it is presumed to measure. To demonstrate validity, the common practice in norm-referenced measurement is to correlate the test of unknown validity with a test of known or

accepted validity (concurrent validity). For example, a new intelligence test might be correlated with the *Wechsler Intelligence Scale for Children–Third Edition* (Wechsler, 1991). If the correlation between the two tests is statistically significant ($p \leq .05$) and is reasonable high ($r \geq 0.35$), one can assume that the tests both measure to some extent the same construct: intelligence. The resource teacher must also become familiar with the characteristics of construct, face, and predictive validity, most of which are associated with norm-referenced tests.

Both content and face validity are important for criterion-referenced tests, because the test items should reflect relevant or nontrivial objectives. Further, because these tests are used extensively in decision making, their validity will depend to a great extent on the proportion of correct decisions they yield. In terms of assessment for instructional purposes, then, resource teachers will need to know that students who fail the criterion need further instruction and students who pass the criterion do not. This is true whether the criterion involved relates to passing a number of items (at the 80% level, for example), or whether it refers to passing or failing a single item of interest for instructional purposes. Such an index of correct decisions usually involves the use of a predicted criterion performance.

In addition to these three questions, both norm- and criterion-referenced tests have a question that should be addressed in the manual. In the case of norm-referenced tests, that question is: *Are adequate normative data available?* Standardized tests usually are given to compare students' performance with that of peers. To facilitate this comparison, most test developers provide tables that include normative information, which concerns the typical performance of typical students. These tables are used to convert a student's raw scores on a test into standard scores, age or grade equivalents, or percentiles. Norms can be based on the test performance of samples of students drawn from the nation as a whole; or from one state or province, region, or locality; or from one racial, ethnic, or linguistic group. In general, the resource teacher should select tests that have norms based on large nationwide samples of children whose social class, age, ethnic background, and sex characteristics adequately reflect the country's population.

For criterion-referenced tests, the manual should provide some information about the question, *How was the criterion established?* Where there is some reported data base for setting the criterion, it is more likely that the criterion recommended is truly appropriate.

To be able to select good tests, resource teachers need to have a basic understanding of the principles involved in test construction and test use. These principles and their relation to special and remedial education are discussed clearly by Salvia and Ysseldyke (1991), Wallace, Larsen, and Elksnin (1992), and McLoughlin and Lewis (1990). Where more detailed information is desired, we recommend Gronlund and Linn (1990) and Nunnally (1978).

It is crucial to a resource program that a resource teacher be able to choose appropriate and effective tests. However, it may not be feasible in terms of either the teacher's time or the school's budget for the resource teacher to actually obtain copies of each test that he or she is considering using. For this reason several useful books that describe and review tests are available. By consulting these reference sources, the resource teacher will be able to more quickly locate psychometrically appropriate tests. The primary sources for critical reviews or available tests are *Tests in Print III* (Buros, 1983), the *Tenth Mental Measurements Yearbook* (Conoley & Kramer, 1989), *Test Critiques,* Volumes I–XI (Keyser & Sweetland, 1984–1992), and *Tests* (Sweetland & Keyser, 1991). Although comprehensive, the material about tests provided in these volumes is often contradictory and subjective. When selecting suitable tests, teachers will find *A Consumer's Guide to Tests in Print* (Hammill, L. Brown, & Bryant, 1992) to be more objective. In this volume, the statistical and standardization properties of most popular tests are rated A (highly recommended), B (recommended), or F (not recommended). Each test was rated by several experts who have training and experience in measurement and who use the same criteria for judging a test's merits.

Resource teachers with school experience probably have administered and scored the standardized achievement batteries that are given routinely at the beginning and end of the school year. These teachers will recognize the similarity between the procedures for that task and for administering norm-referenced tests in the resource program. Resource teachers with a background in special education probably received some orientation to testing in their preservice training. Additional skill can be obtained through inservice training or by enrolling in an educational measurement course at a nearby college.

The resource teacher does not give norm-referenced tests to obtain information with which to plan an instructional program. Again, let us stress that it is not recommended that a resource teacher ever plan a school program for a student based primarily on information derived from this type of evaluation. Better procedures for planning programs are described in the following sections of this chapter.

Much of the recent educational activity surrounding test construction and use has been focused on the test user. Many of the abuses found in testing come about because we do not keep testing in its proper perspective insofar as decision making about individuals is concerned. We agree with Thorndike and Hagen (1977) that significant positive advantages are to be gained from testing. Their guidelines for constructive use of test results can be adopted. This means that the test user should:

> *Examine and become clear about all the values involved.* Most decisions, whether they relate to one single individual or to a whole class or category of individuals, involve a complex of interacting and competing values. . . . Only as the competing values are recognized and weighed can one decide whether or how tests can contribute to better decisions.
> *Recognize that test scores are only indicators or signs of the underlying reality that one is interested in.* A score on a reading test is an indicator of reading ability, not the reading ability itself. . . . But the underlying reality is only accessible to us through the signs that it gives. We become aware of fever through the

clinical thermometer, or more crudely through a hot and flushed face. However, when distorting physical, cultural, or social factors intervene, the significance of the indicator may become modified or blurred.

Recognize test results as only one type of descriptive data. The key words in this statement are *one* and *descriptive.* Thus in relation to any decision there are many other types of information that are relevant in addition to test scores. . . . And the . . . test score can do no more than *describe* one aspect of the person's current functioning. By itself, it does not tell *why* he performs as he does, nor make clear what causal relationships that performance bears . . . to the difficulties that he is having . . .

Relate test results to whatever else is known about the person or group. No test score exists in a vacuum. The score gains meaning in proportion as the constellation of information into which it is fitted is complete and comprehensive.

Recognize the possibilities of error in all types of descriptive data. . . . The user of test results needs continuously to be aware of the approximate nature of any score, and to bracket the score with a band of uncertainty. . . . But it is equally true, though perhaps less explicitly recognized, that all the other kinds of information we have about a person are also subject to error. . . . Our decisions are always arrived at on the basis of partial and fallible information, test scores being fallible along with everything else.

In the light of the above, acknowledge the limits of human wisdom, and maintain tentativeness in decisions, to the extent that to do so is realistically possible. Decisions *do* have to be made. But we make them on the basis of partial and fallible data. . . . But for all decisions, whatever the role that test results may have had in them, let us eternally keep before us the caveat: Maybe we were wrong. (pp. 623–625)

Developing and Using Checklists

Basically, a checklist is a list of statements (actually inferred questions) of various degrees of specificity about a student's performance in a particular area or areas. For example, if the area of interest were penmanship, the items might include:

1. Size of writing
   a. Too large
   b. Too small
   c. Varying in size
   d. Appropriate to paper and task

2. Slant of writing
   a. Too slanting
   b. Not vertical
   c. Irregular
   d. Appropriate

Checklists are second cousins to criterion-referenced tests. Whether the information comes from tests, observations, or analyses of student products, a list of behaviors or skills is checked off as known/not known, or observed/not observed. If an item is not known or not observed, then it is assumed that the skill or behavior should be taught.

Checklists permit a great deal of user flexibility regarding the variety of information that can be determined. They also require considerable practitioner judgment in interpreting the results or even in making a yes/no judgment. Information gathered may be unreliable or of questionable validity, so checklist information should be considered as a basis for forming hypotheses about a student's behavior. These hypotheses then can be recast into forms that can be validated or invalidated using tests or data-based teaching procedures.

Conducting Interviews

An interview has been defined briefly as ''a conversation directed to a definite purpose other than satisfaction in the conversation itself'' (Bingham, Moore, & Gustad, 1957, p. 3). Other authors embellish this definition by emphasizing the use of questions or the need for information exchange, but the need for having a predetermined purpose is always a factor.

Most teachers value the information derived from interviews. They spend a lot of time each year talking with and seeking data from parents, students, and other teachers. The interview approach provides a quick and convenient way of obtaining the perceptions that a person has about a situation or event that is current or historic. For example, by interviewing the parents of a student, the resource teacher can gain some insights as to how the student is perceived and treated at home and what the parents believe is causing or contributing to the problem. These perceptions are usually highly idiosyncratic and subjective and therefore should not be taken at face value. Yet they provide the resource teacher with clues concerning factors that might be influencing a specific situation.

There is a definite art and science to interviewing. Stewart and Cash (1974), Gorden (1969), and McCallon and McCray (1975) have written useful how-to-books. In the sample interview starters shown below, we have adapted some of the information from these sources to show their application to the resource program.

Sample Interview Starters

1. *Summary of the problem:* Useful when the person to be interviewed is unaware of the problem or when he or she might not know the details of a problem.
   Example: ''Bruce Spencer has been referred this year for resource assistance in reading. Since he was in your room last year, I wanted to get some idea of the materials and techniques you used with him and how he responded to them.''

2. *Explanation of how you discovered the problem:* Useful when you can be honest and specific about how you did discover the problem; also requires a summary of the problem.
   Example: ''This past week I have been working individually with Sharon Kessler to get some idea of how to help her with math. It seems that she can actually *do* the problems but has trouble with some of the formats used in this new math series. I would like to get your reactions to some procedures that might help her within the classroom, at least until she becomes used to the different way of presenting the problems.''

3. *Mention of an incentive or reward for assistance:* May imply that you are a ''salesperson''; useful if a real incentive does exist for the teacher.
   Example: ''While I was observing Tyrone Johnson and James Brown, I noticed that some of the other children also are rather quarrelsome. I know that you hesitate to refer so many children, but perhaps some of the techniques we plan to try with Tyrone and James could reduce some of the other disruptive behavior. Could you tell me a little more about times of the day that seem to bring on the most problems?''

4. *Request for advice or assistance:* One of the more common interview openings.
   Example: ''I have just been studying the referral data on Maria Valdez. I can tell that Maria must have some severe problems. Could we use this referral form as a basis for helping me get a more detailed picture of how these problems show up in your classroom?''

5. *Reference to known position of the interviewee:* May explain why you decided on an interview. Use caution and tact to prevent defensiveness.
   Example: ''As a new resource teacher, I need to find out about the kinds of spelling curricula used here in Birchwood School. I understand that you have modified your program because of some of the shortcomings in the Boredom Program.''

6. *Reference to the person who sent you to the interviewee:* Be sure that (a) the person really did send you and (b) the interviewee likes the person you name.
   Example: ''Mr Hafeman suggested that I talk with you about how I might approach Penny DeGraaf's father concerning her hostile attitude toward school. He mentioned that you had worked with the family successfully for some years, but that each year is literally a new one.''

7. *Request for a specified period of time:* Perhaps the most overused starter.
   Example: ''Janet, when will you have 5 minutes to discuss Ruth Wright's progress with the Nuffield Math materials?''

Two basic types of interviews are useful for gathering information for planning individual educational programs. The more common is the one in which the teacher wants to find out about perceptions of a problem situation. The interview can also be used to probe a student's cognitive behavior—how the student thinks either about social or emotional events or about academic tasks. In the former case, Morse (1971) provided a classic structure for these interviews. For academic performance, Opper (1977) provided structured guidelines for probing a student's reasoning. In both cases, any information obtained from such a source must be considered hypothetical or tentative.

Using Rigorous Educational Technology

Education does have its own technology in which a series of educational experiments are carried out with or on behalf of the student. The use of such a technology makes it more probable that statements made about a student or about what works and does not work with a student are reliable and valid. This technology has become known as applied behavior analysis, or ABA methodology. It is usually associated with behavior modification, but it is an entire system for both assessing and teaching either academic or social behaviors. Lovitt (1975a, 1975b) has presented the rationale that underlies ABA and has described how it can be applied to remedial education as well as to curricular research. His discussion of the five ingredients that make up ABA, which are summarized below, is important to an understanding of the system.

> *Direct measurement.* When ABA techniques are used, the behavior of concern is measured directly. If the researcher is concerned with the pupil's ability to add facts of the class $2 + 2 = [\ \ ]$, or to read words from a reader, those particular behaviors would be measured. This form of measurement is contrasted to more indirect methods that use such devices as achievement tests that measure behaviors not of immediate concern.
>
> *Daily measurement.* A second important ingredient of ABA is that the behavior of concern is measured, if not daily, at least very often. If, for instance, the pinpointed behavior is the pupil's ability to add facts of the class $2 + 2 = [\ \ ]$, he would be given the opportunity to perform that skill for several days during a base-line period before a judgment is made. Averaging data for several days would balance out the possibility that on one day the pupil performed very poorly, the next day better, and so forth. Many times in research, the pretest-posttest methodology is used: a test is given before treatment and another is given after treatment. Judgments or decisions derived from such limited data might be pernicious; the consequences for some children could well be disastrous.
>
> *Replicable teaching procedures.* Another important feature of ABA is that generally the instructional interventions are adequately described. In most instances they are explained in enough detail for other interested researchers to be able to replicate their studies. In contrast, other types of research sometimes explain general procedures only very casually. For example, one Brand X research study

that used a phonics training program as an intervention simply said that "daily phonics drills were conducted." It would be impossible for an interested teacher or researcher to replicate such an investigation. In ABA research, if a phonics treatment was used, the reader would be informed not only about which phonics elements were stressed and how they were presented but also about the amount of time used for instruction.

Individual analysis. The very heart of the ABA technology is that the data from individuals are presented. For this reason some have referred to this methodology as the "single-subject" method. In an ABA study, if data are obtained on five subjects, a graph of each subject's performance would generally be shown. By this means, all of the idiosyncratic behavioral patterns become obvious. An inspection of these graphs would likely reveal that although the general effects on all five subjects might be the same, no two graphs of pupil performance look exactly alike. Other research systems report the average data of groups— experimental and control. It might well be that these average scores do not represent the scores of any individual.

Experimental control. In every research study, regardless of the methodology, the researcher is obligated to prove that the effects on the dependent variable are attributed to the scheduled independent variable; we must establish a functional relationship. The reason for establishing such a relationship is extremely important. For if researchers recommend that method C be used by all reading teachers because it was discovered that it improved certain reading skills, the researcher must be certain that variable C and nothing else caused the improvement. (Lovitt, 1975a, pp. 433–434)

The precision teaching model offered by Kunzelman (1970), the responsive teaching model advocated by Hall (1972), and the varieties of formalized behavior modification that use baseline procedures and continuous data collection are all forms of ABA. Lovitt (1977) is a particularly good reference. The most comprehensive book that describes the purposes, technology, and ethics of ABA is Sulzer-Azaroff and Mayer's (1982). All of these references can be used in conjunction with current case studies that employ ABA procedures. These are found in the *Journal of Applied Behavior Analysis,* published through the Human Development Department of the University of Kansas at Lawrence, Kansas.

Conducting Analytic or Diagnostic Teaching Sessions

Many practitioners have devised various methods for analyzing a student's behavior in dynamic, ongoing instruction situations. Information from these analyses is used to hypothesize about the nature of the problem and/or to determine the next steps in assessment or remediation. In assessment, these methods are used to find out how behavior is produced, changed, or maintained; in teaching, they are used to document student progress or to serve as systematic ways of discovering the elements that need to be changed when expected progress is not evident.

Analytic teaching methods have at least four characteristics in common: (a) The practitioner has to observe the student engaged in the behavior of interest; (b) the student's responses must be noted and analyzed within some constant frame of reference; (c) the selection of future steps to be taken depends on the interpretation of the results of the successive response analyses; and (d) the methodologies are flexible enough to be applied to almost all aspects of a student's school performance, including academic, linguistic, emotional, and social areas. Methodologies that share these characteristics are grouped under the heading analytic teaching.

Perhaps the most popular diagnostic teaching approach used in the schools today is the one set forth by Johnson and Myklebust (1967). They base the choice of remedial goals and activities on the teacher's direct observation of a student's performance and on the interpretation of objective diagnostic information obtained from physicians, parents, educators, and other specialists. Data derived in this manner are used to prepare a totally individualized program for a given student. This program is tried and revised repeatedly in response to the pupil's performance. In all cases, the activities are selected to match the student's characteristics and needs; the student never is forced into conforming to a preselected curriculum.

The whole clinical teaching system advocated by Johnson and Myklebust is superimposed over a medical-psychological-process orientation to the field of remediation. By this we mean that they interpret students' problems and learning behavior impairments, and hypothetical neurological constructs, such as intra- and inter-neurosensory learning. Our approach is more behavior oriented; however, we recognize that the basic procedures used in their approach to clinical teaching have merit and deserve to be studied by resource teachers.

Analyzing Permanent Products Made by Students

Permanent products made by students include all academic work done in school or for school purposes. They may also include any nonacademic products that seem important in evaluation, such as art products. These products provide valuable information about the student's approximations to the teacher's expectations and also offer windows to the student's thinking and level of cognitive development. In addition, we have found that many students fail or do poorly in school not because they do not know the content area but because their permanent products do not reflect what they know.

Permanent products are analyzed diagnostically for two purposes: to note patterns of errors, as in mathematics, or to determine how the student structured or interpreted the material, as in the evaluation of compositions. It is more usual merely to be interested in the number of items or units that were right versus the number of items or units that were wrong. Although such analyses do provide measurement information, right-versus-wrong analyses provide no insight or hypotheses about the nature of the student's thinking or motivation. It is this latter type of information that will prove more valuable for instructional purposes.

The information from the analysis of permanent products is highly inferential. For example, we infer the student's understanding of the subtraction process from error patterns such as these:

$$
\begin{array}{r} 14 \\ -\ 7 \\ \hline 13 \end{array}
\qquad
\begin{array}{r} 12 \\ -\ 8 \\ \hline 16 \end{array}
\qquad
\begin{array}{r} 22 \\ -\ 7 \\ \hline 25 \end{array}
$$

Inferences are confirmed or disconfirmed through diagnostic interviews, diagnostic teaching, or the methodology of ABA.

It is often through improvement in permanent products that student progress is judged by classroom teachers and parents, if not by the students themselves. These products, then, are a major focus of assessment activities by resource teachers.

POSTSCRIPT REGARDING ASSESSMENT

As the experience of the resource teachers becomes deeper and broader—that is, as they acquire the ability to study students with increasing sophistication and see more students exhibiting a wide variety of problems—they probably will develop a set of internalized norms. That is, the teachers will become aware of the degree of difference in a student's behavior as compared with that of other students. They also will be sensitive to minimal cues—that is, they will be alert to the subtleties in the qualities of a student's behavior. Often these two abilities mistakenly are called intuition; we prefer to consider them as examples of clinical judgment, a skill that at least to some extent can be enhanced through continuing integrated experience and training.

One final point needs to be made about assessing students in the schools. Within the past several years, many citizens have become sensitive about violating the rights of privacy and using tests that may be culturally biased. Because of these concerns, many school districts have instituted strict policies regarding the evaluation of students. Resource teachers should ask their supervisors or principals if such policies exist in the district; if so, they should become thoroughly familiar with them so that they can behave both ethically and legally. If such policies do not exist, teachers should begin to advocate for adoption of such policies.

Chapter 4

The Teaching Role

In this chapter we address three basic questions: (a) What specific purposes of instruction are associated with resource programs? (b) Why should the resource teacher have any ongoing teaching responsibilities? and (c) What are the basic teaching competencies needed by resource teachers?

SPECIFIC PURPOSES OF INSTRUCTION

Teaching within the resource program does not duplicate teaching in the regular classroom, except that the class size is smaller. Instead, student needs suggest six identifiable purposes for instruction within resource programs:

1. To provide or plan remedial instruction in content or methodology, where the student has not mastered some of the basic skills required for more advanced study;
2. To provide instruction to compensatory skills, where the student must function immediately in other instructional environments (as in general classes);
3. To continue diagnostic instruction, to obtain additional information about the knowledge base and learning habits that students bring to instruction, to see the learning problem from the student's point of view, or to provide data concerning the effectiveness of new programs or program modifications;

4. To teach new skills or strategies that are not ordinarily taught in the classroom environment;

5. To teach new content in a different format that reorganizes it either to assure mastery learning or to provide student motivation; and

6. To supervise study hall tutorials to maintain the student's daily assignment expectations in regular classes.

Many of these functions are as relevant for the resource program that enrolls the gifted and talented as they are for students with a history or expectation of academic failure. Our primary focus, however, is on students experiencing academic difficulty.

Remedial Instruction

Remedial instruction is one of the most needed, yet often overlooked, aspects of resource teaching. Often students in the middle grades and beyond do not know basic computational "facts," common reading words, or spellings; their handwriting may be illegible. The extent of the problem may range from incomplete mastery (too small a range of known material) or lack of automaticity (resulting in work that is simply too slow) to a nearly complete lack of skill or content demonstration in these areas. The student suffers a double disservice, because instruction may proceed at a higher level in which he or she continues to fail in this material, while not having an opportunity to master needed skills or content as well.

Students who have not mastered functional academic skills may also require simultaneous instruction in compensatory techniques for learning new material (e.g., how to use a hand-held calculator) and in different ways to learn new content (e.g., taped lessons) while remedial instruction is implemented. For students who are older and who have more severe disabilities, the compensatory focus will often predominate. This means that we may come to a point where the use of the calculator is more feasible, and certainly more socially acceptable, than any basic remedial program. But for those students who require basic academic skills to function over time in educational settings, the development of an appropriate skill mastery program is a high priority.

Even though many remedial programs are available, few find their way to the students who need them. Chapters in the companion volume of this book suggest the kinds of remedial planning that are effective in resource programs.

Compensatory Instruction

Compensatory instruction does in fact help the student make up for some skill or content needed to participate in the ongoing general program. The use of the calculator has been mentioned; other examples include (a) the use of typewriters or lap-top computers to compensate for illegible handwriting, (b) the use of taped books to compensate for the inability to read well enough or fast enough to complete assignments, and (c) the use of electronic spelling checkers to assure a well-written product.

These are the skills that the student will also use in many environments other than the classroom. Home, community, and vocational settings often require getting the job done in the most efficient way, and that way is rarely "the school way." The generalizability of compensatory skills or strategies makes them valuable contributors to the student's general success with life skills.

Wood (1984), in her book *Adaptive Instruction in the Mainstream*, spoke to the classroom teacher regarding the general practice of using compensatory techniques. She recognized that many compensatory practices require permission from the general classroom teacher before the student can use them, and still others require direct adaptation by that teacher. She also discussed the need for working with the classroom teacher to provide some adaptations within the resource program itself, such as compensating for problems in writing by translating a written test to an oral modality. In addition to general suggestions, such as those of Wood, we discuss specific compensatory techniques in the companion volume.

Diagnostic Instruction

Diagnostic instruction is the hallmark of many resource programs. It serves (a) to uncover subskill problems, inefficiencies, informational content deficiencies, inappropriate learning methods, or overgeneralizations the student may be applying; (b) to see the learning process from the student's point of view; and (c) to provide data concerning the effectiveness of a particular program or program modification.

For example, diagnostic teaching may show that a child has trouble in general with "memory," especially when the items to be memorized are not classified into categories. Several hundred basic math facts are difficult to learn as isolated items, but they are not as difficult when they are arranged in terms of mathematical relationships (Baroody, 1987).

All good instruction includes a diagnostic component, but where the regular teacher may swiftly integrate such information into ongoing instruction, the resource teacher must also record diagnostic notes to assist with future instructional planning and to provide an overall "diagnostic picture" of the individual child. In this sense, it is part of assessment. The line between teaching and assessment is indeed a fuzzy one, and the two often need not be distinguished in practice.

Teaching New Skills or Strategies

Sometimes less-perceptive students do not learn the skills or strategies that good students seemingly intuit. Study routines, social behaviors, test taking, and reading in the content areas are examples of important skills the classroom teacher may not deal with either directly or incidentally, simply because most students already know and use them. The resource program is often the only place that these strategies can be taught directly.

Like compensatory strategies, these skills have wide applicability. However, their successful use is embedded in improvement in other areas such as academic achievement, interactions with peers and with adults, or management of important personal variables such as time budgeting.

Areas such as social skills and study behaviors may be taught directly in the resource program, but they are not considered as learned until they are generalized in naturally occurring environments. This means that before planning for instruction, the resource teacher must know both the demands that require these skills and the student's functional abilities in those natural occurring environments.

Instruction in New Content

At times the resource program becomes the best instructional source for learning new content because (a) a textbook program needs to be reorganized or (b) the regular program is grossly mismatched to identified student abilities.

Most classrooms are highly dependent on textbooks to specify the content of what is learned, the methodology by which the student should learn it, and the organization and management of specific teaching acts. For students with learning problems, the textbook-based program signals almost certain failure. Reading in content areas, study skills, and compensatory skills are useless to the failure-prone student in the face of poorly organized content or poorly managed instruction. Someone must reorganize the content and/or replan the management of instruction for these students, and most often that person is the resource teacher.

In reality, a common practice in the resource program is to provide content classes, especially at the middle school level and beyond, as self-contained components with watered-down content to accommodate the meager background of content or poor reading skills of the students. This practice creates an unfortunate vicious circle, especially where there are alternatives available. Students who are in desperate need of learning new vocabulary items and concepts are removed from the opportunity to do so by well-intentioned teachers who are matching instruction to the skill levels identified through initial assessment, and teaching only to the deficit rather than finding ways to help the student understand the content in spite of the deficit. The restructuring of the mainstream textbook program is one way of accomplishing such an instructional goal.

At times the general program is completely inappropriate for the student, and a new one in the research program must be substituted. For example, if the student has not flourished under a curriculum that does not include children's literature or sustained opportunities for writing, a literature-based literacy (reading and writing) program may need to replace it. The same would be true of a math program that does not provide for functional, problem-solving math skills, and of an oral language program that did not provide opportunities to talk and listen in a variety of contexts.

The decision to replace an entire portion of the general curriculum content is a serious one. Unlike a restructuring of one text for one course or school year, an entire program substitution is often a long-term commitment that requires continuity over time, sometimes for several years, for the student. There must be some assurance of stability in the programs so that the student, who is likely already in academic trouble, does not further suffer from disjointed efforts at "assistance."

Study Hall Tutorials

The sixth instructional purpose of the resource program is one of the most common, yet one we do not often recommend. It involves using the resource program as a study hall, where the resource teacher "tutors" the student in the completion of daily work assignments from the mainstream program. This is an appropriate function when the resource teacher is trying to find out what the requirements of the general program are, and how the student's work is handled by the classroom teacher(s). It is also appropriate when the teacher wants to monitor the student's progress with new skills that are to be applied to classroom work, especially in the case of study skills and test preparation. However, resource programs should not be used as study halls when the classroom work is simply too difficult and the teacher is unwilling or unable to make modifications of content, management, method, or standards to accommodate or encourage individual instructional differences. Nor is a study hall appropriate when the student "goofs off" in the general program, because both teacher and student know that the work can always be done in the resource room.

This instructional function should be used sparingly for several cogent reasons. First, the resource teacher cannot be with the student for the rest of her or his life. The practice creates learned helplessness, in which the student looks to someone else for help rather than relying on her or his own resources. Second, the time taken for a study hall is better spent in one or more of the other activities mentioned previously. And third, the real goal of the teacher helping the student (and often that of the student as well) is to complete the work so that it is ready for the classroom teacher's evaluation. This is not a direct instructional goal per se, only task completion. Whatever indirect instructional goal may exist is buried in the task to be completed, and task completion may or may not contribute to accomplishment of the goal. Students in these circumstances rarely retain what the material was intended to "teach" or practice.

Summary

We have described six purposes of instruction associated primarily with resource programs, and have recommended the first five, and cautioned against the sixth:

(a) planning and or implementing remedial instruction, (b) teaching and assuring the use of compensatory skills, (c) continuing diagnostic instruction, (d) teaching new skills or strategies, (e) teaching new content in a different format, (f) and supervising study hall tutorials. There is no reason that these purposes cannot be fulfilled within the general program as well. Consulting Teacher (CT) models, the restructuring of general education (from within), and the General Education Initiative (GEI) from Special Education, all intend to promote this change of instructional responsibility. However, until such time that this has, in fact, been accomplished, the need for meeting these instructional purposes through resource programming will continue. It is even likely that one of the criteria for success of the GEI, CT model, school restructuring, and similar initiatives to come will be the degree to which the five recommended purposes are incorporated into general classroom programming.

The most practical reason, then, for resource teachers to assume a teaching role is that the education of many students will suffer if they do not. We discuss additional reasons for our inclusion of the teaching role as an important part of resource programs.

ONGOING TEACHING ACTIVITIES

In addition to providing direct assistance to children and continuing to obtain diagnostic information, the resource teacher should participate actively in instructional activities to (a) demonstrate specific activities to other instructional personnel, including teachers and those who will carry out teaching plans (e.g., general classroom teachers, assistants, and peer tutors), (b) become more skillful and insightful in clinical work, and (c) engage in self-education.

Instruction as a Demonstration or Modeling Technique

People rarely like teachers to *tell* them how they should change their instructional practices. They would usually prefer to have someone *show* them how to make such changes, and to assist them with any transitions from old to new practices. The resource teacher who shows others how to carry out a particular plan has a great deal of professional credibility and is usually more effective.

Resource teachers may help demonstrate an entirely different program of instruction (e.g., a new spelling or math curriculum); may simply want to call attention to a particular instructional variable, such as guided practice of the appropriate use of manipulatives; or may wish to demonstrate the reorganization of a classroom for peer tutoring or cooperative learning. Whatever the purpose, resource teachers should be careful not to become aides, or to take full responsibility for a new program located within the classroom. Instead, they should incorporate consultation skills to make sure that the classroom teachers recognize, understand, and are able to eventually employ the techniques.

To accomplish changes in classroom teacher behavior where the resource teacher is integrally involved, we recommend any method that is designed to help the classroom teacher become appropriately independent in the use of the new method, new material, or new measurement or management system. These strategies include team teaching, modeling or demonstration teaching, and peer coaching.

Teaching to Improve Clinical Insight

Continued direct work with students often gives resource teachers an additive, integrated effect on their own clinical competence. Reflective and critical examination of continuing teaching experience helps make most teachers more sensitive to the infinite variations and nuances of student problems. This sensitivity is often referred to as clinical insight. This heightened professional sensitivity provides at least two important professional benefits.

The most obvious benefit from working directly with a variety of students and their perceived problems is the development of substantial internalized norms regarding the range of individual differences in growth and development. Resource teachers who have developed internal norms are able to differentiate truly unique learners from those who are more rightly within the limits of normal variation. A second benefit of improvement in clinical insight is the economy that is effected in developing instructional plans. Experienced teachers are likely to be more accurate in the initial selection of programs, materials, or methods that are appropriate for the individual student.

Teaching as a Means of Self-Education

Reflective experience as a teacher provides a unique opportunity to try out assumptions or principles about a particular academic area, such as spelling or reading, or about human behavior, particularly about children in groups. Especially as new formulations or theories become available, the resource teacher who engages in instruction with real children can find out if these new theories or approaches are theoretically or actually useful. Using one's experience interactively with new ideas is consistent with the current emphasis on the teacher-as-researcher (e.g., Myers, 1985).

BASIC TEACHING COMPETENCIES FOR RESOURCE TEACHERS

Almost every college/university training program, state or province department of education, and local school district has developed lists of instructional competencies for general classroom teaching. These lists tend to be more alike than different, implying that basic "good teaching is good teaching," wherever it may be. We certainly recommend general teaching competencies from such lists. However, we describe here what we believe to be critical skills that have special importance to the resource program: (a) curriculum analysis, (b) analytic teaching, (c) organization of the learning environment, and (d) management of the learning environment. In this section we describe why each of these skills is especially important in the operation of the resource program, and suggest professional resources for further study.

Curriculum Analysis

Curriculum analysis is a tool that enables teachers to take apart any given curriculum to determine its components or attributes. The skill is presently only marginal to general education teachers, who use it primarily when selecting new curricular programs. The resource teacher uses curriculum analysis for several additional purposes: (a) to compare the relative attributes of programs, (b) to select individually appropriate content or methodology, and (c) to fill in gaps in an ongoing instructional program.

Attributes of a specific curriculum, in a commercially available program, are the relevant characteristics that ultimately make the program "good" or "poor." For the resource teacher's purposes, however, a program may be "mostly good," and capable of being "good" with a few changes. Or, it may simply not have enough positive attributes or characteristics to make it worth the effort of modifying it. To know what needs to be replaced or added, to know which programs are similar and which are quite different, the teacher must be able to analyze any curriculum.

As a practical example, the teacher who needs to find a math program that emphasizes language mediation during instruction should know that both *Mathtime 2* (Fullerton, 1987) and *Mathematics . . . A Way of Thinking* (Baratta-Lorton, 1977) share this important attribute, and that most basal math programs do not have this characteristic. Within a single program, too, the teacher should be able to tell when a math series that purports to teach concepts and vocabulary in fact "teaches" only computational algorithms; or when a reading program that states that teaching students how to read in content areas is a major objective provides instructional activities that are indeed consistent with this goal.

The resource teacher selects content and/or methodology to use in both curriculum-based assessment and teaching activities. To make appropriate selections to meet individual needs, the teacher must know the curriculum in the detail that will assure a match between student needs and curriculum content or methodology. Sometimes this means taking parts of one curriculum and mixing and matching with another. For example, the teacher must know that a certain computational drill program in arithmetic is to be used only *after* initial instruction (from another program), and that its goal is only to achieve speed and accuracy leading to mastery of computational processes—not to an understanding of these processes. The teacher must make the selection fit the instructional purpose. As a quite different example, *Focus Units in Literature* (Moss, 1984) is an integrated approach to written and spoken language that teachers may use both for assessment and for individualizing instruction within a larger group. Knowledge of this attribute enables the teacher to recommend it when these attributes and the content are important in a specific instructional situation.

Finally, careful analysis helps the teacher fill in large or small gaps in an ongoing instructional program to make it more appropriate for a student or for a group. For example, a ''guided practice'' component is often a critical missing element in commercial math programs. In spelling, perhaps the program does not provide a means of monitoring student practice, and the student is allowed to practice errors. In both these cases, the teacher must not only know what attributes are missing, but find a means of integrating them into the existing programs.

We suggest two formats for curriculum analysis. The first is a general set of questions to ask about any curriculum, and the second deals with the analysis of computer software programs that are used for educational purposes.

A Sample Cue (Q)-Sheet for Analyzing Curriculum

The Q-Sheet approach (V. Brown, 1975) uses questions that the person or team conducting the analysis addresses (see Figure 4.1). It is especially helpful for the teacher inexperienced in curriculum development and analysis.

Wiederholt and McNutt (1977) stressed several additional points that should be considered when evaluating materials for older students. For example, they noted the importance of the experiential background of the students as it relates to the topics represented in the material. Specifically, the students in most cases should have had either real or vicarious experiences with the topics to understand and relate them to their own lives. They also encourage the use of interviews to obtain the students' own perceptions of the materials being considered.

The dimensions we have called attention to are major variables or characteristics. There is growing professional interest in curriculum analysis, so that it is possible to further analyze it by looking for very specific variables of content, organization, or methodology. Examples of concerns from special education are (a) curricular and instructional variables that support success for low-achieving students (e.g., Christenson, Ysseldyke, & Thurlow, 1989); (b) how to modify curriculum to support student success (e.g., Wood, 1984); and (c) how to construct curriculum (e.g., Engelmann & Carnine, 1982). Within general education subject matter areas, contributions such as Shuard and Rothery's (1984) *Children Reading Mathematics* and Winograd, Wixson, and Lipson's (1989) *Improving Basal Reading Instruction* provide subject-specific insight and direction for detailed curriculum analyses.

Directions: If the process of dissecting materials is new to the teacher, he or she might employ the following techniques. First, take at least two programs that purport to teach the same skills and analyze them simultaneously. Second, several professionals might work together on analyzing material and then compare their perceptions. Third, the teacher might write down the specific examples in the material that cause him or her to make a judgment and have another person check these perceptions. Fourth, specific experts in one area, such as reading or mathematics, may be requested to evaluate the material. Fifth, only one component of an instructional area, such as teaching addition facts in real-life situations, may be evaluated in several different series. Finally, the teacher may develop a different Q-Sheet that relates to specific content knowledge.

Cue Sheet

1. *What is the stated rationale for developing the instructional program?* Look for one or more statements of (a) definition of the content area under study (e.g., reading, mathematics, language, etc.); (b) philosophy regarding instruction in the area; or (c) dissatisfaction with specific aspects of other programs, or perhaps a previous program by the same publisher.

2. *What is the rationale for selection of program elements or content?* Look for comments on (a) tradition; (b) experimental determination (always check this out in greater detail); (c) logic of the subject matter; (d) survey of other programs and their elements; or (e) the assumptions made concerning the content area, such as the linguistic base in a reading program.

3. *How can the quality of the content be checked?* This question is difficult. Usually some credence is given to the reputations of authors and publishers, as well as to supporting reference material. Usually ''expert'' opinion is needed as well as a determination of the internal consistency of *all* program elements.

4. *What is the scope of the program?* Scope tends to characterize the comprehensiveness or the breadth of the program. It determines how much of what is possible to teach has been included in the program at hand. A program of limited scope may be desirable for teaching a specific skill, or as a supplement to an existing program that is weak in a particular area or variable.

5. *What is the sequencing of skills or items or units?* Sequence determines in what order the subject matter or elements are to be taught. Some materials are sequentially dependent so that success at each level is required for continuing on to the next. Sequentially dependent curricula leave little room for flexible use or the pulling out of compo-

Figure 4.1. A Sample Cue Sheet.

nents. Other materials are "spiralled" so that the topic may be left and then returned to later. Paradoxically, spiralling may be helpful or detrimental. Sometimes leaving an area of difficulty for a while has the effect of desensitization. However, it may also be possible that mastery is never actually accounted for in a spiralled curriculum except when the particular topic disappears from "mention." The problem of sequence may also be based upon several factors other than the sequential/spiral question. Logical organization of the subject matter may be a determiner; the curriculum may proceed from immediate to remote life experiences; or it may move from concrete to abstract symbolism.

6. *How is the curriculum paced?* Control of pacing is presently one of the major ways of controlling individualization of instruction. Several bits of information provide clues to intended and actual pacing of the materials or program:

   a. Are there differing starting times for various groups or individuals, and then essentially the same pacing along the way? If so, the modification is not in "pacing" but in "readiness" for the program.

   b. Are "mastery" suggestions made along the way for those who need more or different experiences at various points? How is it suggested that such modifications be managed if in a group situation?

   c. Do suggested instructional timelines presented elsewhere in the program mitigate against modifications in the pacing of instruction?

7. *Are there listed or evident any psychological principles of instruction that are content-free?* Look for reference to the systematic use of notions such as stimulus control, reinforcement, rate of introduction, set induction, et al. (See books that deal with educational psychology.)

8. *What are the specific techniques of instruction for each lesson?* The more highly structured the lessons, the less likely it is that the success of the program depends upon teacher experience and previous training. More highly structured programs may also lend themselves to use by aides and volunteers under the supervision of the teacher. It may also happen that if little teacher variation is allowed or encouraged, the lesson may not be readily modifiable.

9. *What are the specific modifications suggested for individualization?*

   a. Is the individualization on a 1:1 basis, or intended for instruction within the group situation?

   b. What are the bases for the suggestions made?

   c. What range of suggestions is made, or are they all pretty much alike?

   d. What range of differences is accounted for?

Figure 4.1. *Continued*

e. Are the suggestions general, or are they specifically tied to potential instructional problems?

10. *Is a prerequisite skill level or information base needed to administer the program?*
    a. Is there a formalized, separate "package" of instruction available?
    b. Is the training continuous as an integral part of each unit or lesson?
    c. Are there suggestions for determining instructional competency of personnel who would work with the program?

11. *Are there "readiness" behaviors specified that are prerequisites for the student?*
    a. Are assessment strategies included?
    b. How are the behaviors to be acquired or taught?

12. *How is reinforcement used in the program?*
    a. If mentioned at all, note the definition well. In the majority of nonspecial education programs there is a tendency to equate reinforcement with repetition.
    b. What kinds of reinforcement are suggested (e.g., social, tangible, edible, visual . . .)?
    c. Are there suggestions for how to determine what is reinforcing to an individual child?
    d. Is there any consideration of schedules of reinforcement?
    e. Are there specific examples, or generalized suggestions?
    f. Is there a procedure recommended for fading from tangible to social?
    g. Is there any discrepancy between notions of reinforcement and practices such as paper-grading or marking?

13. *What is the format of the material to be presented?*
    a. Is the material in kit, book, worksheet, chart, or some other form?
    b. How are the units organized?
    c. What kind of type is used? Size? Style? Compactness?
    d. If pictures are included, what kinds are there, and what are their purposes?
    e. Are the page arrangements likely to make any difference to the learners?

14. *How independently can the material be used?*
    a. If independence of use is recommended, is there a systematic program to teach the child how to use the materials independently?
    b. How is progress in work habits or independence to be monitored?

15. *Has any effort been made to assess or control the complexity of the language of instruction, either receptively or expressively? Does the teacher have any*

Figure 4.1. *Continued*

way of assessing the appropriateness? For example, in materials for young children, which "Wh___ questions" are introduced and in what sequence? Do these correspond with the developmental sequences in language and cognition?

16. *What is the developmental interest level of the materials?* Materials that are obviously intended for younger children are likely to be inappropriate for older students. On the other hand, it may be necessary for the teacher to actually develop or provide background experiences, information, or interests for some students. It should be noted that statements of "mental age" do not necessarily correspond to the "interest age" or to the "social age" or stage of the child.

17. *Are there behavioral objectives for the program or for the lessons?*
    a. Is there any attempt to justify the objectives or to determine their value?
    b. Are the objectives linked in any way to prior or to subsequent objectives?
    c. Are the statements complete in the sense of meeting behavioral criteria?
    d. What are the consequences of objectives assessment in terms of future instructional procedures?
    e. Is the program built on predetermined objectives, or do the objectives follow from the nature of the program?

18. *What is the nature of diagnostic assessments provided?*
    a. Type?
    b. Frequency?
    c. Pre/post, or continuous during instructional sequences?
    d. Feedback mechanisms to the learner and to the instructional program?
    e. What are the consequences of assessment feedback?

19. *Is this program coordinated with any other programs?*
    a. Is the program part of a series or a unified approach by the same publisher? Can it be readily separated from other components?
    b. Are there recommendations for companion programs, or for previous and subsequent programs?

20. *Have there been any attempts to determine readability or learner interest?* What processes have been used, and are the results available?

21. *What is the comparative cost of the program?* Some attempt should be made to estimate the cost-effectiveness of the program. Where similar materials are available, comparisons may be made. Also, try to determine the feasibility of using "homemade" alternatives that may be made in a workshop or by volunteers.

Figure 4.1. *Continued*

22. *What is the realistic availability of the instructional components?* If the program is desirable because of the variety or specific inclusion of certain components, it should be determined that these are actually available from the publisher or with funds allocated. This is vital for hardware and computer software needs. The budget factor should also be considered as critical when considering the use of consumable materials.

23. *Are testimonial, research, author claims, and publisher claims clearly differentiated?*
    a. Evidence of formative evaluation?
    b. Evidence of summative evaluation?
    c. Is there congruence between the program objectives and activities?
    d. Are the program development processes specified?

24. *What are the target populations for whom the materials were developed?* If the population characteristics are stated it is easier to assess the potential relevance of the materials to a population of interest.

25. *Is it possible to foresee, and does the author describe, any potential problems that might be encountered in using these materials?*
    a. How surmountable are the problems?
    b. How readily can the materials be modified to account for the problems?

26. *Are any of the features of this material or program adaptable or incorporatable into other programs?* Features such as self-correctional procedures, reinforcement techniques, etc., may be noted for use in other instructional situations.

27. *Are any significant modifications in the organization and management of the instructional situation required?*
    a. Are there special space and/or equipment requirements?
    b. Will the time/event schedule of the day need to be replanned?
    c. Will present child groupings be significantly affected? How?
    d. Are the descriptions of how the program is to be organized and managed stated clearly enough so that the program may be readily implemented? . . .

28. *How durable are the materials?* Items that require a great deal of handling should be made of strong materials with protected surfaces. Storage or carrying of materials in kit or package form should also be considered in terms of convenience and sturdiness of the packaging materials.

29. *Is there any apparent or subtle bias toward or against a particular target group (e.g., women, African–Americans, Hispanics, or Native Americans)?* Many states or local school districts will have guidelines available for this kind of analysis.

Figure 4.1. *Continued.*

Analyzing Instructional Software Programs

The past decade has found computers and their educational software to be an integral part of school programs. The resource teacher must often select or help select programs of good quality. This means that software must be evaluated. Owston's (1987) *Software Evaluation: A Criterion-Based Approach* provides a structured scale for doing so through the York Educational Software Evaluation System (YESES). It may be used either by individuals or by teams of evaluators who pool their evaluations.

We present here the YESES scale in modified format (see Appendix E), but recommend a thorough reading of its accompanying manual for more complete descriptions, and to review the samples of completed evaluations it provides. The categories included in YESES are pedagogical or curriculum content, instruction presentation, documentation, technical adequacy, and modeling (or simulation).

Analytic Teaching

Analytic teaching methods have at least four characteristics in common: (a) The practitioner has to observe the student engaged in the behavior of interest; (b) the student's responses must be noted and analyzed within some constant frame of reference; (c) the selection of future steps to be taken depends on the interpretation of the results of the successive response analyses; and (d) the methodologies are flexible enough to be applied to almost all aspects of a student's school performance, including academic, linguistic, emotional, and social areas. Methodologies that share these characteristics are grouped under the heading of analytic teaching.

Many practitioners have devised methods for analyzing a student's behavior in dynamic, ongoing instructional situations. Information from these analyses is used to hypothesize about the nature of the problem and/or to determine the next steps in assessment or remediation. In assessment, these methods are used to find out how behavior is produced, changed, or maintained; in teaching, they are used to document student progress or to serve as systematic ways of discovering the elements that need to be changed where expected progress is not evident.

The adaptive testing techniques of Haeussermann (1958) pioneered the notion of combining behavioral analysis of responses with ongoing instruction. Since that time, many analytic teaching methodologies have become prominent, even though they come from diverse sources. For example, the diagnostic mathematics interview (e.g., Baroody, 1987; Ginsburg, 1982), the psychoneurologically based clinical teaching techniques of Johnson and Myklebust (1967), and the directive teaching approaches associated with curriculum-based measurement (e.g., L. Fuchs, Hamlett, & D. Fuchs, 1990) all share the characteristics we noted earlier.

Diagnostic Interviews

The diagnostic interview usually centers around a dialogue between the teacher (interviewer) and the student to find out how the student does her or his work, and the student's explanations of the processes he or she uses. Figure 4.2 reproduces a diagnostic math interview described by Ginsburg (1982). Ginsburg summarized the results of the interview by noting:

1. The child's errors often derive from systematic but incorrect written procedures. In adding, Bob always carried the smaller number; in subtracting, he always subtracted the smaller number. Both methods are systematic but wrong. Neither is capricious nor random. . . .

2. The child often possesses sound informal techniques for arithmetic. Bob . . . added by counting and by regrouping. Bob subtracted by counting backward. These informal techniques led to correct answers.

3. There often exists a gap between the child's informal and formal knowledge. Using formal, school-derived techniques, . . . Bob . . . did poorly; relying on informal knowledge, [he] did well.

4. Understanding a child's methods for doing arithmetic often leads to suggestions for helping him. Since Bob's informal counting methods were powerful, and since he himself placed confidence in them, they could serve as a useful basis for instruction. For example, Bob spontaneously made use of regrouping. Given 22 + 19, he regrouped into (22 + 10) + 9. This informal knowledge could be used to teach the standard carrying algorithm. The latter regroups 22 + 19 into (20 + 10) + (2 + 9), which is not very much different from Bob's invented method. . . . *School mathematics should be built on the child's intuitions.* (pp. 132–134)

Generalized Clinical Teaching

Johnson and Myklebust (1967) presented a generalized view of the child in their Clinical Teaching model, including social and medical factors as well as learning characteristics. The following paragraph summarizes their emphasis on individualized, teacher-adjusted instruction:

Clinical Teaching does not assume that the same methodologies are applied to every child. Rather, it stipulates that each child presents a problem with its own idiosyncratic characteristics. The teacher is equipped to adjust her approach to the dynamic pattern of the relationships between the strengths and weaknesses peculiar to each individual; she adjusts her approach, the child is not expected to adjust to her methods. She expects him to perform according to his potential but she is aware that chronological age (not mental age alone) and opportunity for learning are influential and must be considered when planning a remedial program. (p. 64)

I = Interviewer; B = Bob

Bob had trouble with problems like this.

I: Can you do this problem with carrying?
He began by adding 8 + 5 + 8 to get 21. He wrote:

$$
\begin{array}{r}
\overset{1}{158} \\
265 \\
98 \\
\hline
2
\end{array}
$$

B: I take the 2 and write it down here [in the units column] and carry the 1 . . . I carried, so I put the big number down here.

Bob's rule was always to carry the smaller of the two numbers obtained by adding the units column. Although this rule has sensible origins, it leads to consistently wrong answers.

Given 18 + 5, he did:

$$
\begin{array}{r}
\overset{3}{18} \\
+5 \\
\hline
41
\end{array}
$$

He got 8 + 5 = 13, put down the 1 in the units column, and carried the 3.

I: Do you think that's the right answer?
B: Yeah.
I: If you had eighteen candies and you got five more, how many would you have altogether?
B: [He counted on his fingers] 18, 19, 20, 21, 22, 23. [Then he looked at his previous answer, 41.] That's wrong!

Unlike many other children, Bob placed greater confidence in his informal, finger-counting method than he did in the written algorithm. He relied on his own intuition, rather than on his misinterpretation of what had been taught in school.

Bob's work with subtraction showed a similar gap between informal and formal knowledge.

I: Do you want to write a take-away problem for yourself?
B: [He wrote 9 ÷ 5 = .] 4?
I: Right. How did you do it?
B: I counted backwards.

The gap is evident at the outset: Bob could not write a proper symbol for minus; and at the same time he solved the problem by a sound informal procedure, namely counting backwards.

Figure 4.2. Diagnostic mathematics interview.

As in the case of addition, he used a regrouping procedure when the numbers were relatively large.

I: If you had ninety-eight dollars and you gave away twenty-nine, how many would you have left?
B: OK. 88, 78, and 9 would be 67.
I: Almost.
B: I mean 69.

Bob had transformed $98 - 29$ into $[(98 - 10) - 10] - 9$. He first subtracted or counted back by tens—98, 88, 78—and then counted back by ones to subtract the final 9. At first he made a minor error in the last step, but he soon corrected it.

Asked to do written subtraction, Bob did poorly.

I: If you had 158 and you took away 96, how many would you have left?

Bob wrote

$$\begin{array}{r} 158 \\ 96 \\ \hline \end{array}$$

Then he corrected it to

$$\begin{array}{r} 158 \\ 96 \\ \hline \end{array}$$

He did 8 minus by 6 by counting backward from 8. Then he said, "9 minus 5 is 4." This gave him

$$\begin{array}{r} 158 \\ 96 \\ \hline 142 \end{array}$$

Next the interviewer gave him a simpler problem.

I: Let's see, now, 21 take away 5.

Bob did

$$\begin{array}{r} 21 \\ -5 \\ \hline 24 \end{array}$$

I: Do you think that's the right answer?
B: [He checked his work.] Yes.
I: If you had twenty-one candies and gave away five, how many would you have left?
B: Oh! I think I added.

Figure 4.2. *Continued*

He seemed to mean that since he got more than 21 he must have added.

I: **Do you still think that's the right answer?**
B: **No. 'Cause five take away from 21 is 16.**
I: **[He pointed to his written 21 − 5 = 24.] But why isn't that the right answer?**
B: **I don't know.**
I: **You had 21 and you took away 5, and you had 24 left. What's wrong with that?**
B: **Oh! I know! It's from this one [the 1 in 21] that it was supposed to be taken away from.**

In other words, Bob recognized that he should have subtracted the 5 from the 1 rather than the 1 from the 5.

In brief, Bob first used an incorrect written procedure for subtraction. This gave him 21 − 5 = 24, where the result is larger than the number he started with. He could easily do the same problem in his head by counting backwards and in this way got the right answer. Bob then realized that his written answer was wrong. "Oh! I think I added." This shows that he knew that in subtraction you should end up with less, not more, than you started with. Then he saw why he was wrong in the first place: He had reversed the order of subtraction.

Figure 4.2. *Continued.* From *Children's Arithmetic: How They Learn It and How You Teach It* (pp. 222–225) by H. Ginsburg, 1989, Austin, TX: PRO-ED. Reprinted with permission.

Directive Teaching with Curriculum-Based Measurement
In *Monitoring Basic Skills Progress: Basic Spelling,* Fuchs et al. (1990) used frequent measurement to help make individualized instructional decisions. Their "Synopsis of decision making based on student graphs," along with illustrative graphs (Figure 4.3), shows how data are used to make relevant decisions to adjust the teaching (Teaching Change) or to adjust the goal (Goal Increase) for the child. Goals are rarely lowered when progress is not apparent. Like Johnson and Myklebust (1967), Fuchs et al.'s emphasis is on changing the instructional program rather than changing or blaming the student.

Organization of the Learning Environment

In organizing the learning environment, the teacher selects, brings together, and arranges both the physical components (usually space, furniture, materials, media, and people) and time frames that are necessary for the realization of particular program goals. This is the "getting it all together" phase of resource program implementation, and it needs systematic attention to assure that all possible support is given to the general learning environment and to each instructional session.

At least 3 weeks have passed and at least 6 new scores have been collected since the last vertical line?

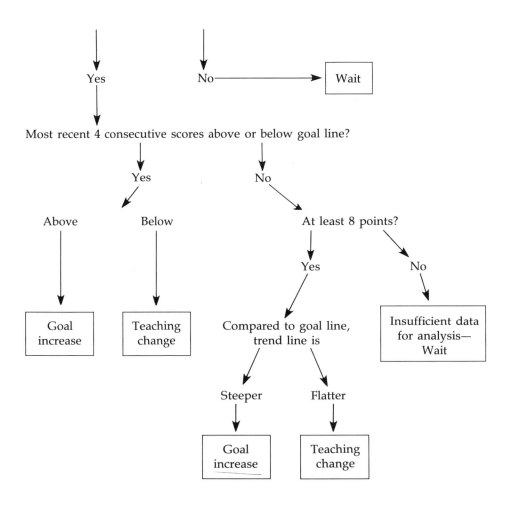

Figure 4.3. Synopsis of decision making based on student graphs.

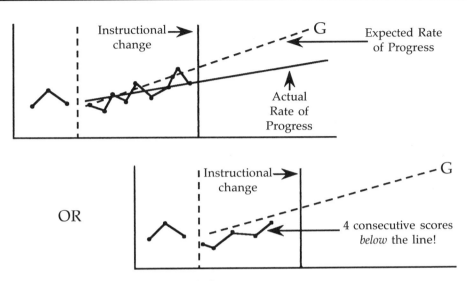

a. Data indicate need for instructional change.

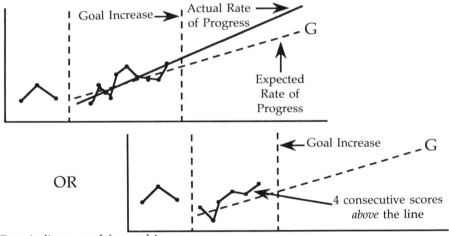

b. Data indicate need for goal increase.

Figure 4.3. *Continued.* From *Monitoring Basic Skills Progress: Basic Spelling Manual* (pp. 33–35) by L. S. Fuchs, C. L. Hamlett, and D. Fuchs, 1990, Austin, TX: PRO-ED. Reprinted with permission.

Most teacher education programs no longer have coursework that directly addresses the organization (and management) of the classroom. Prospective teachers may learn about organization in separate subject areas such as reading or math, but very little about how to organize the environment to support their total program. We believe that "organization" has the power to (a) support instructional goals; (b) help with management routines both for students and for teachers; (c) reduce discipline problems; (d) directly or indirectly influence students' understanding of schools, of teaching, and of the learning process; and (e) encourage independence of thought and action for students. In this section we describe these five ways in which organization influences the teaching situation, and suggest representative sources of information for three of them.

Organization and Student Goals
The way the environment is organized tells us a great deal about the match of instructional goals and the program used to effect them. For example, a child may present problems in developing social relationships, expanding oral language skills, and interacting appropriately with materials. The teacher who organizes the classroom so that each student sits at an individual carrel without opportunities to socialize, to interact using spoken language, or to learn to select and use materials appropriately has not used organizational options to promote what should be goals of the child's instructional program.

Also, it is tempting to organize the class or room to accommodate present problematic behaviors rather than to address positive academic and/or socio-emotional goals. For example, students who are readily distracted are often placed in isolated environments where they do "independent" work all the time. There is a real question of program quality if students continue in this mode far into the school year. It may be a "successful" mode, but students' apparent change in distractibility is environmentally and only temporarily controlled. Because the real world offers all sorts of distractions to all of us, it would seem more appropriate to teach students some means of coping with environmental complexity.

Organizational arrangements may change throughout the year as new objectives assume greater importance. For example, students may move from independent work to competitive groups to cooperative groups. Each plan requires a different structural or organizational pattern.

Resources for relating organization to instructional goals.   Some specific instructional programs directly and in detail consider the role of organization in their successful implementation. For example, Anderson (1984) described numerous organizational options for the whole language classroom. The Direct Instruction series (e.g., Silbert, Carnine, & Stein, 1990) provides explicit direction to the organization of the program in relation to instructional goals. Clark's (1986) model of integrative education, often associated with education of students who are gifted and talented, presents methods of organization and management keyed to developmental age levels and the ensuing instructional goals. Finally, Dudley-Marling and Searle (1988) listed guidelines for creating a favorable language environment that includes assuring that the physical setting (a) promotes talk and (b) provides opportunities for children to learn to interact and use language as they learn.

Organization and Management Routines

Management routines are helped when (a) the teacher organizes the classroom to permit a traffic flow that does not interrupt instructional sessions; (b) the teacher instructs students in how to secure and put away materials in designated places without constant teacher monitoring; (c) students know when and where events will occur; and (d) the teacher or students have all the elements at hand to conduct instruction in a timely manner. If the teacher or students have to look for materials, if the time allocation is inappropriate, or if students (or the teacher!) are not available for instructional interactions, successful management is impossible.

Resource recommendation for management routines. The type of organization the teacher uses to assist program management will depend on the nature of the program. For example, in *Change for Children*, Kaplan, Kaplan, Madsen, and Gould (1980) specifically show the elementary teacher how to organize for individualized instruction, primarily through learning centers. Figure 4.4 shows one of their illustrations of room organization. They accompany their many illustrations with descriptions of management systems.

Organization and Discipline

Organization is most often used to support a particular discipline objective. The most obvious example occurs when a teacher places a student physically to discourage communication and cooperative work. Discipline is equated with power in the hands of the teacher. Many alternatives to this arrangement, along with the implications of each alternative for management, are described in the resources noted below.

Resources relating organization to discipline. We recommend the following sources for both elementary and postelementary settings:

- Charles, C. M. (1988). *Building classroom discipline. From models to practice* (3rd ed.). New York: Longman.
- Emmer, E. T., Evertson, C. M., Sanford, J. P., Clements, B. S., & Worsham, M. E. (2nd ed.). (1989). *Classroom management for secondary teachers.* Englewood Cliffs, NJ: Prentice-Hall.
- Fromberg, D. P., & Driscoll, M. (1985). *The successful classroom. Management strategies for regular and special education teachers.* New York: Teachers College Press.

Organization and Students' Perceptions of School

Metacognition about school simply refers to how students come to think about it, both as it affects their own lives and learning, and as a societal institution. Because

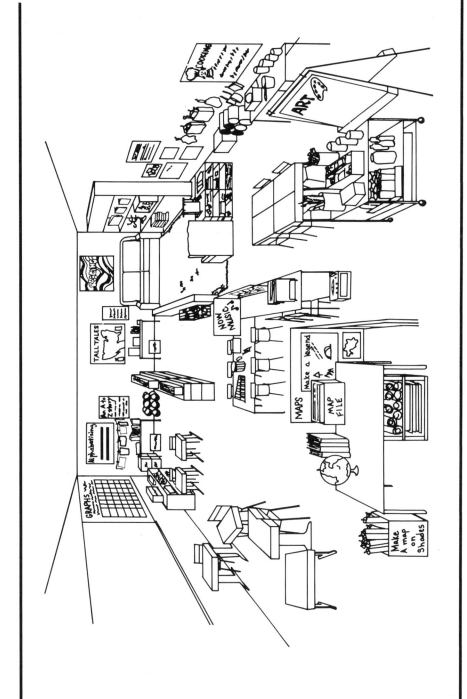

Figure 4.4. Creating classroom sections. Adapted from *Change for Children. Ideas for Individualizing Learning* (p. xi) by S. N. Kaplan, J. B. Kaplan, S. K. Madsen, and B. T. Gould, 1980, Glenview, IL: Scott Foresman. Reprinted with permission.

many students within the resource program have motivational problems, and a high proportion leave school at their earliest opportunity, this question becomes an important one. Ideas about school as a pleasant, neutral, or unpleasant place to be in general are fostered by teachers. However, the organizational plan itself also tells students, directly or tacitly, that school does or does not foster their sense of ownership in learning. Fromberg and Driscoll (1985) described this powerful, though subtle, relationship in connection with a specific skill area:

> By their very existence, areas suggest *positive* activities in which children can engage. When you establish an area for limited purposes, it is useful to ask yourself what you would need if you were a child in that space. It may well be that rulers or writing materials should be available in more than one writing area. Thus, social needs, personal needs to be let alone, and substantive needs dictate the placement of furnishings and materials. (p. 41)

Organization and Independence

Our often spoken desire for seeing students become independent must be matched by organizational structures that facilitate such growth. This is especially true for teachers who may enjoy being "needed." The major rule of thumb is: *Do not do for students whatever they can do—or be taught to do—for themselves.* Teachers are often like many parents, however: It may be easier to do "it" yourself than to teach children how to do it independently. For our purpose, the corollary rule of "nonthumb" is: *Make it easy for students to do things for themselves.* This means that the teacher must keep materials within reach of students, and that students must be taught how to care for, how to obtain, and how to replace materials. Even young children can learn how to mix paints and keep the easel area clean and organized for the next person, just as older students can learn to check homework and to maintain study notebooks.

Management of the Learning Environment

Management, or the skilled handling of the program, is one of the most difficult tasks associated with teaching. It is much like being proud of having learned to cook each part of a meal, and finding that putting the whole meal on the table at one time is a far more complex matter than the sum of creating individual dishes. Only through thorough planning and experience (including failures) does the skill become automatic. In this section we discuss the need to use long-term flexibility in management plans, as well as the relationship of management flexibility both to discipline and to educational growth.

Flexibility and Change in Management

Management plans in most resource programs should be changed throughout the school year, because the goals of the program are likely to change. For example, the teacher may know students only from test scores and Individualized Education Programs (IEPs) at the beginning of the year, and plan accordingly. Through daily interaction, however, different pictures often emerge to suggest changes in both the learning environment and the management plan.

Some teachers never change their organizational patterns simply because such patterns directly affect management. Routines become not only helpful; they become too comfortable. No matter what the instructional goals, the learning environment never varies. In remedial and special education, this sameness is easy to rationalize, because students referred for such education are often characterized as not handling change well, or needing to have their lives structured. We believe that these statements may indeed be true for some students as they *enter* the program; however, one of the purposes of the program should be to help them learn to manage change constructively. Change is a fact of all our lives. Further, it is a rare student who will always have someone around to structure her or his life. Another purpose of the program, then, should likely be to help students learn to structure their own lives around the normative, ever-changing expectations of society. The competent teacher-manager should have the ability to work flexibly around the hopefully changing needs of students.

Discipline and Management
Problems with student discipline are often accompanied by problems with classroom management. Books and films that deal with discipline or "management of student behavior" often direct the teacher or observer to a careful analysis of the learning environment and the way it is organized and managed. Yet, it is not always necessary for the teacher to set up an elaborate system to improve classroom management to achieve or maintain discipline. For example, Smith (1984) noted that, "There is no reason to develop an elaborate point system for improved behavior when merely reviewing behavioral expectations and holding a class discussion about codes of conduct and what they mean specifically will remedy the situation" (p. 7).

Management Flexibility and Educational Growth
Smooth management doesn't necessarily mean good management insofar as educational growth is concerned. Class members may be busy with their tasks, and there may be no disruptions, but broad educational growth may be minimal. At least two related reasons account for this phenomenon.

First, many students in resource programs have a variety of needs, whether they are academically retarded or academically gifted. Socioemotional growth, exploration of interests, the development of independence, and problem-solving behavior may be hindered by apparently smooth management of a room that is always quiet and orderly. It takes a skilled and perceptive manager to orchestrate various groupings and activities that serve the different types of instructional needs of students within resource programs. No one management plan is adequate for multiple goals.

A second consideration is that teaching and learning are not always the didactic matters fostered by smooth, routine management. The learning environment should provide opportunities for students to use what they have learned and to interact socially as they learn. In such an environment, the teacher is much like a coach-manager who observes real, interactive practice and who instructs only as needed. Both observational assessment and corrective feedback are served through varying management plans to encourage student interactions with peers, with adults, and with materials.

Teachers of young children seem to be naturals both at the coach-manager style and at managing for a diversity of student needs. However, teachers of older students may need to work deliberately to make management style contribute to a broader conception of educational growth than is found in too many resource programs. Planned flexibility is not a contradiction of terms.

Sources of Assistance with Management
In addition to the resources we have noted, many useful materials are available to assist with the development of a flexible management style. For example, the Association for Supervision and Curriculum Development (ASCD) has various packaged programs with videotapes and manuals to show examples of elements of good management.

Subject matter methods textbooks are often overlooked by remedial and special educators, because they do not deal directly with their identified students. For example, in *Social Studies for Children: A Guide to Basic Instruction* (9th ed.) Michaelis (1988) deals specifically with planning for individual differences. Most of the ideas in methods textbooks involve management techniques that are useful for the whole class and across instructional areas. For example, Johnson's *Every Minute Counts. Making Your Class Work* (1982) and *Making Minutes Count Even More. A Sequel to Every Minute Counts* (1986) are booklets that address the practical details of management in any classroom.

A second source of information regarding management is in the specialized materials that directly address the creation of differential learning environments. For example, in *Learning Together and Alone. Cooperative, Competitive, and Individualistic Learning* (2nd ed.) Johnson and Johnson (1987) describe both organizational structures and management techniques that are flexible, because they match differentiated instructional activities and goals.

A third source of materials arises from concern for the affective climate of school and its effect on school success. For example, in *Group Processes in the Classroom* (5th ed.) Schmuck and Schmuck (1988) provide a sequential program of classroom management that is directed at fostering improved social relationships. Purkey and Novak (1984) treat classroom climate more personally in *Inviting School Success. A Self-Concept Approach to Teaching and Learning* (2nd ed.).

A final, rich source of instruction on management is in the materials related to teaching and its improvement. For example, in *Effective Teaching. A Practical Guide to Improving Your Teaching* Perrott (1982) gives specific exercises for the teacher to use for self-study in areas such as questioning and affective communication. *Inquiring into the Teaching Process. Towards Self-Evaluation and Professional Development* (Haysom, 1985) is a handbook for teachers to use individually or in small groups to provide focus to the self-study of management.

CONCLUDING COMMENTS

We have discussed purposes of resource program instruction, the rationale for the teaching role within the resource program, and some of the major competencies needed by resource teachers. We need to add that the resource teacher will face many ethical dilemmas in teaching, if only because such dilemmas are often encountered when two or more persons with different perspectives become involved with the same student. There are no easy answers here, but we hope that the resource teacher is always characterized as being a teacher-advocate for the student. It is that central core of professional and personal integrity that most clearly makes the teaching role of the resource program worth doing.

Chapter 5
The Consultation Role

Many people are responsible for providing educational services to students assigned to the resource program, and they all share a mutual interest in having the student be and feel successful. These individuals may, and often do, perform their roles independently, but it is in the student's best interest for them to communicate, to collaborate or work together, and to consult with one another about the design and evaluation of individualized programs.

In this chapter we (a) describe briefly the distinctive differences among communication, collaboration, and consultation; (b) give the rationale for the emphasis placed on collaboration and consultation as major components of the resource teacher's job; (c) describe what is involved in collaborating and consulting; and (d) provide concluding comments about the consultation role and suggest additional resources for study.

COMMUNICATION, COLLABORATION, AND CONSULTATION

Resource teachers spend a great deal of time communicating with others, both about various aspects of the resource program and about individual students. For example, they may:

1. Discuss the educational problems of specific students

2. Describe the methodology being used in the resource program
3. Suggest ideas that teachers can use in their classes to strengthen and supplement the resource effort
4. Find out how to mesh the activities of the resource program with those of the general class
5. Follow up students who are no longer in the resource program
6. Observe and record the classroom performance of students who have been referred for resource assistance
7. Demonstrate techniques by which the teacher might improve the classroom climate, individualize instruction, or manage group behavior
8. Share with others professional information about their respective operations, new programs, and new methods of teaching
9. Assist parents with home-school relationships
10. Share information with community agencies or persons who might have a stake in the progress or programs of individual students
11. Address the questions of generalization of the student's learning

With communication, people send along or exchange information. They might then simply make note of it, or the information may in fact alter the perceptions or actions of those involved. When it does, this joint *use* of information is called *collaboration*. Collaboration, or team effort, is characteristic of schools and of special education services.

In education, those who work collaboratively usually have unique contributions of perspective, experience, or expertise that they bring to the joint solution of instructional problems. In this sense they not only collaborate, but they consult as well. They further work in a triadic relationship where they become *consultants*, working with one or more *consultees* on behalf of the same (student) *client*.

Areas of expertise for consultation in remedial and special education may include (a) any subject matter such as math, reading, or science; (b) behavior change; (c) learning strategies or processes; (d) home-school-community relationships; (e) child development; (f) instructional strategies or organizational patterns; and (g) instructional assessment strategies. The kinds of expertise available in any one collaborative or consultative team are not as much a function of the title of the person (e.g., social worker, school psychologist, mainstream or special education teacher) as it is a function of the history of unique training and experiences of those individuals who are participating.

In the traditional triadic consultation model (i.e., consultant, consultee, and client), the consultant gives her or his report, and then leaves it up to the consultee to decide how much of the advice or interpretation to use. There is no obligation to find out how valid the advice or interpretation happened to be. In what we call collaborative consultation, the consultant and consultee work through the problem together on behalf of the client. They engage in a problem-solving process that ranges from clarifying or behavioralizing the problem to assessing the efficacy of their efforts toward its resolution. In this way, "The outcome is enhanced, altered, and produces solutions that are different from those that the individual team members would produce independently" (Idol & Paolucci-Whitcomb, 1986, p. 1).

The resource teacher who works within a collaboration, consultation, or collaborative consultation framework will find that although the general model may make logical sense, the practice itself is not a simple matter. Nevertheless, this complex aspect of the resource program is being emphasized in both preservice and inservice training for many reasons.

RATIONALE FOR COLLABORATION AND CONSULTATION

The collaboration and consultation functions of the resource program are important for at least five reasons: (a) to prevent unneeded referral to special education, (b) to provide assistance to the mainstream teacher, (c) to assure that all those involved are working toward common goals and to assure program continuity, (d) to develop interagency collaborative consultation, and (e) to multiply scarce resources (i.e., personnel and money).

Prereferral Intervention

First, the present emphasis in schools on "prereferral intervention" (e.g., Chalfant, Pysh, & Moultrie, 1979) is aimed at stemming the tide of referrals for special programs such as learning disabilities and remedial reading. It should not be necessary to refer, identify and classify as educationally handicapped, and subsequently place students in a special program merely to have their classroom activities altered so that they will find success, or so that their teachers can retain their own sanity. For some students there may be positive outcomes that far outweigh the potentially negative effects (e.g., lowered expectations and the stereotyping that comes with labeling) of being placed in a special program. However, for the majority of students with mild learning and behavior problems, a local school problem-solving process can readily provide immediate and effective changes or interventions into the ongoing curriculum and classroom organization and management patterns. The problem-solving process in this case is effected through collaborative consultation between the mainstream educator and those who might be of assistance. When the prereferral processes that try to address the educational problems of individual students with academic and behavioral difficulties are not successful, referral for more intensive services may proceed.

Assistance to the Mainstream Teacher

A second reason for the importance of the consultation function is found in guidelines that follow from P.L. 94-142. General classroom teachers who are responsible for the education of students labeled as in need of special education are entitled to assistance in working with these students within the general classroom. A relationship of ongoing communication, collaboration, and consultation with the special education teacher and any other relevant IEP team members should be in place to assure that the mainstream experience is indeed a positive one for all concerned. Consultation may include not only educational programming, but also methods of promoting social acceptance among peers and long-range planning with parents on behalf of the student.

Assuring Common Goals and Program Continuity

Third, resource teachers may collaborate or consult with mainstream teachers to assure that the student's program is mutually goal directed, consistent, and appropriately generalizable. This means that their respective programs should not take students in vastly different directions; teachers should remove redundancies of content, or unnecessary elements, in either program; and they should assure that specific skills or content learned within either program will generalize. Three examples illustrate what we mean. (a) If both teachers provide reading instruction, it would only be confusing if one were a whole language approach and the other a highly structured phonics program. (b) Students who receive services within the resource program should not have to do ''all work they missed in the general program'' as well. Negotiation is needed around the actual goals of instruction. (c) If the student learns to use a calculator in the resource program, there should be rewarding opportunities to use this skill within the mainstream math program. Sometimes such concerns require only simple coordination, but more often teachers need a formal problem-solving process to resolve these issues and problems.

Interagency Coordination/Collaboration

Another major reason for the need for collaboration and consultation involves personnel from other agencies who might have an official stake in the life of the student or in the student's family. For example, a social worker, probation officer, drug counselor, and/or a worker from the state social services agency might be interested in the development of an individually appropriate set of needed services. These people cannot plan such a program while working independently of each other, and further, their efforts and time commitments are usually uneven because of the press of heavy caseloads. Karp (1990) noted that, ''Without interagency coordination the family must patch together the services . . . and mediate among agencies—each of which has its own set of rules, regulations, priorities, and service patterns'' (p. 55). We do not believe that it should be left to the family to mediate among agencies to obtain services to which the student and family are entitled. Neither the family nor the school can plan an appropriate program of education without considering the impact of other agencies and their representatives. For children of school age, then, the school usually becomes the central point of interagency consultation, with a goal of reducing the educational handicaps of the children.

Formalized interagency agreements are supposed to provide the structure for the coordination of services around an individual case. However, interagency agreements only touch the surface of the collaborative consultation process that is needed to minimize service fragmentation when more than one agency is involved in school matters. Karp (1990) described critical strategies for multiple agency involvement or collaborative consultation through Early Intervention Coordinating Councils created by P.L. 99-457. Her comprehensive overview provides a readily generalizable framework for the resource program as well.

Making Use of Scarce Resources

To the major parts of the rationale for the consultation function of the resource teacher, we can add both the high cost of special services for all referred students and the scarcity of trained professional personnel. These practical reasons, however, should not be emphasized at the expense of the truly professional rationale we have just presented.

WHAT IS INVOLVED IN COLLABORATING AND CONSULTING

The term *consultation* as used in this book refers to components called advising and instructing others, following up on these activities, and formal problem solving. Although we discuss these components individually at this point, we recognize that in practice they cannot be readily separated from each other.

Advising Others

Resource teachers provide advice both for individual change and for system change. In the case of individuals, the activity is roughly analogous to the medical practice situation in which a specialist (a resource teacher) is called on to assist in diagnosing a difficult case or prescribing a course of action that is not usually known to the generalist physician (the classroom teacher). In such instances, the patient (the student) is likely to improve; the consultee (the classroom teacher) may benefit in learning to look at the patient (the student) in a different way; and the consultation ends when a specific decision has been made about diagnosis and treatment.

An educational example of this activity occurs when a classroom teacher requests assistance on a problem that a student has in mathematics. The resource teacher, after careful examination of the student's mathematics papers or by observing his or her work, may call attention to a consistent error pattern, such as trying to calculate from left to right instead of from right to left in two-place subtraction problems. In this case, the student is likely to benefit from this consultation; the teacher may or may not be alert to such a problem in the future; and the specific consultation activity will end when the teacher understands the problem and/or how to deal with it, at least in that individual case.

Also analogous to the medical model, the specialist, or in this case the resource teacher, may serve at times to confirm the soundness of the diagnoses or decisions concerning treatment made by colleagues. Such a situation might occur when a parent or a supervisory person questions the instructional strategies of the classroom teacher.

Resource teachers are in an excellent position to bring about changes in an entire school program or system as they work from an "intervention-to-prevention" model. This means that instead of intervening, or working on the same problems over and over, people take measures to prevent their recurrence. For example, the resource teacher may notice a consistent pattern of problems in the students being referred for service. Perhaps a disproportionate number of students are being referred because of weakness in comprehension or in elaborative reading skills, such as finding the main idea or anticipating outcomes of stories. If the general teachers use a strict sound-symbol correspondence system for teaching phonics and word analysis, the resource teacher may suspect that the students' problems are the direct result of this method rather than of deficiencies within the individual students being referred. In this case, a reevaluation of the approach to reading instruction is desirable; to do this, the principal and faculty must have documented evidence of the possible need for making such a change. Once convinced, the school faculty may decide to augment the word analysis methods with a complementary comprehension program. In this way, many of the students' difficulties can be prevented and valuable resource time is not wasted.

The key ingredients here are that the resource teacher is able to (a) identify a pattern in the referrals, (b) determine its possible source, (c) formulate a course of action, and (d) effectively communicate both the problem and a potential plan for its amelioration to the faculty.

The use of the intervention-to-prevention model is just one instance in which the resource teacher may wish to advise the principal and faculty even though they may not have requested it. On such occasions, advice should be given with considerable care and tact, for resource teachers always should keep in mind that advice is generally received better when it is requested than when it is offered freely. As a rule, therefore, resource teachers should give advice only when their expertise is specifically asked for. As is true of all rules, however, this one is meant to be broken—but judiciously.

Instructing Others

The instructing that a resource teacher does is actually a form of inservice training. The major aim of the activities is to increase other teachers' understanding of the difficulties students encounter in school and to develop plans to prevent or ameliorate these problems. The teacher may use both formal and informal means to accomplish this goal.

Some of the most effective methods of instruction are associated with the informal, almost casual, day-to-day interactions that occur between colleagues. These contacts may assume a variety of forms, ranging from informal conversations concerning strategies for managing a particular student's problem to a quick observation and discussion of a student's behavior within the classroom. In these instances, teachers will readily see the practical significance of any informal "instruction," because it relates to an immediate need.

When formal instruction is needed, resource teachers may (a) use a prepared inservice package and/or (b) become demonstration teachers who model specific activities. The prepared inservice training package usually has the advantages of (a) activities that are already planned and sequenced, (b) objectives that are usually prespecified, (c) the inclusion of useful evaluation procedures, and (d) a good description of the materials and additional resources that will be needed to carry out the training.

A popular example of an inservice training package is the Learning Strategies program developed at the University of Kansas (e.g., Deshler, Warner, Schumaker, Alley, & Clark, 1984). One of its primary purposes is to instruct both students and their teachers in the use of study and learning strategies that will facilitate the acquisition and retention of content material such as science and social studies. Resource teachers who are trained and certified by the program developers can provide training in turn to content area teachers.

The Learning Strategies program benefits not only students who receive resource services; it is also believed to have a beneficial effect on most students in the content classroom. This makes it highly desirable when selecting inservice packages. Only in cases of students with unusual and severe disabilities would an inservice effort be directed at helping just one student. Most inservice programs should effect both an intervention and a prevention function.

Many prepared inservice programs require that those who teach them become "certified trainers." The requirement is not unique to remedial and special education, but holds in other areas as well (e.g., Ferguson-Florrisant Writers Project, 1990). Program developers understandably do not want their program to gain the reputation of being ineffective due to incomplete understanding and implementation. Resource teachers should be alert to opportunities to become certified trainers in a variety of areas.

We have noted previously that the resource teacher should not become an aide to help manage groups or to take responsibility for a new instructional program or procedure located within the mainstream classroom. In these cases, demonstration teaching or modeling may be the best way to assist classroom teachers in assuming increased responsibility for implementing recommended programs within their own settings. Demonstration teaching or modeling is appropriate when the classroom teacher needs to master a specific, critical instructional technique. It is not enough to tell or advise when mastery is the goal; the resource teacher should be prepared to model the instructional behaviors of interest.

For example, the instructional variable of *guided practice* (e.g., Silbert, Carnine, & Stein, 1990) or the correct incorporation of manipulatives in *Mathematics Their Way* (Baratta-Lorton, 1976) seem rather straightforward to those who already understand them. Their truly effective use by someone who is just learning them, however, may require a formal modeling process. Demonstration within the mainstream or other classroom may be informal, but it is more likely to be effective if both teachers follow a formal procedure. Resource teachers can use the checklist in Figure 5.1 to provide a general plan for designing demonstration lessons. We describe this plan below.

1. *Data/observation base for needs assessment*
   a. The exact means of data collection depends on the behavior of interest (e.g., examination of permanent products for comments, or observations made during instruction).
   b. Key the data collection or observation to teacher behaviors that support learning for a specific student or group—for example, changing the nature of teacher feedback to students as they miscue during oral reading.
   c. The ''need'' may be directed by an administrator and centered around teacher evaluation. However, the resource teacher should not become involved in what is more appropriately an administrative function. An exception to this rule is the case of a teacher-peer evaluation program.

2. *Joint specification of skills or behaviors to be demonstrated.* This phase allows for the development of a matching evaluation plan, and also limits the involvement of the resource teacher in the classroom program. Otherwise, there may be a tendency to stray beyond the ''contracted'' effort.

1. Data/observation base for needs assessment
2. Joint specification of skills or behaviors to be demonstrated
3. How the behavior will be demonstrated or taught:
   a. incorporated into ongoing instruction, or
   b. taught as a separate unit
4. Lesson plan with teacher cue sheet
5. Plan for introducing to the teacher
6. Schedule of lessons and consultation times and days
7. Means of "reinstating" the teaching behavior(s)
8. Conference and replanning
9. Cycle repetition to this point if necessary; include cue sheet
10. Teacher and demonstration teacher share lesson responsibility with or without a cue sheet
11. Repeat process until teacher has reached agreed on mastery level
12. Plan responsibility for maintaining vigilance
13. Plan reinforcement for completion of the process

Figure 5.1. General plan for demonstration teaching.

3. *How the behavior will be demonstrated or taught (i.e., incorporated into ongoing instruction or taught as a separate unit).* Wherever possible, incorporate the behavior into ongoing lessons. This is especially important when the behavior *should* be incorporated into the curriculum anyway (e.g., guided practice).

4. *Lesson plan with teacher cue sheet*
   a. The lesson plan format assures that the lesson will be focused.
   b. The teacher cue sheet notes what the teacher should be looking for/at, and has space for recording the observation of the demonstration teacher and for checking off, commenting on, or questioning what was observed.

5. *Plan for introducing to the teacher.* If the teacher has not been involved in planning, then devise a tactful means of introducing the lesson goal.

6. *Schedule of lessons and consultation times and days.* Specific times need to be scheduled, rather than hoping for a "good" time.

7. *Means of "reinstating" the teaching behavior(s).* Video- or audiotape the demonstration teaching so that both teachers can discuss specific instances or examples. Both intended and unintended happenings can be reviewed.

8. *Conference and replanning.* The conference is critical for clarifying and extending understanding. Replanning should focus on what to look or listen for next time.

9. *Cycle repetition to this point if necessary.* The number of trials will depend on the complexity of the behavior and the ability of the teacher to acquire the skill. Include the cue sheet each time the sessions are recycled.

10. *Teacher and demonstration teacher share lesson responsibility with or without a cue sheet.* Shift responsibility as quickly as possible to the person who will continue ongoing instruction.

11. *Repeat process until teacher has reached agreed upon mastery level.* Usually, when the teacher has the "idea," the resource teacher can be on call for coaching when there are questions, or for assuring maintenance of the behavior.

12. *Plan responsibility for maintaining vigilance.* Both the means (e.g., taping) and the person(s) should be scheduled to assure that the behavior maintains. Unless the behavior is one of high continuing priority by the teacher, it will decay quickly without vigilance.

13. *Plan reinforcement for completion of the process.* Reinforcement that is tied to student progress that results from the teacher's new behavior is especially important. In addition, arranging for recognition by someone who is highly regarded by the teacher is simply a nice thing to do.

The process just described is time-consuming, so it should be used only for critical instructional behaviors. It is a powerful tool of behavior change that can actually save everyone's time when considering the continuing expenditure of human resources needed to remedy the unfortunate results of a missing or improper instructional component.

Following Up on Recommendations

Every time resource teachers make a specific recommendation that teachers use a series of drills, techniques for managing undesirable behavior, or strategies of any type, they need to visit the classrooms to see that the teachers are willing and able to implement the suggestions properly. The teachers may not know how to translate the recommendations into actual classroom practice, especially if the suggestion requires reorganization of the instructional program. By following up the recommendations they have made, resource teachers can provide needed assistance or find out why the recommendations have been ignored.

Another important reason for doing follow-ups is to determine the validity of the recommendations that have been made. Resource teachers who assess students, who prescribe programs of instruction for other teachers to use, and who fail to monitor the operation in the classroom will never know the consequences of their suggestions; they are operating in a vacuum and with impunity.

Problem Solving and Collaborative Consultation

We have stressed the importance of formal procedures in collaborative consultation, because they make it possible to be mutually goal directed, and because with them it is possible for two or more people with diverse interests and backgrounds to troubleshoot a common process until it results in satisfactory outcome for their client (student). The collaborative consultation process is a formal means of resolving important problems that arise before or after a student is referred for special services of any kind. The problems may relate either to a student's instructional program or to obtaining and using well the resources that enable the student to benefit from instruction (i.e., related services). Problem solving is the central focus of collaborative consultation.

Example of a Problem-Solving Curriculum

Groups have many choices of problem-solving models, but the most comprehensive training program for problem solving through collaborative consultation is *Collaboration in the Schools: An Inservice and Preservice Curriculum for Teachers, Support Staff, and Administrators* [Learner's Booklet] (West, Idol, & Cannon, 1989). It is designed as a training curriculum "to develop essential communicative/interactive, and problem-solving skills in all concerned professionals" (Introduction). The curriculum itself centers around 47 skills arranged in eight areas of concentration:

1. Consultation theory models
2. Research on consultation theory, training, and practice
3. Personal characteristics
4. Interactive communication
5. Collaborative problem solving
6. Systems change
7. Equity issues and values/belief systems
8. Evaluation of consultation effectiveness

We recommend the entire program, but illustrate its general format by focusing on Cluster 5, Collaborative Problem Solving. Modules 27 through 35 of this skill area concern nine specific skills that the developers define in behavioral terms as shown below.

Regular and special educators engaging in collaborative consultation will:

- Skill #27. Recognize that successful and lasting solutions require commonality of goals and collaboration throughout all phases of the problem-solving process.
- Skill #28. Develop a variety of data collection techniques for problem identification and clarification.
- Skill #29. Generate viable alternatives through brainstorming techniques characterized by active listening, nonjudgmental responding, and appropriate reframing.
- Skill #30. Evaluate intervention alternatives to anticipate possible consequences, narrow and combine choices, and assign priorities.
- Skill #31. Integrate solutions into a flexible, feasible, and easily implemented Action Plan relevant to all persons affected by the problem.
- Skill #32. Adopt a ''pilot'' problem-solving attitude, recognizing that adjustments to the Action Plan are to be expected.
- Skill #33. Remain available throughout implementation for support, modeling, and/or assistance in modification of the Action Plan.
- Skill #34. Redesign, maintain, or discontinue interventions using data-based evaluation.
- Skill #35. Utilize observation, feedback, and interviewing skills to increase objectivity and mutuality throughout the problem-solving process. (West et al., 1989, pp. 278–279)

Within these skill areas the training activities include practice with using techniques and formats such as self-assessments, recording and summarizing data, and process checklists. We show a reproduction of the Problem-Solving Worksheet and Action Plan from Modules 30, 31, and 32 (see Figure 5.2).

The input materials of this program include case studies built around exemplars from traditional curricula and behavioral assessments. The inputs and exemplars, as well as the range of assessment techniques, can be modified by a skilled trainer to represent the local curriculum. The problem-solving process itself is constant.

Regardless of the specific program a collaborative consultation team might wish to use, the resource teacher should receive specific preservice or inservice training in its appropriate implementation. It is preferable if those who work together receive the training together, but if this is not possible, the resource teacher can provide instruction and modeling of many good consultation skills such as the problem-solving component just described.

Metacognition and Problem Solving
As the problem-solving process becomes more readily describable, it makes general classroom teachers more effective as problem solvers. One of the more recent examples of this direction is the long-term work of Pugach and Johnson (e.g., 1990),

PROBLEM-SOLVING WORKSHEET
[Modules 30, 31, and 32]

Resource Teacher _____

Classroom/Content Teacher _____

Date _____

Problem:

Details: _____

Alternative Solutions	Possible Consequences	Priority
1.		___
2.		___
3.		___
4.		___
5.		___
6		___
7.		___
8.		___

Solution to Be Tried First:

Adapted from: Ann Knackendoffel, Institute for Research in Learning Disabilities, University of Kansas.

Figure 5.2. Forms from *Collaboration in the Schools* (West, Idol, & Cannon, 1989). Reprinted with permission.

PROBLEM-SOLVING WORKSHEET, P. 2

ACTION PLAN

Implementation Steps	When	Who
_____	_____	_____
_____	_____	_____
_____	_____	_____
_____	_____	_____
_____	_____	_____
_____	_____	_____
_____	_____	_____
_____	_____	_____
_____	_____	_____
_____	_____	_____

How Will the Plan Be Monitored?

_____

_____

_____

_____

How Will Progress Be Evaluated?

_____

_____

_____

_____

_____

Date and Time of Next Appointment

_____

_____

Figure 5.2. *Continued*

who have used metacognitive training through collaborative consultation as a means of developing internal thought processes and self-regulation of teachers' problem-solving thinking as they (the teachers) "differentiate between problematic student situations they could accommodate effectively and those they could not" (Pugach & Johnson, 1990, p. 186). This sounds quite complicated, but it simply means that two teachers work together in a problem-solving mode to decide which students really need to be referred for special services and which ones do not. One teacher, known as the Initiating Teacher (the one being trained), and the Facilitating Teacher (the one doing the training) initially work together within a framework that involves:

1. Clarifying questions about the student or the problem
2. Summarizing what is known about the problematic situation
3. Generating interventions and predicting their relative merits
4. Evaluating the interventions selected and tried with the student

At each of these stages, the Facilitating Teacher and the Initiating Teacher have a dialogue to discuss the value of the options they have regarding the instructional problem (Johnson & Pugach, 1991). Table 5.1 shows the nature of this dialogue. The ultimate goal is to get the teacher to "talk to her/himself" using the type of "script" shown in Table 5.1, until the entire process is internalized so that it becomes an automatic reflective behavior. "In this manner, teachers might be encouraged to rely less on specialists for so many classroom problems and gain confidence in their own strength as professionals" (Pugach & Johnson, 1990, p. 187).

CONCLUDING COMMENTS

When engaged in consulting activities, the resource teacher must be very percep-tive about sensitivities and possible adverse reactions of regular classroom teachers. Smokoski (1972) stated that teachers do not want other teachers coming to them and saying, in effect:

> "You have failed with this child and I have some secrets which I'll be glad to share with you which will make you a better teacher and which will better enable you to handle all the children in your classroom." Teachers, it seems, don't want to be considered failures. (p. 6)

Of course, few resource teachers would be so impolitic as to express such opin-ions to another teacher. Yet, to some extent these sentiments are implicit in the consulting situation. As a result, resource teachers who consult must guard against incipient friction between themselves and the teachers with whom they work or collaborate.

Table 5.1. *Format for Metacognitive Training in Reflective Problem Solving*

Stage	Initiating Teacher Role	Facilitating Teacher Role
I Clarifying Questions	a. Brings brief, written description of problem to session	Explicit, verbal rehearsal of questioning strategies
	b. Generates and responds to questions aloud to clarify all aspects of the problem	Provides guidance by suggesting different or expanded areas for questioning, using the format: ''Is there a question you might ask about ____?''
		Aimed at broad perspective
	Continue until all relevant issues are exhausted.	
II Summary	Three steps: a. A description of the patterns of student behavior b. Teacher's response to and feelings about the situation c. Identification of variables over which the teacher has some control	
	Consolidating information and thinking about which variables might lend themselves to intervention	Describes requisite parts of the summary.
		Assists partner as he or she describes requisite parts of the summary.
		Assists partner in checking that all parts have been included, and that behavior patterns and classroom variables are consistent.
III Intervention and Prediction	Teachers generate at least three interventions, taking into account variables from the previous step. Predicts potential outcomes for each intervention, and publicly states prediction.	
IV Evaluation		Provides prompts for self-monitoring concerning a. practicality and b. process and outcome data

Note. From ''Peer Collaboration: Accommodating Students with Mild Learning and Behavior Problems'' by L. J. Johnson and M. Pugach, 1991, *Exceptional Children, 57*(5), pp. 454–461. Reprinted with permission of The Council for Exceptional Children.

The emphasis that we give to the consulting role in the resource program model is long overdue in special education. Most teacher-training institutions have been slow to include such skills among their competencies; until the advent of the resource programs, public schools had no practical instructionally oriented arrangement that lent itself conveniently to providing consulting services to teachers. In any event, schools in which the resource teachers are permitted to perform only two duties (to assess and to remediate students' problems) are overlooking a profitable avenue for improving the education of both students and teachers. In fact, in selecting resource teachers, one primary consideration might be their ability to implement tactfully the consulting aspects of the resource program.

We recommend that the resource teacher study two books that describe consultation functions in education. They are both practical, giving many examples of specific intervention techniques as well as information about consultation. Both are based on behavioral principles, yet they are different enough that they complement each other.

- Heron, T. E., & Harris, K. C. (1993). *The educational consultant: Helping professionals, parents, and mainstreamed students.* Austin, TX: PRO-ED.
- Idol, L., Nevin, A., & Paolucci-Whitcomb, P. (1993). *Collaborative consultation.* Austin, TX: PRO-ED.

For additional basic information regarding consultation models other than those we have mentioned, we refer you to:

- Parker, C. A. (1985). *Psychological consultation: Helping teachers meet special needs.* Minneapolis: Leadership Training Institute/Special Education, University of Minnesota.

Finally, the Instructor's Manual and the Learner's Booklet of the West et al. (1989) training program also contain many current references to books and articles (a) regarding the research base for collaborative consultation and (b) further explaining consultation procedures.

Organizing and Managing a Resource Program

The actual details involved in establishing/refining and operating resource programs (the nuts and bolts) are discussed in Part III. The information presented is drawn primarily from our own experiences in implementing and supervising the resource model in the schools, as well as the written observations of others who also have had direct practical experience in resource program operations. Readers can therefore determine how we and other resource administrators and teachers have handled a wide variety of matters associated with the operation of resource arrangements. The matters include enlisting support of school staff and parents for the resource effort, grading student progress, selecting pupils for service, and other activities involved in successfully managing a resource program on a daily basis. This practical information has been organized into six chapters that deal specifically with (a) working with school staff, parents, and the community; (b) equipping the resource room; (c) referral and selection procedures; (d) managing the program; (e) the Individualized Education Program; and (f) homework and grading.

Chapter 6

Working with
School Staff, Parents,
and the Community

One of the more difficult responsibilities that the resource teacher faces is maintaining effective communication with others who have a need to understand what is occurring in the resource room. Communication between the resource teacher and the school staff is critical, as is effective communication between the resource teacher and the students' parents/guardians. Public relations is also an important element of effective communication that the resource teacher should not overlook. Organizations like the parent-teacher association, the Junior League, and so on, are often rich in support for resource programs if the resource teacher will take the time to inform them as to the functions and needs of the program. Support people, in the form of students, aides, mentors, volunteers, other teachers, and parents, expand the effectiveness of the resource teacher and of the program. After reviewing some problems in working with people, we offer suggestions to the resource teacher on how to communicate effectively with (a) the school staff, (b) the parents or guardians of the students, and (c) the community. The chapter concludes with a consideration of the tasks that the resource teacher may delegate to other people.

SOME DIFFICULTIES IN WORKING WITH SCHOOL STAFF AND PARENTS

Witt, Miller, McIntyre, and Smith (1984) noted that one of the most common problems encountered in maintaining a resource program is insufficient communication between the resource teacher and the school staff and parents. The problem of how to prepare and involve teachers and parents for the student's involvement in the resource program, as well as how to maintain productive communication during the student's time in the resource program, is paramount. McNamara (1989) surveyed general educators as to information regarding the resource program that they would find useful. This survey revealed that general educators were not particularly satisfied with the information that was typically provided about the resource program. Further, it was noted that most educators believed that they were not presented with enough specific information. Although resource teachers should realize that it is not feasible to provide all general educators with all of the specific information that they need, they should be aware that most general educators are interested in the resource program, and that requests for information by the classroom teacher are necessary for effective functioning of the program. McNamara (1989) stressed the idea that effective communication between the resource teacher and the classroom teacher is essential for the success of the student. He noted that without the proper preparation of and communication with classroom teachers, ''the efforts expended in the confines of the resource room will be for naught'' (p. 112).

Effective communication may be initially difficult to establish because, for reasons that may not be fully known or articulated, some teachers will be reluctant to work with resource teachers. Also, some teachers may be unwilling to modify their programs to work effectively with resource students. Further, some administrative support personnel may have negative attitudes toward resource programs; perhaps in the past they were oversold on the merits of special programs and have been disappointed with the results. To begin positive communication, as well as to attempt to dispel any preexisting prejudices against the resource program, Brown (1982) suggested a 2-week grace period at the beginning of the school year.

> In some situations, the resource program may be allowed a two or three week grace period. Resource teachers, then, should take the time to: (a) explain carefully to the school staff just what the purpose of the grace period is and what activities will be undertaken in planning and organizing the resource program and (b) assess pupils that are likely to need resource support during the school year. Of course, the resource teacher should be visibly busy at all times, especially during this initial start-up period. (p. 6)

Parents have also been known to resist resource programs. A few parents of students with disabilities may prefer segregated instructional support because they fear their daughter or son may not receive the amount of quality instruction they need in the general classroom. Some parents may resist a particular resource model, such as the cross-categorical program, because they prefer a categorical model, with the teacher trained in a specific disability area. Other parents may be reluctant to having their child removed from the general program for even a portion of the day. Finally, some parents of students in the general classrooms may be reluctant to have their children educated with others who have learning and behavioral problems. Or they may believe that too much teacher time is taken by these students, and as a result, the quality of instruction of their own children may suffer. Consequently, principals, resource teachers, and other responsible professionals need to work thoroughly with the school staff and parents and make every effort to enlist their support. Some strategies for accomplishing this task follow.

WORKING WITH THE SCHOOL STAFF

The major responsibility for working with the staff of a school in which a resource program is operating should be assumed by individual building principals and by resource teachers. Local education agency personnel probably will also assist in this effort in many ways. At the very least, agency personnel should provide principals and resource teachers with the latest written guidelines that describe clearly the rules of the resource operation. These guidelines will help ensure that the operation of the program is consistent with the intent of the funding organization (the local, state, and/or federal agency) and with existing district policies.

We cannot stress enough the importance of these guidelines. Educators are increasingly being held accountable for their activities in providing special services to students. Consequently, principals and resource teachers must be familiar with all regulations that pertain to the resource program.

Once the guidelines are understood, principals and resource teachers can begin to plan the agenda for a faculty meeting called annually to discuss the resource program. The specific information that is presented can be drawn from this book, from related literature, and from a set of written guidelines about the resource program. The best time to conduct the staff inservice meeting is during the first few days of the school year. Topics that could be included in this session are:

1. The continued need for a resource program
2. The resource program model
3. The roles of the resource teacher
4. The roles of the general classroom teachers
5. Referral and pupil selection guidelines
6. Management practices in the program's operation
7. Support services and materials available through the resource room
8. Times that the resource teacher is available to meet with staff

These topics should be presented to the school staff in as interesting and enthusiastic a manner as possible. Nonnegotiable rules and regulations established by district or state policy should be delineated. If possible, some flexibility should be allowed for staff of an individual school to select some of its own operating procedures.

Small-group discussions can give the teachers in the school an opportunity to develop some of the negotiable aspects of the program. After familiarizing the faculty with the operations of the program, the principal and resource teacher can suggest that small groups be formed and that recommendations concerning the operation of the resource program be suggested by each group. This technique often results in useful suggestions and enlists support for an understanding of the resource program. A suggested discussion guide is presented in Table 6.1.

The left side of the table lists some tentative activities of the resource teacher. The right side of the table lists tentative activities of the general staff. Both groups should be encouraged to discuss each block of activities and to add to or delete from the list as well as to specify ways in which these activities can be accomplished.

It is important that the principal and resource teacher be sincere in asking for suggestions. They need to consider carefully the recommendations made by the school staff and deal fairly with them. Therefore, the nonnegotiable aspects of the resource program should first be carefully stated. Also, the benefits of a resource program should be presented optimistically and realistically. The program should not be oversold, however.

A most important consideration in introducing resource support is any potential need for the teacher to modify his or her behavior toward the resourced students (i.e., whether any classroom modifications will be expected). Riegel (1983) suggested ways of discussing, evaluating, and either implementing or modifying classrooms for resourced students. He initially pointed out that whereas the resource teacher (who is the one suggesting the classroom interventions) works with students on a one-to-one or on a small-group basis within a flexible curriculum, the classroom teacher often works with students in large groups teaching preestablished curriculum units. When considering this, it is easy to see how the classroom teacher might consider interventions implausible, whereas the resource teacher might consider the classroom teacher uncooperative for not carrying those interventions out in the classroom. To avoid these misunderstandings, the resource teacher and the classroom teacher should work together in the student's best interests to find educational strategies that will be effective as well as realistically implemented in the classroom. Appendix F presents some of the most effective and commonly suggested classroom interventions, along with many of the complaints that classroom teachers voice regarding the feasibility of these interventions. In the last column, Riegel suggests solutions to many of the complaints, thus making the interventions plausible for the general classroom.

By the end of the first inservice session, the school staff members should be fairly well informed about the resource program. They also should have made some

Table 6.1. *Discussion Guide for Setting Up Mutual Expectations with Resource Teacher and School Staff*

Tentative Activities of Resource Teacher	*Concomitant Activities of Regular Staff*
(priorities to be agreed on)	

A. *With the Student*
   1. Detailed diagnostic assessment with recommendations for programming
   2. Monitor for validity of recommendations. Assist with implementation if necessary.
   3. Consultation in regard to either:
      a. Intensive programs for resource room students
      b. Modest intervention for students without resource room enrollment
   4. Direct work with a student or a group of students
   5. Observation in regular classroom to determine needs and generalization of resource room behaviors
   6. Consultation regarding grades, grade placement, teacher placement and schedules, and related items

A. *With the Student*
   1. Try recommendations
   2. Request assistance with implementation
   3. Provide feedback on validity or modifications
   4. Refer new students when questions occur; or
   5. Request consultation/observation
   6. Attend staffings
   7. Modify grading/credit system if necessary
   8. Encourage observations by resource teacher to determine generalization of behaviors

B. *With School Staff*
   1. Inservice in regard to management, curriculum, or organization
      a. By vehicles such as
         (1) Modeling—involves fading out so that teacher can carry on the target techniques independently
         (2) Direct teaching where appropriate
         (3) Participation in team planning
         (4) Literature distribution
   2. Feedback to the total staff of high-frequency problems for consideration of preventive measures

B. *With School Staff*
   1. Try suggestions
   2. Provide information in regard to the operation of the total resource room program
   3. Consider/generate preventive strategies
   4. Participate in team teaching when new techniques are being introduced

Table 6.1. *Continued*

Tentative Activities of Resource Teacher	*Concomitant Activities of Regular Staff*
(priorities to be agreed on)	
C. *With Parents*	C. *With Parents*
1. Information about the program	1. Participate in liaison with home/school program for continuity
2. Liaison concerning the individual student home/school program	
3. Teaching: management techniques	
D. *General*	D. *General*
1. Schedule or participate in staffings with appropriate personnel	1. Ask questions when you wonder ''Why?''
2. Set up a program evaluation plan	2. Participate in appropriate staffings
3. Provide accountability through	3. Provide necessary data on curriculum or student
a. Time/activity log	
b. Logs on student progress or interventions tried	

suggestions about specific activities for resource teachers to follow. These activities should be carefully recorded at the meeting for the resource teacher to deal fairly with them in refining his or her specific responsibilities during the months of operating the program in the school. Later, the principal and resource teacher should discuss with the faculty the suggestions that were incorporated into the program and those that were not. The reasons that some of the suggestions were not implemented should be explained.

Subsequent or periodic inservice sessions are likely to be needed throughout the school year. Resource teachers should not, however, take up too much valuable time at staff meetings discussing the resource program. Small-group meetings, written communications, and consultation on a one-to-one basis are effective ways to deal with changes, modifications, or problems that are likely to occur.

On a few occasions, principals and resource teachers may find a great deal of resistance, ranging from passive responses (such as apathy or noncommunication) to overt aggressive responses (perhaps verbalized hostility or spoken refusal to cooperate). Almost every resource teacher will find one or two colleagues in the school who respond in such a manner. These cases can be handled on a one-to-one basis with attempts to determine the problem and to delineate and try proposed solutions. In some instances, large numbers of the faculty will be negative toward the program. This negativism may indicate the presence of a serious problem within the school that has little to do with the resource program itself.

Some of these problem schools are characterized by teacher dissatisfaction with their jobs, lack of creativity, complacency, conformity, frustration, and/or poor interpersonal relationships among the faculty and staff. In these schools, because most innovations or new programs meet resistance, the resource program may also come under attack. This attack is a reflection of the school climate and not of the resource program. Some school climates, for either obvious or hidden reasons, are generally unhealthy; other schools, however, have a lively and accepting atmosphere. Sullivan (1987) developed a list of ingredients that are necessary for a wholesome school climate.

Learning Atmosphere

1. Teachers must have opportunities to try to develop an awareness of the context in which schools operate; a concept that is paramount to an understanding of the intricacies of the teaching/learning process.
2. Teachers should be provided with sustained opportunities to clearly identify, discuss, explore, develop, and operationalize their beliefs in their area of discipline.
3. Rules, regulations, and procedures should be established realistically so that students can develop self-discipline by internalizing and interpreting them.
4. The curriculum should be constructed and implemented in such a manner as to address contemporary critical issues, the foremost of which is self-acceptance.

Communication Procedures

1. Students and teachers should be allowed to speak out about their concerns and interests. Provision of a forum for the lively exploration and exchange of ideas rests on a belief in academic freedom. The end result of such discussions should be an understanding, appreciation, and acceptance of others' viewpoints.
2. Students need to be communicated with about their performance levels in a manner that provides a realistic assessment of their efforts to date, and encourages them to seek to improve.
3. The learning environment should radiate many opportunities for learning through the use of displays, props, or other materials that enhance self-concept.
4. Motivational activities should be provided to stimulate and satisfy students' appetite for learning. They should encourage independence and self-discipline.

Pedagogical Pressure

1. Educators should determine the correct dosage of frustration so as to provide enough stress to stretch and challenge, but not to chronically discourage students.

2. Parents, students, and the instructional staff should have periodic opportunities to discuss expectations for students and their respective duties and responsibilities.

3. When students perform as expected, they should be recognized and rewarded for their accomplishments.

Healthy schools are high in personal satisfaction of teachers for their jobs, effective learning on the part of the student, good faculty interpersonal relationships, and a willingness by most to incorporate innovations into the school and into their classrooms. If resource teachers find themselves in unhealthy schools, they are likely to meet with little success in fulfilling their roles unless something is done to change the school climate.

Many professionals have approached the modification of school climate through organizational problem solving. Many problem-solving techniques might be used. For example, the nominal group technique (NGT) of Delbecq, Van de Ven, and Gustafson (1975) has been used in many school and mental health organizations to provide a highly structured and effective means of conflict resolution. The NGT meeting elicits a greater flow of ideas than would be found in traditional meetings. Further, it brings the problem or the task to closure and also ensures the satisfaction of participants. It eliminates the domination of a group by high-status or verbally aggressive members and provides a fair method of mathematically ranking ideas or tentative solutions. The NGT process is explained at length in Delbecq et al. (1975). The book also describes the use of NGT in various planning situations that could be useful to the resource teacher.

Kaiser (1985) provided a thorough description of many communication, decision-making, and problem-solving techniques. He further provided a condensation of the six steps included within NGT:

> *Step 1—Silent generation of ideas in writing.*
> In this step, each member of the group is asked to write down ideas and thoughts related to the issue being considered. The benefits to this step are that members can think freely, interruptions are avoided, undue focusing on a particular idea or content area is minimized, competition, status pressure and conformity are avoided, the group remains problem centered, and the group avoids selecting a choice prematurely.
>
> *Step 2—Round-robin recording of ideas.*
> Each member is asked to provide one idea until all of the ideas are processed. The group leader records each item on a blackboard or flip-chart. Benefits include: equal participation, increase in problem mindedness, depersonalization, tolerance for conflicting ideas, and a written record.
>
> *Step 3—Serial discussion for clarification.*
> Each idea is discussed in turn. During this process, each item can potentially receive adequate discussion, the logic behind arguments can be given, and differences of opinion can be noted without undue argumentation.

Step 4—Preliminary vote on item importance.
Each member independently rank orders, in his or her opinion, the most salient items. From the compiled total list, the most salient items emerge, ranked in order, based on the total frequency of each item.

Step 5—Discussion of the preliminary vote.
Each member is allowed a brief period to comment on the selected items. This allows for discussion of those items that received unusually high or low rankings.

Step 6—Final vote.
The group combines individual judgment into a group decision using a mathematical procedure. (pp. 464–465)

In *Interpersonal Conflict Resolution* Filley (1975) suggested methods for separating problems from persons to turn conflict into creative problem solving. Goal attainment scaling (Garwick, 1978) is a technique that focuses staff efforts on improving the school climate and on measuring progress toward this goal. Goal attainment scaling is a problem-focused set of procedures and a measuring device to be used over time when people from different disciplines, roles, or persuasions must work together.

Strategies for organizational problem solving are becoming an important part of the consulting aspect of resource teaching. Most resource teachers, however, have not been trained in these techniques. Even those who have may have limited success unless the other teachers and the administrators are willing to cooperate. Most formal techniques are adjuncts or crisis tools to use along with the informal but powerful political process. Further, resource teachers are not responsible for the school operations as a whole. This is the responsibility of the building principal, and that person should assume the leadership in the use of organizational problem solving. Resource teachers, however, might point out the need for organizational problem solving and actively support principals in the use of formal techniques in the effort.

WORKING WITH PARENTS/GUARDIANS

In some schools, all parents are automatically advised of any programs implemented in the school and of any major changes or improvements in existing programs that might affect the education of their children. In other schools, only those parents who are actively involved in the operation of the school are notified, such as officers in the local parent-teacher association. Some schools have no policies about notifying parents of program or curricular modifications. The resource teacher should ask the principal if there are any policies governing this matter, and together they should decide what information will be transmitted to parents and how this will be accomplished.

Communication with parents is almost always advisable. For example, if the resource program is to replace a self-contained special education class, the parents of the students to be affected by the change must be consulted. The goals of the program should be described to them carefully; they should be told just how the changes will enhance the education of their children; and their approval should be obtained. In cases where the noncategorical or specific skills resource model is being implemented, the initial notification of parents may not be necessary, though it would certainly be desirable.

Marion (1981) suggested several other points that teachers should tell parents. Teachers should explain why a particular resource model was selected; discuss the source of funding; describe the ages and types of students to be served in the program; and discuss the certification(s) of the teachers as well as their preparation for the position. Finally, the parents' involvement in decision making, program planning, evaluation, and classroom instruction should be agreed upon.

Problems occasionally arise from working closely with parents; however, we believe that a comfortable working relationship between teachers and parents of students with learning and behavioral problems is desirable. Consequently, this book offers throughout many recommendations concerning parental involvement. Some suggestions are mandated by recent court decisions; others are based on the idea that parental involvement in the educational process is a necessity if the difficulties of certain students are to be ameliorated.

Most parents or guardians of students with problems tend to be enthusiastic about the resource program from the beginning, so there is little problem in enlisting their support and involvement. A request by telephone or letter usually will bring these parents to the school for a meeting that will explain how they can help. Occasionally, however, a few parents or guardians will resist the program and/or the resource teacher and will avoid becoming involved.

Resource teachers should seek out parents or guardians and ask them to help implement and maintain the resource efforts. Parental help is important because it can (a) minimize any parental criticism about the program (people are hesitant to criticize programs they participate in or have had ample opportunity to provide input for); (b) seek their approval to provide resource support to their child; (c) enlist their support and possibly active involvement in implementing the instructional plan; (d) obtain their constructive comments regarding program improvements; and (e) help the resource teacher maintain current information about the student's life and changing needs. In this section we make some suggestions for seeking parental and guardian involvement and make some recommendations about how to communicate effectively with parents.

Seeking Parental or Guardian Involvement

The first step in seeking parental or guardian support and participation is to notify them that their child is being considered for resource services. The procedures involved in the initial contact will vary from school to school. In some schools, principals, home-and-school coordinators, guidance counselors, or other staff make the initial contact with parents by telephone or by visiting in the home. The resource teacher will need to ask the building principal about the local policies regarding this matter.

The resource teacher usually is responsible for notifying parents. The initial contact with parents might be by telephone with a conference following or by letter requesting a conference. The letter should be typed on school stationery and bear the principal's signature as a cosigner.

Before writing the letter, the resource teacher should consult both the school records and other faculty members to obtain some information about the parents or guardians, including their awareness of the student's problem and their past experiences with the school. An example will illustrate the importance in getting information about the parents. Let us say that a child, Margaret Farnan, is living with an aunt who has a different surname. A letter sent to Mr. and Mrs. Farnan could be embarrassing for all involved. Another undesirable situation to avoid is sending a letter in English to parents who cannot read that language. In preparing a letter, the resource teacher should keep several points in mind. First, the letter should be individually written; form letters should never be used.

Second, the use of esoteric or pseudoprofessional jargon should be avoided in the letter. For example, if Margaret is having trouble in arithmetic, the resource teacher should say so; he or she should not write that the child has trouble in conceptualizing multiplication as union of sets or in mastering the role of zero. If the student is misbehaving in class, the resource teacher should give examples of the undesirable behavior rather than writing that "Margaret is suspected of being emotionally disturbed because of her hyperactivity." The reason a student has been referred for resource help should be stated simply, accurately, and in plain language.

Third, fear-provoking words should not be used. Such ill-defined terms include *serious, severe, critical, mentally retarded, brain damaged, emotionally disturbed,* and *dyslexic*. Instead, the letter should contain a clear statement that the student is having some difficulty in school and that a special program is available.

Finally, the letter should be friendly in tone, short in length, clear in purpose, and contain some mechanism whereby the parents or guardians may respond. A sample letter about Margaret Farnan, who was referred to the reading resource program, is shown in Figure 6.1.

In most cases, a letter such as this will produce the desired results: The parents or guardian will visit the school to discuss the child. Occasionally, however, this will not happen. The form may not be returned, the parents or guardians may work during the school hours, or they many not be able to leave the home due to health problems or because there are small children in the home. If the form is not returned, another letter should be sent. If there is still no response, a telephone call to the home is in order. Finally, if neither strategy works, the matter should be turned over to the principal, the special education administrator, a social worker, or other appropriate school personnel for a home visit.

(School letterhead)

(date)

Ms. Attie Lyles
(Address)
(City, State, Zip)

Dear Ms. Lyles:

Your niece, Margaret, is having some difficulty with her reading. Fortunately, we have a program in our school that we believe will provide her with the help she needs.

To provide Margaret with the best possible program, we need your cooperation and permission. Could you please come to the school for a short visit, at which time you can talk about the program with Ms. Ruth Angel? Any day during the week between 8 a.m. and 4 p.m. will be fine. If you have questions before that time, please call 494-3765, asking for Mr. Goff.

Please specify the time that you are available to attend the meeting on the form that is at the bottom of this letter, place the form in the attached envelope, and return it to Ms. Angel by mail or by Margaret. Thank you very much. We're looking forward to meeting you in person very soon.

Sincerely,

_____

John Goff, Principal

_____

Ruth Angel, Resource Teacher

— —

Dear Ms. Angel:
I can come to the school on _____ *(date)*

at _____ *(time).*

_____

Ms. Lyles

Comments if any:

— —

Figure 6.1. Sample letter to parents or guardians.

Whenever someone other than the resource teacher is to make the contact with the parents or guardians, the resource teacher should tell him or her all that is known about the student and acquaint him or her thoroughly with the resource program. This information will enable the contact person to speak knowledgeably about both the program and the student. The resource teacher also will want to stress that he or she must eventually meet with the parents or guardians and to request that the contact person arrange such a meeting. Finally, the resource teacher will have to state specifically, perhaps in writing, what he or she wants to be accomplished during this initial meeting.

Communicating with Parents and Guardians

Teachers often view a meeting with parents or guardians as an opportunity to tell them what is "wrong" with their child and what progress the child has or has not made recently. In other words, teachers frequently talk to the parents in a grade card fashion: "Here is what your child is doing in math and here is how your child behaves in school." The parents want this information. But such a meeting also should give the parents a chance to contribute their observations and feelings about their children. They often have valuable information that the resource teacher can use to understand the student better and to develop a more appropriate instructional plan. The resource teacher therefore should plan carefully for the meeting and be prepared to be an active listener.

General Guidelines for Working with Parents

Resource teachers should attempt to build a trusting relationship with the parents or guardians of their students. Margolis and Brannigan (1986) discussed fundamental strategies that the resource teacher should implement to facilitate effective communication with parents.

1. *Accept parents as they are and do not try to induce fundamental changes.* An attempt on the part of the resource teacher to change the parents often abrades the relationship. Once the parents trust the teacher, they often seek advice as to what changes they could make to help their child.
2. *Listen carefully and empathetically for the cognitive and emotional content of the parents' messages.* The resource teacher should be an attentive listener.
3. *Help parents feel comfortable and be willing to share information and resources with them.* A conversational style helps parents feel comfortable. Sharing information builds trust and helps parents see

themselves and the resource teacher as a team committed to helping their child. Evading requests for information has just the opposite effect: It forces parents to see the resource teacher as an external force rather than a team member.

4. *Always prepare for meetings and be prepared to address and discuss issues about the student and the student's progress.* It is important that the resource teacher share information with parents whenever it is necessary and natural. In the meetings, the resource teacher should seem well informed about the issues and clear as to their meaning and implications.

5. *Focus on the parents' hopes, aspirations, concerns, and needs.* The parents should be made to feel that they are an important part of the student's education.

6. *Keep your word.* This shows reliability as well as respect for the parents.

7. *Acknowledge parents' expertise.* Parents have a great deal of information to share about their student. Often, insights into a student's home life, likes, dislikes, or personality can be valuable in helping the resource teacher learn to work effectively with that student.

8. *The resource teacher should be available to parents.* If parents express concerns, questions, or confusions about their child's education, then the resource teacher should be available to address those as soon as possible.

Preparing for the Meeting

In the first meeting, the parents or guardians probably want information about five topics: (a) what specific problems their child is having in school; (b) why it is believed the problems exist or the source of the problems (It is often hard to pinpoint a specific reason for the problems of concern to teachers; nevertheless, parents will want to know how the problems have come about and what the prognosis is for cure. Will temporary help be needed, or is the problem one that will require lifelong accommodations? Any statements made in this regard should be tempered both with truthfulness and with knowledge of our fallibility.); (c) what the resource program is; (d) what type of help will be provided for their child and how long it will last; and (e) what they can do to support the resource effort. Resource teachers should have this information available when the meeting is held.

When discussing the student's specific problems, the resource teacher should let the parents or guardians see assessment results, samples of the student's work, history data on the problem, and so on. The resource teacher also should include examples of what the student does well in school. It is important to give a fair picture of the whole student and not just focus on the negative aspects of performance.

Parents or guardians also will want to know what the resource program is and what type of help it will provide their child. Because the need for such information will be frequent, resource teachers probably should prepare a small handbook or paper describing the program. (This handbook also can be given to other members of the school staff and to community agencies.) The resource teacher should go over each point in the handbook with the parents or guardians. This procedure allows plenty of opportunity for discussion and clarification of points that may be unclear.

Finally, most parents or guardians want to know what they can do to help their child. The resource teacher should know what kind of support she or he wants from them. Does the teacher want them to help in the educational plan? (It is usually wise to consider any instructional plan as tentative until it has been discussed with parents. Their insights and their experience with their child may provide data that will change the best-laid plans. Further, it is hard for parents to believe a request for their help when plans are already cast in school district forms.) How does the teacher want them to reinforce positively the student for work efforts? How does the resource teacher want to schedule regular meetings with the parents or guardians? How often will these be held and for what purpose? Does the teacher want to set up some other type of communication system with the parents or guardians? If so, what type of system?

As is evident, resource teachers will need to plan carefully for the meeting with parents or guardians. Specific information should be readily available and plans for future interactions should be made. Of course, the resource teacher should listen to and consider the parents' ideas throughout the meeting. Resource teachers should be prepared to deal with parents or guardians who claim no responsibility for helping the child and who lay the problems squarely on the school. These parents might assert, often with some hostility, that the school is at fault and that nothing is wrong with their child. Others might blame the child for being lazy, and/or no-good. Occasionally, a few parents or guardians even blame other adults, such as their spouses, grandparents, and teachers. In such cases, resource teachers must call on their consulting skills to the fullest and must be patient, calm, and flexible.

Listening Actively

In conducting parent-teacher conferences, the resource teacher should assume the role of an active listener. The importance of being a good listener when communicating with parents or guardians has been stressed strongly by Kroth (1975) and Lichter (1976), among others. Good listening involves accepting (but not necessarily agreeing with) and interpreting what another person is saying in a nonjudgmental manner while still actively participating in the conversation.

To listen effectively, we suggest that resource teachers develop the four basic attitudes recommended by Gordon (1970). A good listener must (a) really want to hear what the parent has to say and take sufficient time to listen; (b) be able to accept the parents' or guardians' feelings even when these feelings are different from his or her own; (c) trust the parents' ability to find some solutions to the problem their child is having; and (d) have a genuine desire to help. A resource teacher who does not have these basic attitudes probably will not be successful in dealing with parents or guardians.

What are active listening skills? Lichter (1976) presented the following guidelines for being an active listener. First, teachers should listen carefully for the basic message the parent is trying to convey. Second, teachers should restate what the parents say in a simple and concise summary. Third, teachers should observe or ask the parent if their interpretation of what the parent is saying is correct. Finally, the parents should be allowed to correct the restatement by the teacher if it is incorrect.

Two examples of how a teacher might respond to a parent follow. In the first example, the teacher is *not* being a good listener. Instead, he or she is lecturing the parent. In the second example, the teacher *is* being an active listener. In this case, he or she is simply restating what the parent was saying.

Example 1

Parent: Johnny has always been a problem. He is not like his brother at all. His brother never has had any problem with school.

Teacher: You should not compare Johnny to his brother. All children are different from one another.

Example 2

Parent: Johnny has always been a problem. He is not like his brother at all. His brother never has had any problem with school.

Teacher: You feel that Johnny has always had problems with his schoolwork?

Good listening involves more than just restating what another person has said. The possible meaning of the statement also must be interpreted. For example, from the conversations just cited, it appears that the parent is comparing Johnny negatively to his brother. But the parent might be trying to convey that he or she is a good parent; after all, the other son does not have any problems. Teachers always should be attentive to these nuances.

Resource teachers who have not had training in active listening may want to read further on this subject. We recommend Kroth (1975), Gordon (1970), and Lichter (1976) as rich sources of information. We also suggest that two or more teachers role-play several meetings with parents before scheduling a parent-teacher conference.

WORKING WITH THE COMMUNITY

As noted earlier, one role of the resource teacher is consultant. Specifically, we referred to the teacher working with general classroom teachers. In essence, this consulting activity can be referred to as one type of public relations. In these instances, no matter how trivial the communication might seem, resource teachers may improve another person's attitude toward the program by their statements.

Although day-to-day public relations with other personnel in the school is critical, the importance of public relations with community and professional organizations should not be ignored. These community and professional organizations include the parent-teacher association, the Junior League, the Kiwanis Club, the Rotary Club, the Lions Club, the Council for Learning Disabilities, the National Association of Retarded Children, the International Reading Association, the American Speech-Language-Hearing Association, the Council for Exceptional Children, the Orton Society, and local special education advisory groups. These organizations are rich sources of support for the resource program. This support includes one or more of the following: (a) lobbying for money to support the program; (b) providing volunteers to work as aides in the program and/or small donations of monies to purchase materials and equipment; (c) supporting inservice training; (d) delineating competencies for teachers; and (e) delineating ethical standards of practice. Each of these points is discussed below.

Resource programs may be viewed as ancillary services in the schools. Therefore, when money becomes tight or scarce, the financial support for these programs is among the first to be pared down or eliminated altogether. No matter how loud and long resource teachers may complain about the injustice of this action, they alone have little clout in changing or escaping budget reductions; however, local parental, civic, and professional organizations frequently do have a lot of influence in such matters. If they support the resource program strongly, then local school administrators may be careful when considering any budgetary cuts in these programs.

Funding is particularly a problem for the noncategorical and specific skill resource programs. The financial base for special education programs, the categorical and cross-categorical resource models, is usually more stable. However, regardless of the resource model being used, all resource teachers may find that from time to time special lobbying for money to support the program is necessary. They should be prepared for such an eventuality by having already established good public relations with important local organizations.

The second point concerns the provision of volunteers to work as aides or the allocation of monies for special materials and equipment. Many of the organizations mentioned have set up volunteer programs; each volunteer spends a few hours a week in the schools. For example, members of the Junior League often offer their services in this capacity. In other cases, some organizations have varying amounts of monies that they spend on special materials and equipment for the schools. This is particularly true of the Kiwanis, Rotary, and Lions clubs. Donations may be made by these organizations to the resource program—if good public relations have been established.

Professional organizations often provide inservice training to their members. Local and state chapters of the International Reading Association, the American Speech-Language-Hearing Association, the Council for Exceptional Children, and the Orton Society, among others, schedule many meetings each year that deal with interesting and relevant professional topics. Parent and civic organizations, such as the Council for Learning Disabilities and the Junior League, also sponsor speakers on a variety of subjects.

The final point, the delineation of competencies and ethical standards of practice, relates to the professional organizations. Resource teachers should be members of their professional organizations. Many of the organizations have listed the competencies their members should have; some give certificates for demonstrated competency; a few have delineated ethical standards of practice to which their members must adhere; almost all have professional journals and newsletters that keep members informed on new developments in practice. It is professionally indefensible for a resource teacher not to be an active member of one or more of these organizations.

The question remains as to how resource teachers establish public relations with these organizations. In terms of the professional organizations, the answer is quite simple: Resource teachers will need to contact the membership chairperson of those organizations with which they wish to affiliate and pay their dues. The next step is to start attending local and state meetings and to become actively involved in the business and benefits of the organizations.

The problem of establishing public relations with parent and civic organizations requires more attention. Resource teachers should contact organizations that are the most active in their areas and offer to discuss the resource program with members of these organizations at an upcoming meeting. Most of these organizations will gladly welcome such a presentation.

Preparations for such a meeting will have to be considered carefully. Resource teachers will have to describe clearly the objectives of the presentation. Is it just to familiarize the participants with the resource program? Is it to enlist their support in some specific way? Once the objectives have been determined, the manner of presentation will need to be decided. Is it going to be a short lecture? Will any audio or visual presentations be utilized? Will handouts be given to those attending the meeting? How will questions be handled?

At first, some resource teachers may feel uncomfortable about presenting to a group of adults; however, they must recognize that these presentations are an important aspect of the public relations effort and that they will have to engage in many during their career as a resource teacher. Many teachers have found that a slide presentation is helpful. It serves as a guide for the speaker and usually is more interesting to the audience than simply a straight lecture. Some teachers tape an audio presentation to accompany the slide presentation. Resource teachers from several schools often will get together and select one teacher to give the presentations, even though all of them share equally in preparing for the meetings.

There are, of course, some slide and movie presentations of the resource concept. These usually are available from the local special education resource center for short checkout periods. Although these commercially made materials are beneficial in some cases, we believe it is much better for resource teachers to prepare their own presentation using both local teachers and students as participants (with appropriately secured permissions to take and show pictures). Those who view the presentation then can see the relevance of the resource program to their own school and students more clearly.

The resource teacher is responsible not only for effective communication with other people, but also for managing people resources (e.g., assistants, volunteers). Some of the people resources available to the resource teacher are underused, primarily because it takes time to train them. We believe that time can be saved and the effectiveness of the resource teacher and of the program expanded when the resource teacher takes the time to delegate tasks to other people.

The tasks performed by people other than the resource teacher are almost unlimited. They range from the routine (e.g., parking attendance) to the unusual (e.g., showing videos of a European trip). In addition to direct instruction, there are many tasks that should be checked off using a format similar to the one found in Figure 6.2.

Students may also be taught to assume specific responsibilities. In this way, the resource teacher may avoid time unwisely spent in doing for others what they may do or be taught to do for themselves. For example, students can be taught to conference with one another in areas such as writing; they may check one another's work for format and convention; and with a rotating buddy system they may be responsible for explaining assignments after absences.

Johnson (1982) suggested a complete plan for math notebook evaluation that includes self-evaluation (see Figure 6.3). His suggestions may be used for any type of work. It is especially important to delegate to students tasks that are a part of their learning how to learn, and of their learning to self-evaluate their own efforts.

Consider or Code:

A. Who can do this?
   1. Students can/should do this.
   2. Teaching associate (aide) can/should do this.
   3. Peers can/should do this.
   4. Others: _____
B. Plan for instruction/monitoring/revising: How can the person(s) be taught to do the task?

(Categories are arbitrarily limited to 20 items. Please add to or modify both categories and lists to suit your situation.)

Instruction

1. Prepare materials for lessons.
2. Provide direct instruction (with record-keeping/observational system).
3. Monitor instructional program.
4. Coach or tutor individual students appropriately (i.e., being careful not to create a dependency relationship).
5. Record outcomes of instruction (record-keeping).
6. Explain feedback to students.
7. Interpret instructions.
8. Help students organize for instruction.
9. Provide feedback to teacher.
10. Instruct/monitor study behaviors.
11. Monitor/coach metacognition program.
12. Collect observational data on student interactions with peers, adults, and materials.
13. Locate supplementary materials for projects or units.
14. Check conventions and formats used in written assignments.
15. Direct a tutor or volunteer program.
16. Assist students with the use of instructional or mnemonic aids (e.g., computers, calculators, spelling checkers).
17. Monitor and record errors with guided practice.
18. Assist with discussion groups.
19. Collect and record sociometric information.
20. Collect and record observational information in settings outside the resource classroom.

Organization and Management of the Learning Environment

1. Make materials for centers or other areas.
2. Help arrange and maintain classroom areas for specific purposes.
3. Make and maintain displays for students.

Figure 6.2. Delegating classroom tasks: Analysis.

Organization and Management of the Learning Environment (continued)

4. Maintain displays of student work.
5. Provide alternate communication system (e.g., signing).
6. Monitor use of the learning environment by students/adults.
7. Secure materials not ordinarily provided (e.g., extra books, paper, supplies).
8. Monitor housekeeping of the environment; suggest changes.
9. Help arrange and maintain schedules.
10. File and catalog materials (may maintain computer system).
11. Help with computerized data-recording system (instructional and personal information).
12. Help students with projects (e.g., printing, making books).
13. Plan and monitor learning environments outside the classroom (e.g., general class, field trips, or lunchroom).
14. Assist with routines such as attendance or lunch money.
15. Order materials.
16. Teach students to use environment appropriately (e.g., manipulatives in math).
17. Learn new skills to teach others (e.g., use of video camera).
18. Provide assistance to students needing alternative communication systems as they learn to operate in the learning environment.
19. Help maintain student records.
20. Evaluate the learning environment in terms of stated goals for students; suggest modifications.

Miscellaneous

1. Help plan for parent meetings.
2. Prepare information for parents/guardians.
3. Prepare for conferences with agency personnel.
4. Provide liaison with homes, agencies, or community.
5. Provide liaison with other school personnel.
6. Help with program evaluation.
7. Monitor medication.
8. Prepare and organize day's materials.
9. Operate machines.
10. Provide appropriate reinforcements (e.g., words of encouragement, comments on growth, or tangibles).
11. Escort students if needed.
12. Assist students who have been absent.
13. General errands.
14. Prepare information about the program.
15. Talk with students to maintain personal contact.

Figure 6.2. *Continued*

Miscellaneous (continued)

16. Assist with research projects.
17. Monitor journals and libraries for new ideas for instruction, organization and management, or child development.
18. Monitor libraries and journals for new books or other materials of possible use for students/teachers.
19. Monitor libraries and journals for ideas to be used in consultation activities.
20. Help prepare reports.

Figure 6.2. *Continued.*

Notebook checks. I expect students in my standard and enriched course sections to check their own notebooks. After the first few days of class, I hand out a self-evaluation checklist to these students. They conduct the self-evaluation outside of class, correct the format of their work where necessary, and place the self-evaluation checklist in the front of their notebooks. After the first 2 weeks, I use this same checklist when I evaluate each notebook and give each one a grade.

MATH NOTEBOOK—SELF-EVALUATION CHECKLIST

Check you notebook regularly. Follow these 12 guidelines:

☐ 1. Begin each day's notes on a new side of paper.
☐ 2. Each day, use a heading that states the objectives for that day.
☐ 3. Write vocabulary in proper form.
☐ 4. Include sample problems with steps and reasons.
☐ 5. After each sample problem, write the reason for putting it in your notes.
☐ 6. Include comments in your own words to make your notes meaningful and helpful.
☐ 7. Include a summary statement at end of each day's notes.
☐ 8. Highlight the major points.
☐ 9. Keep updating vocabulary.
☐ 10. Number the pages.
☐ 11. Be neat!
☐ 12. Keep all notebook evaluation sheets in your notebook.

Figure 6.3. Plan for self-evaluation of notebooks. Adapted from *Every Minute Counts. Making Your Math Class Work* (pp. 48–49) by D. R. Johnson, 1982, Palo Alto, CA: Dale Seymour Publications. Reprinted with permission.

Chapter 7
Equipping the Resource Room

In this chapter we discuss matters relating to equipping a suitable resource room. In particular, the resource teacher should consider such matters as (a) the physical facilities that are available, (b) the equipment and materials that will be required, and (c) the budgetary limitations. Several books are available that deal with the first two topics. For example, Loughlin and Suina (1982) provided excellent suggestions that are useful at both the elementary and the secondary level. Additionally, Hays (1986) set out specific, constructive guidelines for space allocation and room arrangement of resource rooms.

PHYSICAL FACILITIES

Most resource teachers should be assigned a classroom of their own—the resource room. Obviously, the physical attributes of this room will vary from school to school. Room size, furniture, lighting, storage space, ventilation, and expansion possibilities are some of the attributes that will vary from resource room to resource room. Unfortunately, special services, of which the resource program is but one, are often given a low priority in the allocation of space. We know of some resource teachers who have been assigned to the furnace room, to a part of the library, to an already inhabited classroom, to the storage closet, to the stage in the auditorium, to part of the hallway, to the cafeteria, or to a portable trailer parked outside of the school. Occasionally, resource teachers are given no space at all and are expected to carry their materials from room to room.

In most instances, the resource teacher will have to make do with the space that is available. In some cases, however, the initial space designated for the resource room may not be the only space available, and new and more appropriate quarters can be acquired. Where adequate facilities are allocated, it may be possible that some remodeling can be done. For example, new paint, room dividers, portable chalkboards, and better lighting and ventilation can increase the suitability of a given space as a resource room. State regulation about per-pupil classroom space should always be kept in mind as a guide to judging needed space.

To avoid any unnecessary stigma, as well as to promote the idea of the resource program as part of mainstream education, the program should not be housed in a classroom that has recently functioned as a special education classroom. Additionally, placement of the resource room among a conglomeration of special education classes, or in the special education wing, encourages thinking of the resource program as part of special education, and should therefore be avoided. Further, Hays (1986) pointed out that,

> Ideally, the resource room should be located so that little or no stigma attaches to its placement. If possible, it should be placed near the highest grade level classes it serves, rather than the lowest. This may actually help improve the resource room's status. The younger kids are likely to enjoy going to a room near the ''big kids,'' and the older students won't complain about going to a room in the ''baby section.'' (p. 455)

Once a suitable room has been obtained, the resource teacher should attend to its physical characteristics. First, lighting and ventilation should be in accordance with guidelines provided by the state department of education. Second, the room should be large enough to permit student movement. In other words, the room should not be so small or crowded that the resource teacher and the students have difficulty in moving about. Third, sufficient space should be available for the storage of materials. Fourth, an office space for the resource teacher (and possibly an aide as well) should be present, though often this office is limited to the teacher's desk. Fifth, space should be available for students to work individually, as well as in small groups.

Where the amount of space allotted to the resource room is insufficient and does not allow for each of these factors properly, the teacher will need to consider carefully the efficient use of horizontal and vertical space in the room, as well as expansion possibilities. For example, in the vertical use of space, higher cabinets may be installed for storage of materials. If room for a teacher's office is not available, a large closet attached to the classroom may be converted for that purpose. In some cases, the resource teacher may ask to use the space immediately outside of the classroom (the hall) for storage of equipment.

Consideration should also be given to the arrangement of the furniture. Three floor plans with furniture arrangements are shown in Figures 7.1, 7.2, and 7.3. Figure 7.1 represents a large room; it contains three learning centers, two com-

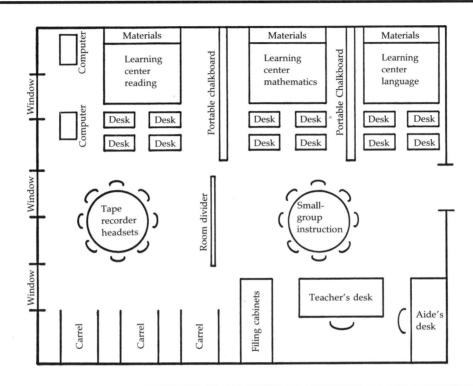

Figure 7.1. Sample floor plan for a resource room.

puters, two round tables, three carrels, a teacher's desk and filing cabinet, a room divider, and two portable chalkboards. The learning centers relate to specific content areas or to types of instruction under one content area. The materials used by the resource teacher and students are stored in these centers. This room also has a space available for small-group instruction in various components of the program. Another round table is available for a tape recorder, and headsets and carrels are placed out of the way for students who are easily distracted. A room divider, filing cabinets, and teacher's desk round out this particular resource room floor plan.

Figure 7.2 illustrates the use of the hall and the closet. This room would be too small to be used as a resource room if the closet were not so large or if the hall were too narrow to allow for storage cabinets.

In Figure 7.3, the resource room is part of an open classroom. In this situation, the resource teacher is given a space rather than a traditional classroom with four walls. Many schools are now built in such a manner, and the resource teacher will be expected to function in such a setting. This type of space arrangement has many

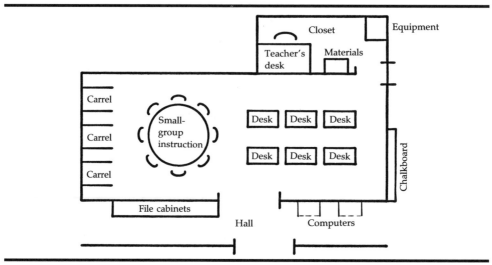

Figure 7.2. Sample floor plan for a resource room.

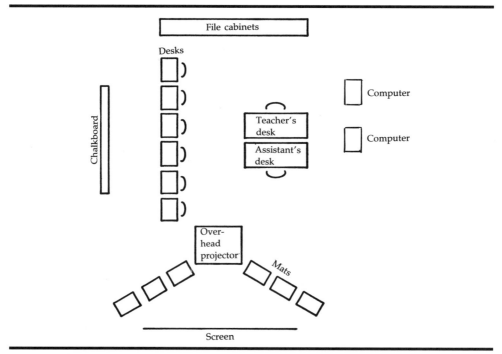

Figure 7.3. Sample floor plan for a resource room.

advantages. First, students are really not segregated to the extent that they would be if they were required to go to a separate room. Second, the resource teacher has ready access to other teachers, their materials, and their equipment. Third, unsupervised travel from room to room is also not a problem in these schools. Finally, the relaxed and informal nature of this arrangement can be highly conducive to learning.

Figure 7.3 is also an example of a floor plan for use when a resource teacher is required to share a room with another teacher. In some cases, several special services operate out of one large room. For example, the speech therapist, the reading teacher, and the resource teacher may share a room. As in the open classroom, the resource teacher is given a space rather than a room.

Most physical facilities will vary from these three examples. The figures are presented to stress the importance of the resource room's physical setting as well as to give some general guidelines to the reader. We have visited resource rooms in which a creative use of space and furniture arrangement has made them very functional. Teachers are encouraged to expend the energy and time to make the most effective use of whatever space is available.

EQUIPMENT AND MATERIALS

In addition to the basic furniture requirements noted in the floor plans, specific types of equipment also are helpful for the successful operation of a resource program. At the very least, a tape recorder, headsets, and an overhead projector should be acquired. The tape recorder can be used with commercially available tapes or teacher-made tapes. This particular piece of equipment greatly enhances individualized instruction. For example, let us say that a resource teacher is providing remedial instruction to a group of students using the Merrill Linguistic Series. One of the skills a student must be able to perform in the program, *I can*, is to write certain words and sentences from dictation. The words include "cat," "bat," "tag," "wag," "jam"; the sentences are "Dan sat," "Nan can bat," and so forth. The resource teacher may dictate these on tape, allowing sufficient time periods for the student to complete each task. At the end of the session, the child may be given the correct responses on a sheet of paper and allowed to monitor his or her own errors and to receive quick feedback.

In many school districts, resource teachers now have access to computers for use in the resource room. Okolo, Reith, and Bahr (1989) interviewed special education teachers, drawn from a random sample of teachers in a large urban school district, about the use of computers in their classrooms. They found that all but one of the teachers surveyed had access to computers, and that the majority of teachers who had access to computers actually had the computers in their classrooms. However, almost half of the respondents reported that they had not used the computers within the last year. A significant relationship was found between the location of the computer in the classroom and the amount of time that the computer was used. Cosden and Abernathy (1990) also reported a relationship between computer location and computer use. It seems important to situate computers so that they are integrated into the classroom, but where they also are isolated enough to allow students the space to work independently. Often, computers are located at permanent stations around the periphery of the room. This placement seems to optimize both the teacher's need to supervise the computers and the student's need to be able to attend to the computer rather than to the activities going on in the classroom.

Cosden and Abernathy (1990) also reported that this arrangement of stationing computers around the periphery of the classroom is particularly beneficial for resource rooms. Often several students in resource rooms are working simultaneously in different content areas or on different assignments, depending on their individual needs and goals. Thus, it does not disrupt the class structure to allow students to use class time to work on the computer. Language arts and mathematics drill-and-practice programs constitute the bulk of educational software available. These programs are particularly useful in aiding instruction because these are areas that are often taught through drill and rote memorization. Computers can also be particularly beneficial to resource teachers because they add novelty and variety to tasks that are often considered dull by students. Also, many resource teachers report that computers are useful in building independence and self-confidence. At the beginning of the school year, the resource teacher may need to choose the program that a student is to use, as well as load that program into the computer for the student. However, as the year progresses, students will learn to perform these tasks for themselves.

The resource room also needs other materials. First, a complete set of the general classroom's standard educational programs that relate to the problems for which students have been referred should be available in the resource room. This usually includes the reading, mathematics, spelling, handwriting, language, and/or content area series. Of particular importance and use will be the teacher's guides that accompany most programs. These guides often provide a wealth of information regarding means for individualizing and supplementing instruction for students using the series.

Second, the resource teacher will need additional materials that relate to the specific types of problems the resource students are encountering. For example, if most students are being referred for reading and behavior problems, then special materials dealing with these areas will need to be purchased. The materials that we recommend for these and other areas of difficulty are described in many popular texts. We suggest, therefore, that when reading these sources, teachers make special note of materials that they believe will be useful in their resource rooms.

We cannot help but reflect here on the type of materials found in some of the resource rooms that we have visited. Often there is no evidence that the materials used in these rooms are geared to teaching the skills necessary to do well in the programs used in the general class. For example, parquetry sets, flash cards containing nonsense symbols, walking boards, specialized faddist language approaches, eye exercise activity sets, perceptual materials, trampolines, and other questionable apparatus are on occasion found in great abundance in some resource programs. Surprisingly, these special education/process types of materials and equipment are being used by resource teachers with students who are referred because they need help in reading, writing, spelling, calculating, behaving, and/or talking.

We, among others, have concluded that the educational value of such techniques has not been established sufficiently to warrant their continued use, especially when their purpose is to teach academics or language. A careful review of the current research literature is likely to lead the reader to the same conclusion. Rather than belabor this point here, we recommend the programs and materials that emphasize the direct teaching of academic, language, and behavior skills.

The decision concerning which materials resource teachers should purchase is difficult. We suggest that they follow the same procedures in selecting educational materials that they would use in their own personal shopping. That is, they should (a) prepare a list of types of materials needed; (b) arrange the items from highest to lowest priority; (c) compare prices on materials; (d) evaluate and compare the ingredients of each material; and (e) determine if it might be possible to make cheaper and equally good materials from scratch.

To aid the resource teachers in this often tedious task, we suggested earlier that they follow the guidelines developed by V. Brown (1975). Brown proposed using a basic questioning approach, which she calls a Q-Sheet. The Q-Sheet approach lists several questions that provide a framework for the teacher to analyze materials so that appropriate evaluations can be made. The Q-Sheet is shown in its entirety in Figure 4.1.

Most individuals who use a Q-Sheet approach in analyzing materials find that the time required is formidable. In addition, the competence of inexperienced professionals to use such a sophisticated approach often is questionable. Brown has suggested that if the process of dissecting materials is new to the teacher, he or she might employ the following techniques. First, he or she might take at least two programs that purport to teach the same skills and analyze them simultaneously. Second, several professionals might work together on analyzing material and then compare their perceptions. Third, the teacher might write down the specific examples in the material that cause him or her to make a judgment and have another person check these perceptions. Fourth, specific experts in one area, such as reading or mathematics, may be requested to evaluate the material. Fifth, only one component of an instructional area, such as teaching addition facts in real life situations, may be evaluated in several different series. Sixth, the teacher may develop a different Q-Sheet that relates to specific content knowledge. Finally, the material under study may be tried with a few students, and various modifications in instructing may be attempted. In this last example, the material is experimented with to determine the conditions of use within a specific program.

Wiederholt and McNutt (1977) also earlier stressed several points that should be considered when evaluating materials for older students. For example, they noted the importance of the experiential background of the students as it relates to the topics represented in the material. Specifically, the students in most cases should have had either real or vicarious experiences with the topics to understand and relate them to their own lives. They also encouraged the use of interviews to obtain the students' own perceptions of the materials being considered.

Wilson (1982) also provided guidelines for selecting educational materials and resources. Various professional organizations have also worked together under the leadership of Daniel Stufflebeam (1981) to develop a common, detailed handbook, *Standards for Evaluations of Educational Programs, Projects, and Materials.* Its content should be useful to the resource teacher in materials evaluation or in the provision of inservice sessions related to the topic.

CURRICULUM ANALYSIS

The particular type of resource program and the function of instruction within that program determine the extent to which the teacher will need competence in curriculum analysis.

In general education, the curriculum is usually well established, and the role of the teacher is to implement it. It may be so standardized that it is divided up into specific pieces to be covered in predetermined time frames. There is little leeway for modification of content, pace, class organization, or methodology. Students who do not match this normative expectation are often referred for special services, and the remedial or special educator's role involves getting the student to fit within the bounds of curricular normality.

In this case, the resource teacher may, of course, merely help each student on a lesson-to-lesson basis, figuring out the assignment with the student, and never getting to know where each lesson fits into the curriculum. We have suggested that this is a role best suited for an associate (aide) or a tutor, perhaps under the resource teacher's direction, but rarely as a major instructional responsibility.

The resource teacher who works primarily with general education may instead capitalize on the professional strength of the role. In this case, curriculum analysis is crucial to modifying or changing the curriculum to accommodate the normally wide variation of student characteristics found within the general classroom.

Resource teachers who deal primarily with the general education curriculum usually work across grade levels and in a variety of subject areas. As they assist students who are having difficulty, they should be able to detect any general patterns of problems, and suggest or demonstrate specific ways to modify the curriculum. Curriculum modification brings some low-achieving learners into the normal range and prevents future students from having some of their same problems.

Silbert et al. (1990) showed how the resource teacher may analyze commercial math curricula according to their characterization of the needs of low-performing students. The five steps they suggested in modifying a math unit guide the teacher in modifying instruction to accommodate these needs:

1. Prioritize the objectives of the unit and set mastery levels.
2. Select problem-solving strategies.
3. Construct teaching formats for the major skills (and for preskills when necessary).
4. Select practice examples.
5. Design worksheets or select pages of the text to provide review of previously taught skills. (p. 20)

Judy Wood (1984) provided a somewhat different model for adapting components of general class lesson plans for students with mild disabilities (see Table 7.1).

We have discussed the curriculum modification function primarily in terms of low-achieving students, but it is obviously desirable for both low- and high-performing students. For example, Renzulli and Smith (1980) showed how to develop individualized plans for compacting and streamlining the regular curriculum to meet the needs of high-performing students. Their plan is designed ''to relieve gifted students of the boredom that often results from unchallenging work in basic skill areas, and at the same time, to *guarantee* the student, his or her parents, and subsequent grade-level teachers that the child has mastered standard competencies necessary for later achievement'' (p.25). Figure 7.4 shows a sample plan sheet for IEP modification for the student in special education, or for any student for whom such an approach is warranted.

BUDGET LIMITATIONS

Most resource programs are allocated a certain amount of money for equipment, supplies, and materials. The particular amount varies greatly from one state to another and often even among schools within the same district. It is important for the resource teacher to understand the budget policies and processes of the state and of the district and even more important to seek out personally and actively all those who have a hand in the budgeting, ordering, or distribution of budgeted items.

In ordering, priority should be given to ordering items that have value across ages, time, and subjects. Very specialized, novel, or consumable materials are usually not as well regarded as more universally applicable items because of their high cost. However, a high-cost item of proven effectiveness may be the better choice in the long run if it helps teach a student to read, write, or calculate.

Before ordering specialized materials, the teacher should check to see if they are already available someplace within the district. Novel items or difficult-to-use programs may have been relegated to the back of a closet after brief use. Or perhaps a new teacher who has no interest in or understanding of a complex material may

Table 7.1. *Adapting Components of a General Class Lesson Plan*

Lesson Plan Components	Application of Chapters 3 and 4
	Procedure

Introduction

State what student should learn:	Select instructional objective for lesson. List subobjectives. Use task analysis to break down all subobjectives. State objectives for mildly handicapped students in the appropriate taxonomy levels.
Demonstrate what student should learn:	Provide model of completed assignment (whole-part-whole method). Provide sequential directions. Check Table 4.11 for alternative teaching techniques in demonstration mode.
Use mind-capturer or activator:	Use manipulative or hands-on activity to boost interest. Note whether or not students have prerequisite skills for mastering objective. Alter objective at this point, if necessary.
Link to past lessons or students' experiences:	Ask questions (on students' taxonomy levels) about past lessons. Provide example from own experience and relate to lesson (the modeling technique). Ask students to share similar experiences; relate student comments to present lesson.

Development

Select and describe activities designed for lesson's instructional objective:	Assign peer tutors to mildly handicapped students. Organize creative groups for instruction. Select grouping arrangements.
Select activities designed for acquisition, retention, and transfer:	Teach for acquisition by selecting appropriate instructional activities and implementing each activity with appropriate instructional strategy (see Table 3.3). Use task analysis to break down all activities for teaching for acquisition. Teach for retention by selecting appropriate instructional activities and implementing each activity with appropriate instructional strategy (see Table 3.3).

Table 7.1. *Continued*

Lesson Plan Components	Application of Chapters 3 and 4
	Use task analysis to break down activities for teaching for retention.
	Teach for transfer by selecting appropriate instructional activities and implementing each activity with appropriate instructional strategy (see Table 3.3).
	Use task analysis to break down all activities for teaching for transfer.
Organize all activities according to taxonomy level:	List all activities.
	Organize all activities, from lowest level of difficulty to highest level of difficulty.
	Present activities on student's functioning level.
Identify and modify content of, and teaching technique for, each activity:	State *content* of each activity and use suggestions in Chapter 4 to adapt or modify presentation of that content.
	State *teaching technique* for each activity and use models in Chapter 4 to select alternate technique or adapt stated technique.

Summary

Conclude lesson:	Select closing activities on instructional level of mainstreamed students.
	Assess student's mastery of concept(s).
Students describe what they have learned:	Assist mainstreamed students in selecting what to share.
	Students tell about what they have learned.
	Students draw pictures of what they have learned.
	Students present projects.

Resources

Compile materials for presenting lesson:	Assess instructional level of materials.
	Select variety of materials to address different perceptual learning styles.
Select appropriate media for lesson:	Use suggestions in Chapter 4 to adapt media.
	Select variety of media.
	Match media to perceptual learning styles.
Prepare resources for adapting learning environment:	Create bulletin boards for incidental and intentional learning.
	Design learning centers to enhance instruction.

Table 7.1. *Continued*

Lesson Plan Components	Application of Chapters 3 and 4
	Evaluation
Teacher assesses student learning:	Use model in Chapter 7 to adapt regular classroom test for mildly handicapped students.
	Assess effectiveness of instructional objective.
	Assess instructional level of activities.
	Assess activities not mastered and consider further adaptations of plan.
Student assesses self:	Give student self-correcting materials for immediate reinforcement.
	Provide models to which students can compare their work.
Students assess each other:	Provide one-on-one peer tutor to give feedback.
	Oversee student assessment of peers (peers' criticism of mildly handicapped student can harm handicapped student's self-concept).
Teacher assesses self:	Were all students included in lesson plan's activities?
	Did each student experience success?
	Was I aware of the instructional level of each student?
	Did each student reach expected learning outcome?
	Did I effectively manage student behaviors?
	Was the learning environment adapted to meet students' learning needs?
	What changes should I make the next time I present the lesson?

Note. From *Adapting Instruction for the Mainstream. A Sequential Approach to Teaching* (pp. 132–140) by J. W. Wood, 1984, New York: Macmillan. Reprinted with permission.

have discarded it. For these reasons, some districts hold sales or materials exchanges each fall to increase the useful life of high-cost, low-use materials.

The new teacher who is looking for materials should find out if it is the district's policy to collect all materials at the end of the school year and redistribute them again in the fall. Further, the resource teacher should find out if the district makes an inventory of all equipment, supplies, and materials. Such a list is useful in locating items.

Students in special education programs are entitled to the basic materials, supplies, and equipment that are budgeted and provided for every other student. This is especially important at the secondary level, where supplies are often allocated by departments such as English or math. The special education department should

The Compactor

Prepared by: Joseph S. Renzulli
Linda H. Smith

NAME _____ AGE _____ TEACHER(S) _____ Individual Conference Dates And Persons Participating in Planning of IEP

SCHOOL _____ GRADE _____ PARENT(S) _____

CURRICULUM AREAS TO BE CONSIDERED FOR COMPACTING Provide a brief description of basic material to be covered during this marking period and the assessment information or evidence that suggests the need for compacting.	PROCEDURES FOR COMPACTING BASIC MATERIAL Describe activities that will be used to guarantee proficiency in basic curricular areas.	ACCELERATION AND/OR ENRICHMENT ACTIVITIES Describe activities that will be used to provide advanced level learning experiences in each area of the regular curriculum.

☐ Check here if additional information is recorded on the reverse side.

Figure 7.4. Individual educational programming guide. From *Individual Educational Programming Guide* by J. Renzuli & L. Smith, 1978, Mansfield, CT: Creative Learning Press, Inc. Reprinted with permission.

have its own allocation or else work out a mutually agreeable arrangement to be sure that the special materials, supplies, and equipment are indeed over and above those to which the student is normally entitled.

Gallagher (1979) has also noted other matters regarding budget. Some budgets specify the allocation of funds to specific categories, such as equipment or instructional materials. In addition, some schools provide consumable items to students, others do not. Finally, some schools require teachers to complete requisitions for supplies, and in other buildings teachers can simply take materials as needed.

In any event, a budget for all special programs, including the resource operation, usually has been decided on, and resource teachers should ask their administrators and supervisors how much money has been allocated for use in their program. They also should determine when and how this money can be spent. In some cases, materials may be ordered only at the beginning of the school year. This restriction causes some difficulty in that most resource teachers do not know which materials are needed until they have become familiar with the requirements and problems of the referred students. If they are unsure as to how much money is available and when they can order materials, they should request specific materials and see what happens.

In requesting materials, professional behavior usually pays handsome dividends. A typed, formal request to the principal in which the materials, publisher, and cost are listed and a written statement about the need and usefulness of the instructional package for a specific student or students are more likely to result in a positive response than is a haphazard verbal request. If the teachers also can state how they have used the materials in the past or how other teachers have used it with success, the probability that the request will be honored is further enhanced.

Resource teachers should set some money aside in their own personal budget to be used in building a professional library. The actual dollar amount will depend on the financial status and interests of the teacher but generally will range from $50 to $200 a year. In 3 or 4 years, the teacher can acquire a comprehensive and useful collection of books, journals, and materials. In addition to their private libraries, resource teachers can always use the facilities of the public library system, instructional materials, and/or media centers, and they can tap the the small budgets that most schools keep to buy selected books for teacher use.

Finally, it should be noted that there are several good sources of inexpensive materials. For example, the periodical *Intervention in School and Clinic* regularly publishes a "Yours for the Asking" article. Materials listed are either free or cost less than $5. An example of the September 1990 issue of that journal is found in Figure 7.5. Additionally, Kaiser (1985) cited a list compiled by Stowitschek and Gable of various centers and organizations that are consistently reliable sources of materials for special educators. The list includes the center name, its primary goals, a description of it, and guidelines as to who can and how to access the materials that they have. A copy of this list is included in Figure 7.6.

YOURS FOR THE ASKING

Here are a variety of practical materials that are free or cost $5.00 or less. Please request the items directly from the specified advertisers. If you would like to list posters, brochures, or other materials, send advertising copy to PRO-ED Journal Advertising, 8700 Shoal Creek Blvd., Austin, TX 78758. Phone: 512/471-1608. There is no charge to advertise in this column. All listings are subject to publisher's approval; publication does not imply endorsement by the editor or publisher.

ASHA Research Division Posts Grant Announcements on SpecialNet

The Research Division has expanded its Grant Information on ACTIONLINE service by posting the three weekly grant and contract announcements on the SpecialNet bulletin board ASHA. UPDATE. Subscribers to Special-Net will now be able to receive weekly postings of current grants and contracts available to researchers in the field of communication sciences and disorders. The information currently available by calling ASHA's ACTIONLINE telephone number 800/638-6868 will now be available by reviewing the SpecialNet bulletin board listing. The information provided includes:

- granting/contracting agency;
- title and scope of research;
- dollar amount and number of grants/contracts available;
- deadline date;
- name and address of contact person.

For further information, contact the Research Division at ASHA, 301/897-5700.

Educate the Educators Program

PC Today magazine announces a new program aimed at helping educators, trainers, and librarians understand more about IBM-compatible computers. Any educator can obtain a free subscription to *PC Today* by calling the toll-free number below and requesting a free trial subscription form. Principals, department heads, and other faculty members may request additional forms if they want their school library or additional faculty members to receive subscriptions. The program extends to all elementary and secondary schools, colleges, trade schools, public libraries, and corporate training departments. To enroll in the Educate the Educators Program, contact *PC Today* at 1-800-424-7900.

Guide for Parents

Helping Your Child Succeed in School—A 36-page guide for parents—contains practical ideas about helping children, preschool through high school, make the most of learning opportunities. Produced by the School Division of the Association of American Publishers. $1.50 each; 10 to 99 copies, $1.25 each; 100 or more copies, $1.00 each. New York residents add sales tax. Send check, payable to School Division, AAP, to: AAP, School Division, 220 East 23rd St.,

New York, NY 10010. Free *Discussion Leader's Guide* available upon request with order of 10 or more booklets.

Guide to Learning Disabilities

This booklet was developed as an introductory guide to help parents, teachers, special services personnel, psychologists, and others responsible for evaluation and treatment of children with learning disabilities. It will assist in the recognition of behavior problems, attentional deficits, and cognitive symptoms and how they may be related to neuropsychological profiles. The *Guide* describes subtypes of learning disabilities and provides ideas for educational treatment of each. Included is a list of tests used for diagnosis and a list of educational and psychological terms. Written by Michele J. Eliason, PhD, and Lynn C. Richman, PhD. Send $3.50 plus $.85 for shipping. To order more than 20 booklets, $3.00 each plus 10% of total cost for shipping. Checks payable to LD Guide. Mail to Educational Assessment Marketing Services, PO Box 1151, Iowa City, IA 52244.

Pen Pal Program for LD Students

The National Learning Disabilities Network (NLDN) is the sponsor of a unique pen pal program that matches students by approximate age level, written expression level, and sex. The pen pal club is free to NLDN members. NLDN also offers many other teacher-usable ideas to LD educators. To obtain a class sign-up form and information sheet, write to: NLDN Pen Pal Club, 82 S. Townline Rd., Sandusky, MI 48471.

Figure 7.5. A source for resource room materials.

Dyslexia Handbook

What's This Thing Called Dyslexia? An encouraging 30-page read-aloud handbook for students diagnosed as having dyslexia. Its purpose is to inform and explain this learning disability and to motivate the dyslexic. Fully illustrated by three students and one adult who are successfully living with their dyslexia. Cost: $2.95 plus $.65 for first book; each additional book is $3.25. Two or more copies sent postage free. Texas residents add sales tax. Send checks to Ray Ham/ Publisher, 6417 Ponderosa Lane, Colleyville, TX 76034.

Free from the National Federation of the Blind (NFB)

The Blind Child in the Regular Preschool: a fact sheet that addresses common questions of preschool teachers and administrators. Is specialized training required? How will the other children react? How will she get around? *Blindness and Disorders of the Eye:* a booklet that explains normal function of the eye and common disorders that can lead to vision loss. NFB, 1800 Johnson St., Baltimore, MD 21230; 301/659-9314.

Free! National Head Injury Foundation

The *NHIF Catalogue of Educational Material*—Listings of over 250 head injury articles and audio- and videocassettes available from the National Head Injury Foundation (NHIF). Articles cover all aspects of head injury and head injury rehabilitation, as well as psychosocial issues, legal issues, community reentry, financial issues, pediatrics, prevention, education, and research. Audiocassette recordings of NHIF conference proceedings and videotapes on a variety of head injury topics are also available. Request from NHIF, 333 Turnpike Rd., Southboro, MA 01772.

The Orton Dyslexia Society

The only national organization directed exclusively to dyslexia research and treatment. Send $3.00 for eight informational brochures and a list of discounted publications to: The Orton Dyslexia Society, 724 York Rd., Baltimore, MD 21204.

Learning Disabilities

Two booklets, $5.00 each, including postage. "Guide to Learning Disabilities" and "College and the High School Student with Learning Disabilities." Send check to: Learning Disabilities Association of America, 4156 Library Rd., Pittsburgh, PA 15234.

Using Whole Language Software

A free quarterly newsletter/ catalog featuring teacher-selected software. The focus is on ways that "off the shelf" software titles, carefully selected from the offerings of hundreds of major publishers, can help integrate literature, writing, reasoning, and

creativity into every K–8 subject. The catalog includes these software categories: desktop publishing/word processing, modeling and simulation, role playing, creativity and creative writing, graphics, and teacher-presentations. Call 800/628-4623 or write Willy Billy's Workshop, PO Box 6104 P, Cleveland, OH 44101.

New!

Summer Speech Book, by Phyllis P. Kupperman, gives the child practice in using speech sounds correctly in words, sentences, and conversation. New activities and illustrations have been added to enhance the edition. Single copies $2.00, Item #3654. Write: PRO-ED, 8700 Shoal Creek Blvd., Austin, TX 78758.

Coping with Tourette Syndrome

Coping with Tourette Syndrome in the Classroom and *Coping with Tourette Syndrome in Early Adulthood*—two booklets addressing the problems of dealing with Tourette Syndrome.

Figure 7.5. *Continued*

[Yours for the Asking, cont.]

The booklets are only $2.00 each and may be obtained from Tourette Syndrome Association, Inc., 42-40 Bell Blvd., Bayside, NY 11361-2861; 718/224-2999.

Free 1990 Complete Catalog

The 1990 PRO-ED catalog features tests, books, materials, and journals in remedial and special education. For a free copy contact PRO-ED, 8700 Shoal Creek Blvd., Austin, TX 78758 512/451-3246.

Assistive Technology Design in Special Education

Assistive Technology Design in Special Education, a new publication of the ERIC/OSEP Special Project, examines the design principles and features of assistive devices. The publication is based on a series of interviews conducted with assistive technology designers who directed projects funded by the Office of Special Education Programs of the U.S. Department of Education. The projects developed a wide range of devices, including alternative communication systems, robotics, and microcomputer-based writing and interface systems. The project directors identified a number of design issues that are discussed in this publication, including analyzing user needs, identifying the full range of decision makers, enhancing accessibility and ease of use, and designing for flexibility. *Assistive Technology Design in Special Education* also addresses important principles of technology transfer and design and performance standards.

The ERIC/OSEP Project, which is operated by the Council for Exceptional Children under a contract with the Office of Special Education Programs, publishes a variety of summaries and syntheses of special education research. *Assistive Technology Design in Special Education* is available from CEC Publication Sales, The Council for Exceptional Children, 1920 Association Drive, Reston, VA 22091. The cost is $5.00 per copy, prepaid, to cover shipping and handling. Discounts for multiple copies of this title sent to 1 address are 10–49 copies, 20%; 50 or more, 25%.

Figure 7.5. *Continued.* From *Intervention in School and Clinic, 26*(1), pp. 62–64. Reprinted with permission.

Stowitschek, Gable, and Hendricksen (1980, pp. 51–55) compiled the information listed below.

NCEMMH

Organization: National Center for Education Media and Materials for the Handicapped (NCEMMH)

Stated Goal: The goal of NCEMMH is to assist and support personnel working with students with handicaps in choosing and locating educational materials and media.

What It Is: It is a national center to help regions, states, and localities provide media, materials, and educational technologies. The center consists of four parts:

1. Media, Materials, and Technology (MMT), which facilitates the distribution of instructional and training materials;
2. Information Services (IS), which deals in information retrieval (see separate section on NIMIS);
3. Coordination Services (CS), which sees that all parts operate together; and
4. Administration and Central Technical Services (ACTS), which administers to the whole.

Who Can Use It: It is available to handicapped learners, teachers (public and private), parents, school administrators, librarians, media specialists, resource center personnel, medical center staff, rehabilitation center staff, researchers, and preservice teachers in special education programs.

How to Use It: Order materials and media in the NCEMMH catalogue directly from the manufacturer. Call Information Services (IS) for information not covered in the catalogue. Order other catalogues and in-house publications from the Ohio State University Press.

Costs: Catalogue and services are free; publications are available at a modest price.

NIMIS I

Organization: National Instructional Materials Information System (NIMIS I) (NIMIS I is a subcomponent of NCEMMH.)

Function: The function is to provide abstracts of materials and media from a data base. These abstracts are designed to aid in a search for appropriate materials when designing Individualized Education Programs (IEPs).

Figure 7.6. Resources for special educators.

Form: Thirty-seven abstracts are accessible through 41 hard-bound bibliographies divided into seven areas: Learning Disabilities, Early Childhood, Mildly Handicapped, Trainable Mentally Handicapped, Severely Mentally Handicapped, Hearing Impaired, and other topics. A computer printout may also be ordered.

Additional Publications: NIMIS Data Preparation Manual (approximately $6), *Instructional Materials Thesaurus for Special Education* (approximately $7). Note: New Service— Special Materials Analysis and Review by Teachers (SMART). Teachers provide information on materials they have used for possible entry into NIMIS I.

Prices: Individual abstracts (approximately $3–$5; entire set of abstracts (approximately $162); computer services (prices vary according to services).

Contact: Publications Sales Divisions, Ohio State University Press, 2070 Neil Avenue, Columbus, OH 43210.

NICSEM

Organization: National Information Center for Special Education Materials (NICSEM)

Function: The function of NICSEM is to aid in the search for appropriate materials by collecting abstracts from a data base along parameters defined by key words.

Forms: Numerous indexes are offered for sale (see NICSEM for a complete list). A computer search is also available through NICSEM. There is an on-line interface with Lockheed (DIALOG) and BRS systems. Over 80,000 abstracts are available.

Prices: Index prices are quoted under NICSEM section. On-line computer service prices vary with the type of service. Note: NICSEM is currently working to assist state education agencies in preparing and utilizing NICSEM products and services in their respective states.

Where to Order Indexes: University of Southern California, NICSEM, University (RAN) 2nd Floor, Los Angeles, CA 90007, Information Officer (213) 741-5899.

HLMDC

Organization: Handicapped Learner Materials Distribution Center (HLMDC)

Stated Goals: The goals of the HLMDC are to serve as a back-up source in the event that materials are otherwise unavailable for loan. Materials may be used for evaluation for possible purchase or for actual use.

Figure 7.6. *Continued*

What It Is: It is a storehouse of materials for use with learners with handicaps. Materials are accessible through catalogue orders for short-term loans.

Who Can Use It: Any organization, institution, or agency working with individuals with handicaps or training workers with individuals who have handicaps can use it. Also, it can be used by parents of a child with handicaps.

How to Use It

1. Determine the materials desired; the materials must be unavailable through local loan services.
2. Order them by mail, phone, or in person (a 3-week notice is preferred).
3. Use the materials for 1 to 7 days (longer loans are available on request).
4. Return the materials to HLMDS (the user is responsible for return postage).

Cost: There is no charge for loans. A catalogue is available on request. Note: The user does accept responsibility for the condition of the material returned to the HLMDC. Extensive guidelines are listed in the catalogue and the newsletter (Vol. 1, No. 1, 1979) available from HLMDC.

How to Order Materials

1. Obtain a catalogue from Handicapped Learner Materials Distribution Center, Indiana University, Audio-Visual Center, Bloomington, IN 47405, (812) 337-1511—Circulation Department.
2. Obtain a HLMDC account number at the same address and phone number.
3. Order needed materials 3 weeks in advance (some orders may be handled faster if phoned).
4. Return materials to HLMDC (the user pays return postage).

Figure 7.6. *Continued.* From "Multidisciplinary Teams and Group Decision Making Techniques: Possible Solutions to Decision Making Problems" by S. M. Kaiser, 1985, *School Psychology Review,* 14(4), pp. 58–62. Reprinted with permission.

Chapter 8
Referral and Selection Procedures

Questions about identifying the students who will receive resource services and the procedures by which they will be declared eligible for those services must be answered before a resource program is implemented in a school. This chapter will assist resource teachers in the important task of managing referrals and selecting students. First, we make some comments regarding the qualifications of students for the program. Second, we offer some recommendations regarding procedures to be followed in seeking and processing referrals. Third, we discuss the resource teacher's role in multidisciplinary staffing, because the final decision concerning placement is often made in such staff meetings.

STUDENT SELECTION: WHO QUALIFIES?

Before implementing any kind of resource program, the resource teacher should clearly understand the rules and regulations governing the identification, selection, and qualification of students for resource help. Prior to outlining the major issues related to qualifications and evaluation of students needing resource support, we address prereferral interventions that may be implemented in an attempt to avoid an overreferral of students with mild problems to the resource room. Second, we discuss due process and other regulated mandates that apply to the education of students with disabilities in the United States. Last, we address the issues involved in evaluating students who do, in fact, need resource support to supplement their education.

Prereferral Interventions

In the United States, The Individuals with Disabilities Act mandates a "free and appropriate education" for all students with disabilities. A central component of that mandate is the concept that all students should be educated in the least restrictive environment possible. This least restrictive environment stipulation means that each student's education should be as "normal" as possible. Therefore, if a student who is experiencing some difficulties in a general classroom can, with the aid of intervention from either the classroom teacher or a team of outside consultants, continue to successfully function within that classroom, then the student should not be placed in a more restrictive environment (i.e., resource program, self-contained classroom, etc.). Overreferrals and overcrowding in resource rooms are common problems that may be solved by the introduction of prereferral intervention programs prior to referring a student to special education.

Most, if not all, of the students who attend the resource program will be initially referred to the program by their classroom teacher. This initial decision to refer a student for special services may, in fact, be the single most important decision in the process of qualifying students for resource support, because most of the students who are referred are subsequently placed in some sort of resource program. Ysseldyke (1983) cited a nationwide survey of directors of special education that indicated that when 3% to 5% of a school population is referred, 92% of the students who are referred are evaluated, and 73% of those evaluated are placed in special education. In prereferral programs classroom teachers are encouraged to look for interventions for students who are experiencing difficulties that can be successfully implemented in the general classroom; thus, an attempt is made to reduce the number of students who are referred for resource help. If practitioners in prereferral programs are able to suggest interventions and remediations that can be effectively carried out by the general classroom teacher, then the number of referrals to the resource room will be decreased. Decreasing the initial number of referrals to the resource room serves two important purposes: (a) It helps ensure that students are being educated in the least restrictive environment possible, and (b) it helps to solve the problem of overreferral or overcrowding in the resource room. In schools where prereferral programs are in effect, students with very mild difficulties are not formally referred for special education evaluation until interventions in the general classroom have been attempted and have failed.

In suggesting the implementation of prereferral programs, we are not stating that all students with learning difficulties should be educated solely in the general classroom environment, but rather we believe that through the use of carefully planned interventions in the classroom, some students who might otherwise attend the resource room could remain in the general classroom. Almost always it is general classroom teachers who first notice that a student is performing differently from other students in the classroom. Upon noticing a student's aberrant performance, there are several things that classroom teachers should check to begin to determine what might be done to solve the student's difficulties. First, the teacher should consult with colleagues to verify that the student is experiencing difficulty in other settings as well. Second, the teacher might want to contact the student's parents to determine whether special circumstances at home may account for the student's current performance at school. Next, the teacher, either alone or with the help of other school personnel, should attempt to modify instruction methods for the student to see if the problem can be remedied in the classroom.

There are several types of formal prereferral intervention teams that are set up expressly to aid the classroom teacher in designing modified instruction for students with difficulties; Teacher Assistance Teams are among the most common and successful types of prereferral program. Teacher Assistance Teams are based within a particular school and are made up of faculty members from within the school including the general classroom teacher whose student is being considered. Fundamental to the Teacher Assistance Team is the idea that the classroom teacher is an equal member of the team who works in conjunction with the other members to attempt to develop effective techniques for combating problems within the classroom. Generally, the classroom teacher who has perceived a problem with a student begins by noting both the student's difficulties and some goals for the student that would enable that student to remain in the classroom. More formal interventions are then decided on by the team, and specific strategies to meet these goals are developed.

Chalfant and Van Dusen Pysh (1989) conducted several studies to determine the effectiveness of Teacher Assistance Teams in developing effective intervention goals, as well as to determine the success of these goals in the classroom. In these studies, students' performance was measured before, during, and after the teacher's intervention. The team was then responsible for coming to a consensus as to the amount of progress students made toward achieving the goals. Table 8.1 summarizes Chalfant and Van Dusen Pysh's findings as to the efficacy of interventions for 200 students whose teachers requested help from Teacher Assistance Teams. The students considered attended kindergarten through ninth grade and were from Arizona, Illinois, or Nebraska. Also, 116 of the students in the study did not have any disabilities but were markedly underachieving in their academic work. Chalfant and Van Dusen Pysh found that the interventions were successful for 103 (88.7%) of the students without disabilities. All of the mainstreamed students who had some identified disability were helped by the interventions. The Teacher Assistance Teams were unsuccessful in helping 54 students; however, all of those 54 students were referred to special education and all of them were found to be eligible for services.

Chalfant and Van Dusen Pysh's (1989) findings on the efficacy of Teacher Assistance Teams seem to support our belief that these teams are able to improve students' academic performances through the team's consultation with the general classroom teacher. Therefore, we believe that prereferral screening procedures should be utilized before a student is referred to the resource room.

Table 8.1. *Effectiveness of Teacher Assistance Teams, K–9*

Target Population (1981)	Number of Students Staffed	Number Helped Within Building	Number Referred to Special Education	Percentage of Requests Helped Within Building
Educationally underachieving and problem students	116	103	0	88.7
Mainstreamed students with handicaps	30	30	0	100
Students referred to special education	54	0	54	0
Total	200	133	54	66.5

Note. From "Teacher Assistance Teams: A Model for Within-Building Problem Solving" by J. C. Chalfant, M. V. Pysh, and R. Moultrie, 1989, *Learning Disabilities Quarterly*, 2, p. 53. Reprinted with permission.

We would like to make one final point relative to the situation where an overwhelmingly large number of students are referred for resource help. This occurrence may suggest that the instructional program in the general classes is not meeting the needs of a sizable percentage of the student body. It is also likely that overreferring in a school occurs because the criteria for selecting eligible students have not been carefully explained to teachers. Regardless, a flood of referrals should be viewed by the principal and the resource teacher as an indication that some sort of general intervention within the school is needed.

The outcome of this intervention should be that the classroom teachers better understand the operation of the resource program and that their skills in adapting curricula more effectively to accommodate those students who are having difficulty in school have been sharpened. Of course, before providing any intervention, a careful assessment of teacher needs should be undertaken to determine factors that cause or contribute to the overreferral of pupils in the school. The content of the intervention sessions would then be planned to focus on these identified factors.

The Referral Process

Rules and Guidelines

Once the classroom teacher has attempted classroom interventions and determined that the student is still performing markedly below all of the other students in the classroom, then the classroom teacher will likely decide to refer the student to special education. Later in this chapter, we will outline the referral process in detail; however, at this point we want to discuss the workings of due process as it applies to students being screened for or receiving special education services in the United States. Because it is legally required that parental permission be obtained *before* a student is tested for special education placement, the resource teacher should clearly understand the rules and regulations governing the identification, selection, and qualification of students for resource help before he or she begins taking referrals.

Outlining the structure and function of the resource program in terms of current, specific, and appropriate guidelines can be difficult. It should be noted that even when guidelines are available to the resource teacher, they may be (a) out of date and consequently not reflective of current thinking, (b) lacking in specificity, (c) in the process of being modified, or (d) inappropriate for a given school implementing a new type of resource program. In examining the guidelines for a resource program, resource teachers should first familiarize themselves with the basic workings of due process. Due process is a right guaranteed to each citizen of many countries by law. As applied to education, this means that no student can be denied the right to an appropriate education. In the case of a student with disabilities, due process usually refers to the right to be made aware of and to protest decisions made by school, state, or federal agencies that affect that student's education.

Although it is not necessary that resource teachers become familiar with the details of the due process codes, they should be generally familiar with the ideas, as well as have a working knowledge of what parents and schools can do to initiate due process proceedings. Turnbull, Turnbull, and Strickland (1979) concisely outlined due process proceedings by analyzing the legal requirements and defined four major components of due process.

1. *Due process hearings.* These can be initiated by either parents or the local education agency if they believe that the student is not receiving the services that he or she requires.
2. *Individual educational evaluation.* Evaluation consists of procedures conducted by trained personnel to determine whether a student has any handicapping condition that would render him or her eligible for special services.
3. *Written notice.* The student's parents and guardians are legally entitled to written notice whenever a change is made in a student's identification, education, or class placement.
4. *Parental consent.* Parental consent must be obtained in writing before a teacher, school, or local education agency may conduct any placement evaluations on a student.

Fundamental to the workings of due process is the idea that parents must be informed of any change in the student's placement in school and that they must provide written consent for the student to be evaluated for special services. Neither the classroom teacher nor the resource teacher should test or evaluate a student for entrance into the resource program without first obtaining permission to do so from the parents of the student.

Evaluation and Eligibility Issues

Once parental consent has been obtained, a school may proceed in evaluating students to determine their eligibility for various resource programs. However, because policies and procedures for placing students in resource programs differ from school to school, we will not attempt to outline specific criteria that could be used to qualify students for the various types of resource programs. Obviously, the criteria that any teacher uses must be consistent with the policies of the particular area, state or province, district, and school; and it should be mentioned that rules and regulations vary widely across these boundaries. For example, in most places, "normal intelligence" is specified as a necessary criterion for eligibility in a learning disabilities resource program. Yet there is little agreement among professionals or policies as to what constitutes normal intelligence, or even as to how intellectual status is to be determined for placement status. In some regions, normal intelligence is defined in regulation as being a score on an intelligence test that is within two standard deviations of the mean. In other regions, it is defined as any score that is within one standard deviation of the mean. In at least one locale, examiners are not allowed to use any standardized test of intelligence at all, but rather are required to diagnose normal intelligence on the basis of their clinical judgment.

The amount of underachievement or nonachievement that students must manifest to qualify for resource help is another area in which the guidelines are inconsistent. In some locales, performance that is one standard deviation or one grade level below expected achievement is grounds for qualification; whereas in other areas, two standard deviations or two grade levels below is required. In regard to learning disabilities, some locales require a significant discrepancy between ability and underachievement in relation to peers. In other locales, a significant discrepancy is also required, but students may be performing decidedly better than their peers. Also, there is no consistency regarding the procedures by which poor school achievement is to be documented. Different tests that purport to measure a particular ability are often used to assess quite different aspects of those skills. In the case of reading, for example, one test might measure the student's ability to recognize sound blends and identify words, whereas another test of reading might measure oral reading and comprehension. Yet both tests yield a score for reading.

In addition, the average performance of students on achievement tests varies markedly from school to school; consequently, some guidelines specify that resource students be severely underachieving in relation to their school peers. For example, if Sally, an underachieving sixth grader of normal intelligence who is enrolled in a school characterized by high academic achievement, moves to another part of town, her educational status might be changed. Sally might find that she is suddenly doing better than her new peers and therefore would no longer be regarded as underachieving. Even more surprising, it is possible that she might now be seen as a good student.

In support of the above statements, Ysseldyke and Algozzine (1983) studied commonly used definitions and standards for diagnosing learning disabilities and then applied those definitions to both normal students and students with learning disabilities. They found that 75% of the normal students could be labeled learning disabled, whereas they were unable to classify 25% of the students with learning disabilities as such. This lack of reliability in special education placement is problematic. It does, however, affirm our belief that placement procedures should be consistent both within a school and with what research reveals about the effective diagnosis of students with disabilities.

Evaluation Tools

Although specific criteria for evaluating students for entrance into and exit from resource programs will differ from school to school, in all instances thought should be put into the tools used in the evaluations to ensure that a student is being fairly and accurately screened. Often, the evaluation of students will contain standardized tests as well as observations and teacher input. When administering standardized tests, thought should be put into the instruments used in the evaluations to ensure that the testing instruments are being used to measure what they are intended to measure in a student. For example, it would be inappropriate to administer a vocabulary test to a student and attempt to infer from the student's performance an IQ score. Furthermore, care should be taken to ensure that the instruments that are administered are administered properly by a trained examiner. One book that is useful in assuring that these evaluation criteria are met is *A Consumer's Guide to Tests in Print* (Hammill et al., 1992). This volume reviews technical characteristics, administration procedures, usefulness, and types of results obtained for many current testing instruments.

The *Consumer's Guide* can be used in two ways. First, the book can be used as a starting point for selecting tests to use in a district, school, or classroom. For this reason, the authors have compiled a taxonomy that classifies each test included in the book according to the attribute or skill that it measures. The taxonomy is divided into four general domains: Achievement, Aptitude, Affect, and General Intelligence. These four domains are then subdivided into more than 60 discrete categories. Also, an overall rating is included next to the test's name. This rating is based on the adequacy of the test norms, reliability, and validity. A rating of A indicates that the test is highly recommended, B that the test is recommended, and F that the test has one or more serious flaws and is not recommended. Several pages from this reference are included in Figure 8.1 to show how the tests are broken down, as well as the form in which the information is presented.

2153 Gross Motor Abilities, Coordination

F	Bruininks-Oseretsky Test of Motor Proficiency	Bilateral Coordination
F	Bruininks-Oseretsky Test of Motor Proficiency	Upper-Limb Coordination
F	Luria-Nebraska Neuropsychological Battery: Children's Revision	F3
F	Miller Assessment for Preschoolers	Coordination
F	Purdue Perceptual-Motor Survey, The	Angels-in-the-Snow
F	Purdue Perceptual-Motor Survey, The	Jumping
F	Purdue Perceptual-Motor Survey, The	Obstacle Course
F	Purdue Perceptual-Motor Survey, The	Walking Board
F	Southern California Tests of Sensory Integration-Revised	Bilateral Motor Coordination
F	Test of Gross Motor Development	Gross Motor Development Quotient
F	Test of Gross Motor Development	Locomotor
F	Test of Gross Motor Development	Object Control

2154 Other Gross Motor Abilities

F	Bruninks-Oseretsky Test of Motor Proficiency	Running Speed & Agility
F	Scales of Independent Behavior	Fine Motor
F	Sensory Integration & Praxis Tests	Bilateral Motor Coordination
F	Sensory Integration & Praxis Tests	Manual Form Perception
F	Sensory Integration & Praxis Tests	Oral Praxis
F	Sensory Integration & Praxis Tests	Postrotary Nystagmus
F	Sensory Integration & Praxis Tests	Praxis on Verbal Command
F	Sensory Integration & Praxis Tests	Sequencing Praxis
F	Southern California Sensory Integration Tests—Revised	Crossing Mid-Line of Body

Figure 8.1. Sample pages from the *Consumer's Guide.*

2154 Other Gross Motor Abilities (cont.)

F Southern California Sensory   Right-Left Discrimination
   Integration Tests—Revised

2200 Verbal Aptitude/Developmental Abilities, General

A Test of Early Language Develop-   Total, Forms A & B
   ment, 2nd Edition
B Clinical Evaluation of Language   Total
   Functions—Screening Test—
   Advanced Level
B Clinical Evaluation of Language   Total
   Functions—Screening Test—
   Elementary Level
B Clinical Evaluation of Language   Receptive Language
   Fundamentals—Revised
   (8–16 yrs.)
B Clinical Evaluation of Language   Total Language
   Fundamentals—Revised
   (8–16 yrs.)
B Detroit Tests of Learning   Verbal Quotient
   Aptitude—Primary
B Detroit Tests of Learning   Verbal
   Aptitude—Primary, 2nd Edition
B Developmental Indicators for the   Concepts Area
   Assessment of Learning-Revised
B Screening Children for Related   Language
   Early Educational Needs
B Stanford-Binet Intelligence Scale, Verbal Reasoning
   4th Edition
B Test of Early Language Devel-   Language Quotient
   opment
B Wide Range Assessment of   Verbal Memory
   Memory & Learning
B Woodcock Language Proficiency   Oral Language
   Battery—Revised
B Woodcock-Johnson Psycho-   Memory Cluster
   Educational Battery—Part 1
B Woodcock-Johnson Psycho-   Long-Term Retrieval
   Educational Battery—Revised—
   Tests of Cognitive Ability
B Woodcock-Johnson Psycho-   Oral Language
   Educational Battery—Revised—
   Tests of Cognitive Ability

Figure 8.1. *Continued*

2200 Verbal Aptitude/Developmental Abilities, General (cont.)

B	Woodcock-Johnson Psycho-Educational Battery—Revised—Tests of Cognitive Ability	Processing Speed
B	Woodcock-Johnson Psycho-Educational Battery—Revised—Tests of Cognitive Ability	Short-Term Retrieval
B	Woodcock-Johnson Psycho-Educational Battery—Revised—Tests of Cognitive Ability	Test 8: Visual-Auditory Learning
F	Analysis of the Language of Learning	Total
F	Carrow Auditory-Visual Abilities Test	Auditory Battery
F	Clinical Evaluation of Language Functions—Screening Test—Advanced Level	Processing Items
F	Clinical Evaluation of Language Functions—Screening Test—Advanced Level	Production Items
F	Clinical Evaluation of Language Functions—Screening Test—Elementary Level	Processing Items
F	Clinical Evaluation of Language Functions—Screening Test—Elementary Level	Production Items
F	Language Processing Test	Total
F	McCarthy Scales of Children's Abilities	Verbal
F	Miller Assessment for Preschoolers	Verbal
F	Psycholinguistic Rating Scale	Auditory
F	Psycholinguistic Rating Scale	Auditory Association
F	Psycholinguistic Rating Scale	Auditory Closure
F	Psycholinguistic Rating Scale	Auditory Reception
F	Screening Assessment for Gifted Elementary Students	Program Related-C/Normal & Gifted Norms
F	Screening Test of Adolescent Language	Total
F	Test of Auditory-Perceptual Skills	Auditory Processing
F	Visual Aural Digit Span Test, The	Aural Output
F	Visual Aural Digit Span Test, The	Oral Expression
F	Visual Aural Digit Span Test, The	Total

Figure 8.1. *Continued*

2200 Verbal Aptitude/Developmental Abilities, General (cont.)

F	Woodcock-Johnson Psycho-Educational Battery—Revised—Tests of Cognitive Ability	Test 16: Delayed Recall-Visual-Auditory Learning
F	Word Test, The	Total Test
F	Word Test—R: Elementary, The	Total
F	Word Test: Adolescent, The	Total

2210 Verbal Cognition, Reasoning

B	Clinical Evaluation of Language Fundamentals—Revised (8–16 yrs.)	Word Classes
B	Scholastic Abilities Test for Adults	Verbal Reasoning
B	Scholastic Aptitude Scale	Verbal Reasoning
B	Screening Assessment for Gifted Elementary Students	Reasoning/Normal Norms
B	Stanford-Binet Intelligence Scale, 4th Edition	Absurdities
B	Stanford-Binet Intelligence Scale, 4th Edition	Comprehension
B	Stanford-Binet Intelligence Scale, 4th Edition	Verbal Relations
B	Wechsler Adult Intelligence Scale—Revised	Comprehension
B	Woodcock Language Proficiency Battery—Revised	Verbal Analogies
B	Woodcock-Johnson Psycho-Educational Battery—Part 1	Analogies
B	Woodcock-Johnson Psycho-Educational Battery—Revised—Tests of Cognitive Ability	Test 7: Analysis-Synthesis
B	Woodcock-Johnson Psycho-Educational Battery—Revised—Tests of Cognitive Ability	Test 21: Verbal Analogies
F	Career Maturity Inventory Competence Test	Part 5: Problem Solving
F	Cognitive Levels Test	Verbal Reasoning
F	Hahnemann High School Behavior Rating Scale	Reasoning Ability
F	Illinois Test of Psycholinguistic Abilities	Auditory Association
F	Language Processing Test	Associations

Figure 8.1. *Continued*

2210 Verbal Cognition, Reasoning

F	Language Processing Test	Categorization
F	Language Processing Test	Differences
F	Language Processing Test	Similarities
F	Luria-Nebraska Neuropsychological Battery: Children's Revision	F11
F	Pictorial Test of Intelligence	Similarities
F	Screening Assessment for Gifted Elementary Students	Reasoning/Gifted Norms
F	Screening Test of Adolescent Language	Language Processing
F	Screening Test of Adolescent Language	Proverb Explanation
F	Test of Auditory-Perceptual Skills	Auditory Quotient
F	Test of Language Competence	Composite
F	Test of Language Competence	Making Inferences
F	Test of Language Competence	Partial
F	Test of Language Competence	Recreating Sentences
F	Test of Language Competence	Understanding Ambiguous Sentences
F	Test of Language Competence	Understanding Metaphoric Expressions
F	Test of Problem Solving	Avoiding Problems
F	Test of Problem Solving	Determining Causes
F	Test of Problem Solving	Determining Solutions
F	Test of Problem Solving	Explaining Inferences
F	Test of Problem Solving	Negative Why Questions
F	Test of Problem Solving	Total
F	Wechsler Intelligence Scale for Children—Revised	Comprehension
F	Wechsler Intelligence Scale for Children—3rd Edition	Comprehension
F	Wechsler Preschool & Primary Scales of Intelligence	Comprehension
F	Word Test, The	Associations
F	Word Test, The	Semantic Absurdities
F	Word Test—R: Elementary, The	Associations
F	Word Test: Adolescent, The	Brand Names
F	Word Test: Adolescent, The	Signs of the Times

Figure 8.1. *Continued.* From *A Consumer's Guide to Tests in Print* (2nd ed., pp. 151–154) by D. D. Hammill, L. Brown, and B. Bryant, 1992, Austin, TX: PRO-ED. Reprinted with permission.

Once the taxonomy has been consulted and one or more appropriate instruments have been identified, the reader is referred to an alphabetic listing of tests, which summarizes the administration and scoring characteristics, examiner characteristics, test format characteristics, and nontechnical, descriptive information about each test. The A, B, and F rating system that was employed in the general taxonomy is used to rate the norms, reliability, and validity of each instrument.

The list also provides information regarding ages and/or grades for intended use of each test; whether the test is administered in a group or to an individual; the average testing time, in minutes; and which types of scores are obtained from the test administration (i.e., age equivalents, standard scores, percentile ranks, etc.). Any examiner qualifications that are necessary to administer the test are reported (EA = easily administered; ST = specialized training required to administer; R = restricted to trained psychological examiners). An example is found in Figure 8.2.

Standardized tests are not the only way that students are evaluated for special services. In fact, we recommend that several assessment techniques be employed prior to making a placement decision for a student. Observations are widely used as assessment tools. They can be either formal observations where specific behaviors are methodically recorded, or informal observations in which the observer notes his or her impressions of the observed student. Classroom behaviors, academic strategies, and interpersonal skills can all be the focus of observation.

SEEKING AND PROCESSING REFERRALS

Prior to beginning to seek and process referrals, resource teachers should familiarize themselves with the issues discussed in the previous sections of this chapter: (a) They should consider the benefits of prereferral intervention programs, (b) they should know the regulations governing special services and they should become familiar with due process as it pertains to the resource program, and (c) they should be aware of the issues and difficulties associated with evaluating students for special services.

Events in the Selection Process

The specifics of referral and placement procedures will be determined largely by the needs and requirements of the school as well as by the preferences of the resource teacher. However, the basic procedures that are followed and the general course of events that transpires during the referral and placement of a student are fairly consistent from school to school. White and Calhoun (1987) interviewed veteran resource teachers about the procedures regarding the referral and place-

| | | Technical Characteristics | | | | | | | | | Ages/Grades for Intended Use | Nontechnical Characteristics | | | | | | | | | | | | | | | | | | | | | |
| | | Norms | | | | | Reliability | | | Val. | | Admin. | | Scores | | | | | | Test Formats — Input | | | | | Test Formats — Output | | | | | | | |
Taxonomy code	Overall rating	Scores	Size	Demographics	Recency	Total	Internal consistency	Stability	Total	Total		Group/Individual	Testing time	Age equivalents	Grade equivalents	Percentile ranks	Standard scores	Other	Examiner qualifications	Third Party	Listen	Read print	Look at stimuli	Other	Speak, minor	Speak, major	Manipulate objects	Mark answer sheet	Point	Draw	Write print	Other
TEST OF MATHEMATICAL ABILITIES (1984)																																
Total Math Quotient — 4000	**B**	A	B	B	B	B	F	B	B	A	8-6/18-11 yrs.	I	60				•		EA		•	•			•	•					•	
Attitude Towards Math — 3210	**F**	A	B	B	B	B	F	F	F	F	8-6/18-11 yrs.	G	7			•	•		EA		•	•			•	•			•			
Vocabulary — 1230	**B**	A	B	B	B	B	B	F	B	B	8-6/18-11 yrs.	G	22			•	•		EA		•	•									•	
Computation — 1220	**B**	A	B	B	B	B	B	F	B	B	8-6/18-11 yrs.	G	22			•	•		EA		•	•									•	
General Information — 1230	**B**	A	B	B	B	B	A	B	B	A	8-6/18-11 yrs.	I	22			•	•		EA		•				•	•						
Story Problems — 1210	**F**	A	B	B	B	B	F	F	F	A	8-6/18-11 yrs.	G	22			•	•		EA		•	•									•	
TEST OF NONVERBAL INTELLIGENCE (1982)																																
TONI Quotient, Forms A & B — 2110	**B**	A	B	B	B	B	B	F	B	A	5-0/85-11 yrs.	I	7			•	•		EA				•						•			
TEST OF NONVERBAL INTELLIGENCE, SECOND EDITION (1990)																																
TONI Quotient, Forms A & B — 2110	**B**	A	B	A	B	B	A	B	B	A	5-0/85-11 yrs.	I	15			•	•		EA				•						•			
TEST OF PICTURES/FORMS/LETTERS/NUMBERS/SPATIAL ORIENTATION AND SEQUENCING SKILLS (1991)																																
Spatial Relationships (Pictures) — 2131	**F**	A	F	F	A	F	F	F	F	B	5-0/6-11 yrs.	I	2			•	•		EA		•		•						•			
Spatial Relationships (Forms) — 2131	**F**	A	F	F	A	F	F	F	F	F	5-0/8-11 yrs.	I	2			•	•		EA		•		•						•			
Reversed Letters & Numbers — 2250	**F**	A	F	F	A	F	F	F	F	B	5-0/7-11 yrs.	I	2			•	•		EA		•	•							•			
Reversed Letters in Words — 2250	**F**	A	F	F	A	F	B	F	B	B	5-0/8-11 yrs.	I	2			•	•		EA		•	•							•			
Reversed Letters from Non-Reversed Letters — 2250	**F**	A	F	F	A	F	B	F	B	B	5-0/8-11 yrs.	I	2			•	•		EA		•	•							•			
Reversed Numbers from Non-Reversed Numbers — 2250	**F**	A	F	F	A	F	B	F	B	B	5-0/6-11 yrs.	I	2			•	•		EA		•	•							•			
Letter Sequencing — 2250	**F**	A	F	F	A	F	F	F	F	F	5-0/8-11 yrs.	I	2			•	•		EA		•	•							•			
TEST OF PRACTICAL KNOWLEDGE (1983)																																
Total — 1000	**F**	A	A	F	B	F	A	F	B	A	gr. 8–12	G	45			•	•		EA		•	•							•			
Social — 1910	**F**	A	A	F	B	F	B	B	B	A	gr. 8–12	G	22			•	•		EA		•	•							•			

Figure 8.2. Sample pages from the list of tests in the *Consumer's Guide.*

	Taxonomy code	Overall rating	Norms: Scores	Size	Demographics	Recency	Total	Reliability: Internal consistency	Stability	Total	Val: Total	Ages/Grades for Intended Use	Admin: Group/Individual	Testing time	Age equivalents	Grade equivalents	Percentile ranks	Standard scores	Other	Examiner qualifications	Third Party	Listen	Read print	Look at stimuli	Other	Speak minor	Speak major	Manipulate objects	Mark answer sheet	Point	Draw	Write print	Other
TEST OF PRACTICAL KNOWLEDGE (1983) (cont.)																																	
Personal	1910	**F**	A	A	F	B	F	B	B	B	A	gr. 8–12	G	22			•	•		EA			•	•					•				
Occupational	1830	**F**	A	A	F	B	F	B	F	B	A	gr. 8–12	G	22			•	•		EA			•	•					•				
TEST OF PROBLEM SOLVING (1984)																																	
Total	2210	**F**	A	B	F	A	F	B	F	B	B	6-0/11-11 yrs.	I	25	•		•	•		EA		•					•						
Explaining Inferences	2210	**F**	A	B	F	A	F	F	F	F	B	6-0/11-11 yrs.	I	5	•		•	•		EA		•		•			•						
Determining Causes	2210	**F**	A	B	F	A	F	F	F	F	B	6-0/11-11 yrs.	I	5	•		•	•		EA		•					•						
Negative Why Questions	2210	**F**	A	B	F	A	F	F	F	F	B	6-0/11-11 yrs.	I	5	•		•	•		EA		•		•			•						
Determining Solutions	2210	**F**	A	B	F	A	F	F	F	F	B	6-0/11-11 yrs.	I	5	•		•	•		EA		•		•			•						
Avoiding Problems	2210	**F**	A	B	F	A	F	F	F	F	B	6-0/11-11 yrs.	I	5	•		•	•		EA		•		•			•						
TEST OF READING COMPREHENSION (1978)																																	
Reading Comprehension Quotient	1310	**F**	A	B	F	B	F	B	F	B	A	7-0/17-11 yrs.	G	60				•		EA			•	•					•				
General Vocabulary	1310	**F**	A	B	F	B	F	B	F	B	A	7-0/17-11 yrs.	G	22			•	•		EA			•	•					•				
Syntactic Similarities	1310	**F**	A	B	F	B	F	B	F	B	A	7-0/17-11 yrs.	G	22			•	•		EA			•	•					•				
Paragraph Reading	1310	**F**	A	B	F	B	F	B	F	B	A	7-0/17-11 yrs.	G	22			•	•		EA			•	•					•				
Sentence Sequencing	1310	**F**	A	B	F	B	F	B	F	B	A	7-0/17-11 yrs.	G	22			•	•		EA			•	•					•				
Mathematics Vocabulary	1230	**F**	A	B	F	B	F	A	F	B	A	7-0/17-11 yrs.	G	22			•	•		EA			•	•					•				
Social Studies Vocabulary	1500	**F**	A	B	F	B	F	A	F	B	A	7-0/17-11 yrs.	G	22			•	•		EA			•	•					•				
Science Vocabulary	1400	**F**	A	B	F	B	F	B	F	B	A	7-0/17-11 yrs.	G	22			•	•		EA			•	•					•				
Reading the Directions of Schoolwork	1000	**F**	A	B	F	B	F	B	F	B	A	7-0/17-11 yrs.	G	22			•	•		EA			•	•					•			•	•
TEST OF READING COMPREHENSION — REVISED (1986)																																	
Reading Comprehension Quotient	1310	**B**	A	B	B	B	B	A	F	B	B	7-0/17-11 yrs.	G	60				•		EA			•	•					•				
General Vocabulary	1310	**B**	A	B	B	B	B	A	F	B	A	7-0/17-11 yrs.	G	22			•	•		EA			•	•					•				
Syntactic Similarities	1310	**B**	A	B	B	B	B	A	F	B	A	7-0/17-11 yrs.	G	22			•	•		EA			•	•					•				
Paragraph Reading	1310	**B**	A	B	B	B	B	A	F	B	A	7-0/17-11 yrs.	G	22			•	•		EA			•	•					•				
Sentence Sequencing	1310	**B**	A	B	B	B	B	B	F	B	A	7-0/17-11 yrs.	G	22			•	•		EA			•	•					•				
Mathematics Vocabulary	1230	**B**	A	B	B	B	B	A	F	B	A	7-0/17-11 yrs.	G	22			•	•		EA			•	•					•				
Social Studies Vocabulary	1500	**B**	A	B	B	B	B	A	F	B	A	7-0/17-11 yrs.	G	22			•	•		EA			•	•					•				
Science Vocabulary	1400	**B**	A	B	B	B	B	A	F	B	A	7-0/17-11 yrs.	G	22			•	•		EA			•	•					•				
Reading the Directions of Schoolwork	1000	**B**	A	B	B	B	B	A	F	B	A	7-0/17-11 yrs.	G	22			•	•		EA			•	•					•			•	•

Figure 8.2. *Continued.* From *A Consumer's Guide to Tests in Print,* 2nd ed., (pp. 111–112), by D. D. Hammill, L. Brown, and B. Bryant, 1992, Austin, TX: PRO-ED. Reprinted with permission.

ment of students as well as about their roles and responsibilities in those procedures. In seeking to answer the questions, What are the events of the process from
referral to placement as experienced by special education teachers? and, What do
resource teachers perceive their responsibilities to be at each stage of the process?
White and Calhoun identified 11 basic steps that were consistently apparent in
the referral process. These basic steps, as well as the resource teachers' perceptions of their roles within these steps, are outlined below.

1. Initial Contact with a Classroom Teacher

Informal contact with a classroom teacher who is having a problem with a student
in the classroom is generally the beginning event in the referral process. The
resource teacher should feel a responsibility to make this contact as productive as
possible as well as to listen to the classroom teacher and take the informal referral
seriously.

2. Considering the Referral

At this point, the resource teacher generally considers the information that he or
she has been given about the student by the classroom teacher. The resource teacher
must consider that information in trying to make preliminary decisions regarding
the eligibility of the student. White and Calhoun (1987) pointed out that, over time,
most resource teachers develop a standard battery of questions that they ask the
teacher during this initial contact. At this stage it is also important that the resource
teacher call on his or her knowledge regarding the rules governing placement criteria in that particular school.

3. Providing Instructional Recommendations

At this point, it is generally beneficial for the resource teacher to offer instructional
suggestions for the classroom teacher to implement in the classroom. These instructional recommendations serve two purposes. First, if the student's problem is
moderate enough, then often specific, thoughtful suggestions made by the resource
teacher and implemented in the classroom will be sufficient. This eliminates the
need for further referral of the student, and thus helps to reduce crowding in the
resource room. Second, a significant length of time often passes between the classroom teacher's initial mention of a student and the evaluation of that student. For
this reason, helpful suggestions as to how to effectively manage that student in
the interim are often appreciated.

4. Formal Referral

A formal request for evaluation and referral always follows the informal contact
between a classroom teacher and the resource teacher. White and Calhoun (1987)
found that in all of the cases they considered, the completion of the formal referral
form was the responsibility of the classroom teacher requesting the referral. They

also pointed out, however, that resource teachers felt responsible for assisting teachers with that task.

5. Parental Permission
Special education programs require parental consent prior to the formal evaluation of a child for placement into special education services. Consequently, parental permission must be sought before proceeding.

6. Academic Screening
White and Calhoun (1987) found that all of the resource teachers surveyed reported that they personally conduct this screening. Further, respondents perceived this screening to be their major professional responsibility in the referral process.

7. Considering Psychological Evaluation
At this point in the process, the resource teacher has informally talked with the referring teacher and also made some initial contact with the student in question. It is now time to decide whether the student will be referred for a psychological evaluation. Resource teachers are called on to use their professional judgment to determine whether a psychological evaluation would result in the placement of the student, because school administrations do not like to process large numbers of ineligible psychological requests. Resource teachers reported that their ability to accurately predict the outcome of psychological referrals was highly valued.

8. Informing the Teacher
When requests for psychological evaluations are denied, then the resource teacher often feels responsible for soothing the disappointed classroom teacher. At this point, the resource teacher may want to suggest instructional or behavioral modifications that can be implemented in the classroom.

9. Referral to Special Services
If the psychological results warrant placing the student into a special service, then the student's parents must be informed of the results of the evaluation, the label assigned to their child, and the type of placement that the student will receive. White and Calhoun (1987) reported that "resource room teachers are very involved in informing parents of the chronology of events that has transpired since their consent to have the student tested" (p. 462–466).

10. Developing the Individualized Education Program
In the United States, prior to a student's actual placement within a special services program, an Individualized Education Program (IEP) must be written for that student. The resource teacher is primarily responsible for developing the IEP, although input from parents and teachers should be considered. The IEP is a docu-

ment that outlines the activities for the resource room program and further presents a plan specifically designed to remediate the referred student.

According to Section 121a.346, "Content of Individualized Education Program," in the Code of Federal Regulations published August 23, 1977, at 42 Federal Register 42474–42514, the individual education program for each student must include:

1) A statement of the student's present levels of performance.
2) A statement of long term goals, including short term objectives.
3) A statement of the specific types of educational and related services to be provided, including the extent to which the student will participate in both the resource and regular educational programs.
4) The projected dates for initiating the services and the anticipated duration of the services.
5) Appropriate objective criteria and evaluation procedures and schedules for determining whether the short term objectives are being achieved.

The IEP Conference

The purpose of the IEP conference is to present the IEP to the student's parents and teachers and discuss it with them. White and Calhoun (1987) reported that the major responsibility of the resource teacher during the conference was obtaining the parents' signatures on the IEP. Once this final parental consent is obtained, then referral and placement are concluded and the intervention begins.

Examples of Referral Approaches

White and Calhoun (1987) observed that almost all referral processes they surveyed had similar skeletal qualities, and that resource teachers had very definite perceptions of their roles within that process. However, they did not present any one specific referral outline that should be followed during the referral process. As was pointed out earlier, many factors affect the specific procedures that a resource teacher will choose to adopt for dealing with referrals. Therefore, resource teachers will need to investigate carefully these factors before beginning to develop their own procedures. We will present examples of different approaches to processing referrals.

The first referral and identification approach to be discussed was developed by Ysseldyke and Algozzine (1990). The process is presented in a flowchart in Figure 8.3. Because the process of assessing the special education needs of most students begins in the general classroom with the general classroom teacher noticing some difficulty that the student is having, the flowchart begins with the student's enroll-

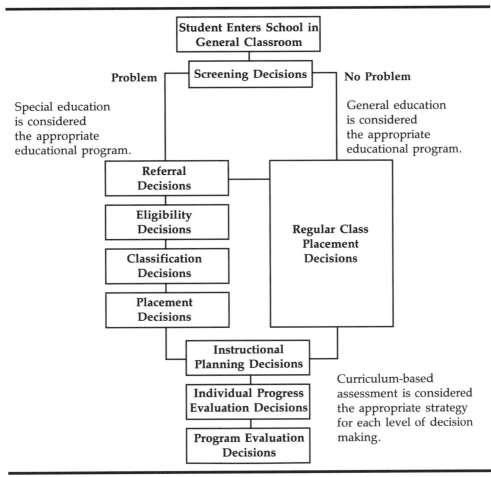

Figure 8.3. Flowchart representing a referral approach. From *Introduction to Special Education* by J. E. Ysseldyke and B. Algozzine, 1990, Boston: Houghton Mifflin. Adapted with permission.

ment in the general classroom. Once a difficulty has been recognized by the general classroom teacher, a screening phase begins. This screening phase involves the general teachers and the Teacher Assistance Team. During this period, data are gathered on the student and interventions within the general classroom are attempted. These interventions are to determine whether more intensive assessment of the student is necessary. This phase is important because most schools do not have enough psychological services to test each student who is having difficulty in the general classroom setting. Further, often minor modifications can be made in the general classroom that allow the student to function quite well in that environment. If the general teacher is able to modify instruction so that the student can function well in the general classroom, then a decision is made that general class placement is most appropriate for that student at the present time.

If it is decided that more extensive evaluation is required, then the student is referred for psychoeducational assessment. This process involves more extensive testing and observation of the student. During this process, three decisions must be made: (a) It must be officially determined whether or not the student is exceptional; (b) if it is decided that the student is exceptional, then the student must be classified (e.g., learning disabled, emotionally disturbed, etc.); and (c) particular placement decisions must be made. In other words, it must be decided where services are going to be provided (e.g., a resource room, a self-contained classroom).

Once it has been decided where the student is going to be served, then the student's skills, strengths, and weaknesses are evaluated and specific instructional planning decisions are made. It is during this phase that the student's Individualized Education Program is constructed and specific goals are set for the student's progress. Once the student's educational interventions begin, then progress is periodically monitored through individual progress evaluations. Parents, teachers, and the student himself or herself need to know if progress is being made. This evaluation is based on tests of specific skill acquisition as well as teachers' observations and impressions as to the student's performance, effort, and attitude.

Figure 8.4 presents another example of a referral procedure system. This referral process is easily adaptable to any type of resource program, including categorical, cross-categorical, noncategorical, or specific skill programs. The steps in the flowchart in Figure 8.4 are numbered to make the process easier to understand. A description of the particular duties of the resource teacher at each step in the referral process follows.

Step 1

At the first step, the principal and the resource teacher tell others about the nature of the program and the procedures to be followed in referring students. This is usually done at a general faculty meeting at the beginning of the school year. At this faculty meeting, the principal and/or resource teacher (a) states as clearly as possible who will and who will not be considered eligible for resource services; (b) specifies and if necessary justifies the number of students to be served; (c) explains the procedure that a classroom teacher should follow in referring a student; and (d) distributes any specific referral forms or other printed material that need to be given to teachers.

The content and format of these referral forms will differ according to the type of resource program being implemented, the policies of the school and the school district, and the personal preferences of the resource teacher and the school administration. For example, the referral form for a resource program designed to serve students who have been identified as mentally retarded would be different from a referral form that was designed for use in a resource program set up to remedi-

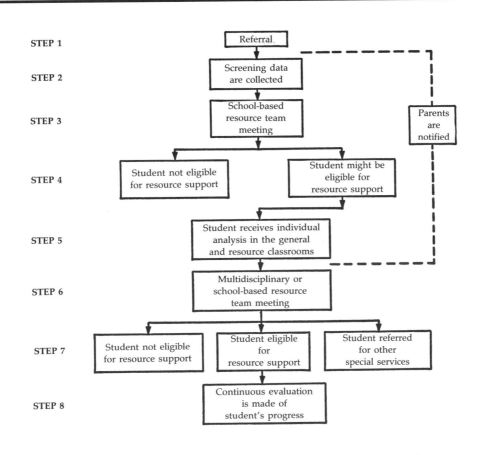

Figure 8.4. A proposed referral process.

ate students with reading difficulties. Three types of referral forms are shown in Figures 8.5 through 8.7. The form in Figure 8.5 is for use in programs where students must be formally classified as disabled to qualify for services. This form could be adopted for use in either a categorical or a noncategorical program. The second form, Figure 8.6, is designed for use by a teacher operating a noncategorical resource program. The third referral form, Figure 8.7, would be appropriate for use in any type of resource program. This particular form has the further advantage of being based on the assumption that the general education staff has been aware of and concerned about the student and that prereferral resources have been exhausted.

Resource Program—Mental Retardation

Referring Teacher: _____

Student's Name: _____

Criteria for Placement: Low Intellectual Functioning
                        Maladaptive Behavior

1. Why do you suspect the student is of low intelligence?

	YES	NO
A. An intelligence test score	____	____
B. Poor functioning in: Reading	____	____
Arithmetic	____	____
Spelling	____	____
Handwriting	____	____
Spoken language	____	____

2. Is the language of the home standard English?

   YES   NO   UNCERTAIN
   ____   ____   ____

3. In what areas does the student demonstrate maladaptive behavior?

	YES	NO
A. Socialization with: Adults	____	____
Peers	____	____
B. Attention	____	____
C. Self-Control	____	____
D. Self-Concept	____	____
E. Other (specify): _____		

4. What can the student do that is "normal" for his or her chronological age? _____

   _____

   _____

5. Additional comments: _____

   _____

   _____

   _____

Figure 8.5. Example of a referral form.

REFERRAL FORM
Resource Program—Noncategorical

Referring Teacher: _____

Student's Name: _____

1. In what area does the student perform inadequately?

	YES	NO	UNCERTAIN
Reading	____	____	____
Arithmetic	____	____	____
Spelling	____	____	____
Handwriting	____	____	____
Spoken language	____	____	____

2. Does the student have appropriate independent study habits?

	YES	NO	UNCERTAIN
	____	____	____

3. Does the student demonstrate appropriate classroom behavior?

	YES	NO	UNCERTAIN
Socialization with: Adults	____	____	____
Peers	____	____	____
Attention	____	____	____
Self-control	____	____	____
Self-concept	____	____	____
Other (specify) _____			

4. Additional comments: _____

_____

_____

_____

Figure 8.6. Example of a referral form.

REFERRAL DATA

THIS IS A REFERRAL FOR: (Check appropriate)

_____ Reading   _____ Spelling   _____ Social Behavior
_____ Mathematics   _____ Writing: Mechanics   _____ Other:
_____ Oral Language   _____ Writing: Composition   _____

Student Name   Student No.   D.O.B.   Grade   School

Parent   Address and Zip Code   Phone   Home School

Date Referral Received   Date Parent Permission Was Received

1. What is the presenting problem?
   SOCIAL BEHAVIOR   ACADEMIC BEHAVIOR

2. Give available data (std. or informal testing, interview, school history, etc.—include date of testing and tester)

3. What are the student's strengths?
   BEHAVIORAL   LEARNING

4. What resources have been used?   5. Effectiveness of resource:

5. What has been done by regular staff to meet the student's needs?
   BEHAVIORAL   LEARNING

6. What has worked?
   BEHAVIORAL   LEARNING

7. What hasn't worked?
   BEHAVIORAL   LEARNING

8. What might work?
   BEHAVIORAL   LEARNING

Adapted from the Madison, Wisconsin, Public Schools, Division of Specialized Educational Services, 1976.

Figure 8.7. Example of a referral form.

As with all other suggestions in this chapter, these sample forms are offered as a point of departure for teachers developing referral forms. They should not be seen as the only possibilities, nor do we recommend that they be adopted blindly into any type of resource program. Resource teachers should consider developing their own forms with the specific needs of their program, their own personal tastes, and the characteristics of the school(s) that the resource program serves in mind.

We recommend that resource teachers keep their referral forms as direct as possible. The form should be short and easy to complete, and its format should be easily understandable. In considering the structure of the form, it should be kept in mind that two types of information must be obtained: (a) information that is legally required and (b) information that is specific to the resource program to which the student is being referred. In time, the resource teacher may want to modify or change the forms if some of the information they require is not being used, or if necessary information is consistently missing. When change is being contemplated, suggestions from other faculty members should be solicited and taken into consideration.

Step 2

All referral forms should first be sent to the building principal. The principal can thus keep a record of referring teachers, the names of students who are referred, and any other information that may be desired by the school administration. Having reviewed the referral, the principal passes it on to the resource teacher. The resource teacher then initiates a meeting with the referring teacher to discuss the student being referred. In addition, any pertinent information about the student that is readily accessible should be accumulated, such as school records, test results, and other documented histories of the student. The purposes of the activities at this step of the screening are to begin to hypothesize as to the nature of the student's difficulties and to accumulate all the information that will be useful in diagnosing the student.

Step 3

At Step 3, selected school personnel meet to discuss the referred student. Those who attend this Teacher Assessment Teams meeting include the building principal, the resource teacher, the referring teacher, and any other members of the school faculty who might be able to make suggestions regarding effective services for the student. These other faculty members might include the nurse, the counselor, the school psychologist, or the special education teacher.

Because these meetings must be held regularly if they are to be effective, some of the team members may initially resist the idea. The most common reason cited against regular team meetings is the problem of freeing the necessary faculty during the school day. For this reason, resource teachers are encouraged to suggest that the meetings be held before or after school, or during lunch. If school faculty, including principals, classroom teachers, and counselors, are willing to commit some time to this program, then those who are resisting will generally go along. Because many states require these meetings by law or by policy, organizing a team meeting may not present a problem.

Two points need to be considered in establishing a team. First, the meetings should be short, and well organized around specific objectives. When inconsequential or irrelevant information is introduced, it is the resource teacher's responsibility to insist that the agenda be strictly adhered to. This can often be accomplished by providing a written format for each of the participants. Administrators and teachers are busy people; they do not want to attend meetings that are too long, poorly organized, wasteful, or indecisive.

The second point deals with the question of who the team comprises. Only members of the school staff should be included on the team on a regular basis. In general, including outside professionals such as district personnel and community specialists is not helpful. Because the faculty members within the school will interact with the student on the most regular basis, they should be primarily responsible for making the decisions about the placement of that student. However, when additional help is needed, or when specific rules or regulations must be satisfied, then outside personnel must be contacted.

Step 4

At Step 4, there are two options. The team may decide that the student is not eligible for resource support at the present time. It may be that the student's difficulties do not appear severe enough to warrant removal from the general classroom. If this decision is made, the referring teacher will want the team to suggest interventions that could be attempted in the general classroom. However, if the student seems a possible candidate for resource support, then the process continues to the next step.

Step 5

An analysis of the student in the general classroom and an individualized supplemental analysis of the student are undertaken. If the student must be officially classified as disabled to qualify for resource support, then a certified district employee will probably have to make the diagnosis. Resource teachers should realize that this sort of assessment is necessary primarily for administrative and funding purposes, and they should proceed with their own education-based assessment.

Step 6

This step calls for another meeting. If the student is suspected of being disabled, the meeting will probably be a multidisciplinary staffing, which includes specialists who are required to examine and to label students with disabilities. If, on the other hand, regulations do not require that any special professionals certify the diagnosis of the student, then the initial members of the team will attend the meeting.

Step 7

At this step, an official placement decision is made. Three options are possible: (a) It may be decided that the student is not eligible for resource support; (b) it may be decided that the student is eligible for resource support, in which case the general classroom teacher and the resource teacher will begin to implement the recommendations generated at Step 6; or (c) it may be decided that the student would benefit most from special services other than resource support. This decision is made when the student's difficulties are so severe or complex that special education self-contained placement is considered desirable.

If at this point it is determined that the student is eligible for special services, then a carefully planned Individualized Education Program (IEP) is prepared for the student. Although the specific legal guidelines for developing the IEP are discussed earlier in this chapter, we want to reiterate the importance of careful attention to the IEP. Also, we want to point out some practices to be avoided in developing an IEP. First, administrators and teachers are becoming increasingly concerned about the amount of paperwork and time involved in generating individually tailored programs for each student. As a result of this concern, shortcuts are being developed and explored. For example, some resource teachers have begun to rely almost exclusively on one or two published lists of arbitrary objectives and/or curricula. Although these objectives and curricula often lack empirical support, resource teachers often simply transpose them into written programs for individual students. Little, if any, attempt is made to individualize the program from student to student. As a result, all programs are the same or similar for every student receiving support from the resource unit. The use of computers in generating the individualized plan is also being introduced. In these instances, the student's deficit is fed into the computer, which in turn provides a list of instructional objectives and teaching strategies.

We find both of these practices highly questionable and believe that they violate the spirit and the nature of the Individualized Education Program when they are used without any additional information. We believe that the number of instructional and human variables that must be accounted for in comprehensive instructional programming planning can never be accommodated by consulting one or two lists of arbitrary objectives.

Many administrators and teachers are also concerned about the number of regulations that apply to special services within the school, particularly those relating to students with disabilities. This problem is made more manageable if professionals take the time to separate the regulations as they are required by law from the elaborate recommendations that often accompany the implementation of those regulations. There is a great deal of misinformation and misunderstanding as to the actual requirements and regulations. In addition, laws are being reinterpreted constantly and regulations are frequently modified. We strongly support the idea that an Individualized Education Program should be written for each student receiving resource support, regardless of whether that practice is mandated.

The education of students with disabilities cannot proceed systematically and expediently without careful planning. A carefully considered IEP can help guard against irrelevant goals for the student. Further, because the IEP documents what a student can and cannot do as well as outlines goals for the improvement of the student's personal and academic skills, the IEP offers grounds for common understanding of the goals and interventions for a particular student among parents, general educators, and the resource teacher. This sort of consistency and communication is crucial for effective education.

Step 8

At this point, students have been placed in a resource program and their educational plans have been implemented. The results of these plans will need to be carefully and critically monitored. This monitoring must be continuous to ensure that any program continues to be as beneficial as possible for the students and their teachers. Good teaching requires continuous evaluation.

We want to reiterate one point about seeking and processing referrals. In Figure 8.4, a space to the right refers to the notification of the student's parents. This is an extremely important component of due process and of the referral and selection process. In most cases, parents must be notified, and usually their permission must be obtained before any type of assessment or programmatic services can be provided to the student. If the resource program is a specific skill program or a noncategorical program, then the parents may or may not need to be notified, but if the student is being considered as a possible candidate for special education, or if there is any chance that the student might be labeled as disabled, then the parents or guardians must be notified. This point is addressed specifically in Public Law 93-380 (the Educational Amendment of 1974). The language of this act mandates that in providing special education support, the state must

> provide procedures for insuring that handicapped children and their parents or guardians are guaranteed procedural safeguards in decisions regarding identification, evaluation and educational placement of handicapped children including, but not limited to (A) (i) prior notice to parents or guardians of the child when the local or state educational agency proposes to change the educational placement of the child, (ii) an opportunity for the parents or guardians to obtain an impartial due process hearing, examine all relevant records with respect to the classification or educational placement of the child and obtain an independent educational evaluation of the child, (iii) procedures to protect the rights of the child when the parents or guardians are not known, unavailable, or the child is a ward of the State including the assignment of an individual (not to

be an employee of the State or local education agency involved in the education or care of children) to act as a surrogate for the parents or guardians, and (iv) provision to insure that the decisions rendered in the impartial due process hearing required by this paragraph shall be binding on all parties subject only to appropriate administrative or judicial appeal. [Public Law 93-380, Title VIB, Sec. 612(d) (13 A)]

We purposely have not designated the exact point in the referral and placement process when parental permission should be secured. It will vary from place to place. Resource teachers must ascertain the local policies relative to securing parental agreements and involvement. Regardless of the local rules, the resource teacher should make sure the due process is followed with regard to the labeling and placement of students with disabilities. If resource teachers are unfamiliar with their due process responsibilities, we strongly urge them to consult *A Primer on Due Process* by Abeson, Bolick, and Hass (1976). This publication will provide a suitable background on the legal aspects of due process, the sequence of procedures that must be followed, an overview of the structure and operation of hearings, the role of the surrogate parents, and sample forms.

The referral and selection process often is a complex, cumbersome, time-consuming, and law-governed procedure. Consequently, care must be taken to ensure that all local and state rules and regulations that relate to providing special services to students are followed to the letter. The rights of students and their parents probably will be drawn more sharply in the future as more court cases are decided. Resource teachers are strongly encouraged to keep abreast of any changes in these legal rights and to alter their procedures to comply with pertinent court decisions.

MULTIDISCIPLINARY STAFFING

Historically, the multidisciplinary staffing model was developed in clinical settings where children with severe physical, social, and/or emotional problems were involved and where complex and highly restricted treatment procedures were employed. For example, a child with severe problems might need medication, very specialized individualized educational programming, and/or highly specific psychiatric treatments. The multidisciplinary staffing model was created to address the problem of communication among a group of relatively specialized professionals who generally work independently in these cases. Such a model allowed professionals to determine interrelated treatment possibilities, to establish treatment priorities, and to discuss and monitor the progress of persons with severe disabilities over time.

We view the multidisciplinary model as a necessary and valuable component of treating these individuals with severe disabilities. For most students referred to the resource room, however, we question the value of using such an approach.

Although the idea of a multidisciplinary team (MDT) is philosophically attractive, upon more careful consideration, it proves to be laden with several inherent flaws. Pfeiffer (1980) identified four areas of concern with MDTs. First, the small amount of data available on MDTs indicates that they tend to reduce the role of parents and teachers while simultaneously increasing the roles of specialists and professionals who may be unfamiliar with the student in question. Second, there seems to be no specific standard or set of guidelines as to the information that should be collected in making placement decisions. Third, there is no evidence to support the idea that the potentially positive effects of MDTs are being realized. Fourth, and perhaps most importantly, Pfeiffer suggested that MDTs often do as much to promote interpersonal rivalry as they do to promote cooperation.

During their preservice training, resource teachers have likely been told about the importance of multidisciplinary work with individuals who have learning and behavior problems. Consequently, these teachers may be inclined to enlist the aid of psychiatrists, social workers, psychologists, guidance counselors, curriculum experts, and other specifically trained personnel to enhance the resource program effort. For most students referred for resource program help, this is an inefficient and unrewarding practice. Most of the referred students will have mild to moderate learning and/or behavior problems and will require academic and behavior treatments that the resource teacher should be able to implement without any assistance other than that of the general classroom teacher and the student's parents. A competent resource teacher should have had sufficient training and experience to manage most of the referred students successfully.

In a few cases, some specially trained individuals may need to be consulted. For example, some resource students may need medication, and a properly trained physician should be consulted on that matter. Or, in other cases, substance or sexual abuse may be suspected and personnel with expertise in those areas should be notified. If the home life of a student seems questionable, then a social worker may be asked to further investigate the problem. In all cases, however, the resource teacher should be intimately involved and adequately informed and should participate to the utmost extent feasible.

Occasionally, a resource teacher may be unfamiliar with techniques for dealing with a student who has a particular problem. For example, an individual student who is bilingual may have been assigned to a resource teacher who knows little or nothing about such cases. In these instances, the resource teacher will have to call on a specialist for assistance. However, resource teachers should always attempt to increase their competence so that they have to rely on others less and less. Further training, reading, and practice are needed on a continuing basis to round out the resource teacher's skill.

In sum, we suggest that multidisciplinary staffing for most resource students is unnecessary but may be undertaken occasionally when needed. Specifically, we believe that individuals other than those housed in the school in which the resource program is located generally should *not* be part of developing and implementing programs for referred students. Only when a student's problem is outside the domain of authority or skill of a resource teacher should ancillary professionals be called on. Although rules and regulations specify that specialists other than the resource teacher must certify a student as eligible for special support, the resource teacher should recognize that this labeling process will relate very little to the daily instructional program of an individual student in a specific school and classroom. The planning, implementing, and evaluation of daily programs for the resource teachers must be the responsibility of the resource teacher, local school staff, and the parents.

In this chapter, we have given an overview of the referral and selection procedures relative to the resource concept. In addition, guidelines regarding the development of an individual educational plan and suggestions on multidisciplinary staffings were included. The legal requirements, the detail and scope of the referral process, the specificity of the individual educational plan, and the sheer amount of talent and competency needed by professionals to adhere to these matters may be somewhat overwhelming at first. However, there are few shortcuts to defensible professional practices, and resource teachers will usually find, after a period of study and implementation, that these matters can be smoothly and efficiently incorporated into their own personal skills and competencies.

Chapter 9

Managing the Program

As with most other educational enterprises, a great deal of attention must be directed toward planning and managing the daily operations of the resource program. Without careful planning and management, even the most instructionally competent resource teachers will find that their programs are disorganized and ineffective. The information in this chapter will help resource teachers develop a management system applicable to the unique requirements of operating resource programs. The suggestions in each section of this chapter are not comprehensive enough to solve all the problems that arise in the day-to-day operation of resource programs; instead, we have attempted to deal pragmatically with management difficulties that usually crop up in any resource program. The areas discussed are (a) elementary and secondary schools; (b) start-up procedures; (c) scheduling; (d) movement between classrooms; (e) evaluation of the program management; (f) peer tutoring and cooperative learning; and (g) personal time management.

ELEMENTARY AND SECONDARY SCHOOLS

Up to this point, we have described the resource program concept, resource teacher roles, methods for initial implementation of the program, and referral and selection procedures. Little attempt has been made to differentiate these descriptions for elementary and secondary schools. This is because there is not much differentiation on the topics discussed. The concept of resource programs does not change from elementary to secondary; the same categorical programs, cross-categorical programs, and the others exist at all levels in schools. Nor do the roles of the resource teacher change. At both levels they are expected to assess, teach, and consult. The procedures employed for initiating a program and selecting students for both systems are also very similar. The organization and curricula of the systems are somewhat different, however, and as a result different management strategies are sometimes needed at the two levels. In this section, the major differences in organization and curricula are described.

The person responsible for the entire operation of an individual school is the building principal, who in turn is responsible to the district superintendent and a board of education. There is considerable variation of titles and line authorities throughout school districts. For example, some districts employ a great number of directors, supervisors, assistant or associate superintendents, and other administrators, and their relationship to principals may be somewhat different from locale to locale. All teachers, including resource personnel, should become very familiar with their district's administrative structure. Knowing who makes decisions and who is responsible for certain aspects of the educational endeavor is useful information.

There is considerable difference between elementary and secondary principals in their day-to-day relationship with teachers. In a typical elementary school, the principal relates directly to teachers on administrative and instructional matters. Secondary schools, however, are traditionally much larger than elementary schools. Consequently, secondary-level principals often do not deal directly with each teacher; instead, they delegate responsibility to guidance personnel, athletic directors, and department heads. Resource teachers need to determine who within their own school is responsible for specific administrative tasks.

There is considerable variation between elementary and secondary resource teachers in their relationship to other teachers. At the elementary level, resource teachers share major responsibility for an individual student with only one other teacher—the regular classroom teacher—because in most elementary schools, each classroom teacher is responsible for all of his or her students throughout the school day. Auxiliary personnel, such as gym teachers, art teachers, and counselors, are usually available to assist classroom teachers for a period or two a day, but for the most part, the general classroom teacher bears the major responsibility for each child's instruction throughout the school day.

At the secondary level, however, resource teachers are likely to find that students assigned to their program see as many as five or six teachers per day—homeroom teachers, mathematics teachers, history teachers, vocational education teachers, science teachers, and so forth. Each of these teachers may have a department head who is also vitally interested in what is happening with each student in his or her area. Resource teachers therefore must consult with many more professionals in the secondary schools. As a result the management of each student's program will take more effort.

Another difference between elementary and secondary schools relates to the curricula. At the elementary level, teachers focus on the development of basic reading, writing, and computational skills. At the secondary level, teachers focus on content-area subjects such as science, distributive education, history, and foreign language. This is not to say that content is not taught at the elementary level or that basic skills are not taught at the secondary level. Rather, there is a shift in emphasis between the two systems. Management will require more effort at the secondary level because of greater variety of course offerings for students.

The resource program at the primary school level is used almost exclusively to remediate students whose skills are behind those of their peers. However, as students in the resource programs enter junior high and high school, different resource program options emerge. The two most common features unique to resource programs at the junior high and high school levels are (a) they begin to address students' problems in learning specific course content, and (b) they begin to teach basic living skills and/or vocational education.

Resource programs in junior high and high school that serve students whose disabilities affect their performance in general school coursework may want to implement a program that parallels the general school curriculum, but adapts the presentation format and/or the evaluations of the students. Some examples of adaptations that can be made in the resource room include using films and/or audiovisual material to present course content, allowing students to tape lectures and review the tapes in the resource room, or reinforcing the content presented in the general classroom during resource time. Ysseldyke and Algozzine (1990) presented the following scenario to illustrate this type of reinforcement:

> Some of Larry's students have learning disabilities. In the regular classroom, they are reading *MacBeth*. In the resource room Larry has them read from the *Illustrated MacBeth*, then tests their comprehension using verbal quizzes and discussions after each scene in the play. (p. 48)

This type of content adaptation and manipulation allows junior high and high school students with learning disabilities the opportunity to advance through the general curriculum with their peers.

Another consideration in resource rooms at the junior high and high school level that is not present in elementary school programs is the teaching of life skills. Zeigmond and Sansone (1986) discussed this type of resource adaptation as the *novel curriculum:*

> The major emphasis in the novel curriculum is on equipping students to function in society after graduation from high school. The regular curriculum in the high school is seen as largely inappropriate, and the students are taught a different curriculum that is better suited to their needs. (p. 15)

The novel curriculum may focus on consumer information, completion of job application forms, community awareness, or prevocational and vocational training.

Obviously, the above suggestion would be appropriate for junior high and high school students only. At the elementary level, development of basic academic skills should be the major focus both in the general classroom and in the resource room.

That there are differences between elementary and secondary schools should not imply that these organizational structures are discontinuous. As far as the individual student is concerned, the program begun in the elementary years should account for transition between school levels. For example, during the last year of the elementary program, the primary emphasis of the resource program should shift to assessing and teaching the skills that will be needed in the next environment. Whether a sixth grader reads at Level 10 or Level 11 in a particular series is likely irrelevant to the demands of the junior high school.

Serious considerations must be given by the district and especially by the resource teacher to the transition needs of students who move from one major program structure to another. (This is also the case when students move horizontally from one school to another rather than vertically through the grades.)

To provide transition programming, resource teachers at both ends of the transition must know each other's structure. The elementary teacher must understand the structure and demands of the secondary program to prepare students, and the secondary teacher must understand better the extent to which students have been prepared at the elementary level for realities of the secondary school.

In sum, the basic differences between elementary and secondary resource programming relate to administrative organization and curricula. Resource teachers will need to devote some time to investigating their own school's unique organization, as well as the course offerings. In addition, teachers should consider the offerings of the school their students come from, as well as those they might eventually attend.

START-UP PROCEDURES

If possible, no students should be assigned to a new resource program during the first 2 or 3 weeks of its operation. There are several good reasons for this delay.

1. The delay gives the resource teacher ample time to reassess and plan programs for students who were in the resource program the previous year, many of whom will still need special resource services.
2. The delay allows general and special teachers an opportunity to implement their own programs and to identify students in their classes whom they may want to refer.

3. The time interval can give the resource teacher, especially a new one, a chance to meet the other teachers in the building, to learn about the curricula used in the school, and to prepare the resource program for the coming year.

Before deciding about the kind of organization and management patterns that should be associated with a particular resource program, the resource teacher should collect information about the school's administrative and political context. This essential information will help determine both possibilities and constraints that will affect the program. We discuss two major considerations: (a) the general information about the school and community that will be needed regardless of level or setting to describe the general administration of the school and (b) the striking differences between a continuing and a ''new '' program, involving both administrative factors and school politics.

General Information About the School and Community

The first step in collecting information about the context of the resource program is to find out about all characteristics of the school situation that are likely (a) to assist or hinder the operation of the program and (b) to affect the school careers of individual students within that program. These characteristics include school policies and procedures, the instructional programs used throughout the school, demographic indicators of the community, record-keeping practices, and any other special programs operating in the building. Figure 9.1 lists specific information that will be useful.

The better informed the teacher is before beginning the resource program, the less likely that the program will need major revision later on. For example, duty schedules and expectations for attendance at meetings make a great difference in time allocations. If instructional teams meet infrequently, a great deal of time must be spent in such meetings to prevent the resource teacher from losing contact with ongoing student programs and teacher expectations.

Continuing an Ongoing Program Versus Starting a New Program

As the resource teacher plans the program, one of two basic situations will prevail. Either the program will be new, or it will be a continuation of a previously established program. These two circumstances require somewhat different approaches to initial program planning, even though many elements are the same.

A. General School and District Policies

☐ 1. School organization, including grade levels and sections
☐ 2. School hours
☐ 3. Use of secretarial services
☐ 4. Ordering and use of supplies and materials
☐ 5. Budget and budgeting process
☐ 6. Meeting attendance
☐ 7. Social amenities and customs
☐ 8. Duty schedules
☐ 9. Workroom use
☐ 10. Lunchroom schedules and policies
☐ 11. School schedule: annual; reporting period; weekly; daily
☐ 12. Substitute teacher policies and preparation
☐ 13. Lesson plan requirements
☐ 14. Student transportation
☐ 15. Field trips
☐ 16. Required permissions
☐ 17. Liability questions
☐ 18. Schedules of special instructional personnel (e.g., art, music, physical education, or remedial reading)
☐ 19. Schedules of special support personnel (e.g., school psychologist, social worker, or speech and language clinician)
☐ 20. Policies regarding aides or teaching associates
☐ 21. Committee structure: purposes; membership; meetings; and processes
☐ 22. Emergency procedures, such as medical, fire, and disaster
☐ 23. Library or instructional materials center use, resources, and personnel
☐ 24. Floor plan of the school
☐ 25. General achievement levels and expectations
☐ 26. Playground policies and schedules at the elementary level
☐ 27. Off-campus regulations for postelementary settings
☐ 28. Between-class movement policies and regulations
☐ 29. Parking
☐ 30. Restroom locations and use policies
☐ 31. Parent organizations and level of involvement
☐ 32. School history
☐ 33. Faculty evaluation: rationale; procedures; schedules
☐ 34. Bus schedules and routes

Figure 9.1. Checklist of information about school and community.

☐ 35. Regulations concerning releasing children during or after school hours (e.g., to which adults? whose signatures needed? where are restrictions on release noted?)

☐ 36. Professional organizations: structures; influence; regulations

☐ 37. Supervisory personnel: authorities and responsibilities

☐ 38. Student transfer policies

☐ 39. Extracurricular activities and policies governing participation

☐ 40. All federal, state, and local regulations and guidelines concerning the operation of the resource program

B. Special Program Policies and Procedures

☐ 1. Personnel assigned to various units; persons in charge

☐ 2. Written and unwritten policies regarding operation

☐ 3. Forms and procedures, or governing regulations

☐ 4. Expectations for involvement of resource teacher

C. Interagency Agreements/Relationships

☐ 1. Agencies involved (e.g., family services, juvenile court, psychological services)

☐ 2. Contact persons

☐ 3. Nature of involvement with individual students

☐ 4. School agreements/policies

D. Instructional Program

☐ 1. Mandatory curriculum content or methodologies

☐ 2. Scope and sequence of each relevant curriculum offering

☐ 3. Textbook series or curriculum guide names and editions

☐ 4. Grouping practices

☐ 5. Standardized testing program: schedules and uses made

☐ 6. Record-keeping

☐ 7. Grading and/or reporting practices

☐ 8. Accountability expectations or curriculum evaluation

☐ 9. Availability of required resources

☐ 10. Supplemental assistance available

☐ 11. Retention policies

☐ 12. Behavioral expectations and policies

E. Individual Student Information

☐ 1. Rationale for current schedule or teacher assignments

☐ 2. Cumulative records: specific information; uses made; accessibility; confidentiality regulations

Figure 9.1. *Continued*

☐ 3. Parent or guardian contacts and attitudes

☐ 4. Other sources of information about the student

F. Classroom Information

☐ 1. Specific curriculum scope, sequence, content, and methodologies unique to any teacher or class

☐ 2. Time/event schedule for each relevant classroom

☐ 3. Floor plan with potential distractors identified

☐ 4. Seating chart with current student names

☐ 5. Policies or customs idiosyncratic to that classroom

☐ 6. Resources available for individualization (e.g., computers or peer tutoring programs)

☐ 7. Teacher preferences in organization and management of the instructional program (e.g., cooperative groups or whole group instruction)

☐ 8. General experience and educational history of the teacher(s)

☐ 9. Assessment procedures: academic; sociometric; attitudinal; behavioral

☐ 10. Discipline policies

☐ 11. Independent work expectations and evaluation practices

G. Community

☐ 1. School boundaries and adjacent schools

☐ 2. Names and locations of schools to which students are promoted, and schools they have previously attended

☐ 3. General community characteristics (e.g., housing appearance, open space, street lighting, and crime index)

☐ 4. Community landmarks (e.g., stores, laundromats, parks, churches, and fire station)

☐ 5. Community health and social services (e.g., recreational programs, mental health centers, hospitals, and clinics)

☐ 6. General attitude toward schools and education

☐ 7. General economic indicators

☐ 8. School/business partnerships

Figure 9.1. *Continued.*

The Continuing Program

Even with a continuing program, it is not possible simply to begin from where the old year or the previous teacher left off. Too many factors intervene. The major reason for finding out about an ongoing program is that there are already established political factors that influence decisions the resource teacher might like to make in regard to the program and its management. Logic may not be as important as discretion in school politics. We describe below four major considerations in restarting or revising a continuing program.

1. *Understanding the old program.* If the resource teacher steps into a program that has been in operation for some time, the mutual agreements concerning that program are usually well defined. However, "well defined" does not mean that they will be available in written form, or that they will be readily acknowledged. Instead, the teacher must ask questions about the previous program to determine how it was organized and managed. Further, in some cases there will be positive feelings about it, and in others the feelings will be negative. It is important to pick up on these feelings, and to determine their apparent causes. This is potentially a complicated matter for several possible reasons.

First, there may be a split between how the program was/is perceived by the administrator and by the teachers. For example, the principal may wish to have more time spent on in-class activities rather than in a pullout program, whereas the teachers may believe that it is best for the total instructional program to have low achievers sent to a special program during classroom instruction. The resource program may have become the battleground for these conflicting notions of how to accommodate the instructional needs of low achievers, or for a philosophical conflict about grouping practices. Certainly, ongoing collaborative consultation should be used so that neither students nor the resource teacher suffer from discrepant philosophies.

A second reason that makes understanding the old program complicated is that, regardless of whether the program was effective or ineffective, it may be viewed by the school staff as the only way a resource program should be run. Perhaps because no other models were available, or perhaps because people were comfortable with the old program, a program may become ingrained within the school; this will be difficult to change when the new resource teacher comes along with his or her own expectations about how it should operate. In such cases, care must be taken to put any proposed changes in program elements on a "data base" to measure the effectiveness of the proposed changes.

Regardless of the difficulties involved, the resource teacher must take the time to find out everything he or she can about the old program so that decisions can be made early on about any changes that are to be recommended. Further, an understanding of the politics of the situation can help with the diplomacy that may be needed to accomplish any proposed changes in organization and management.

2. *Changes in the school program.* Note any changes in the school program in terms of the effects such changes might have both on individual children and on the resource program itself. Several examples illustrate the importance of this factor.

First, if the school is changing from a basal series reading curriculum to one that is literature based, it is likely that far different assessment information and instructional planning will need to be done on behalf of individual children within the resource program. Further, the relationship between the general program and the resource program must be redefined in a mutually satisfactory manner. Or if the school has reorganized so that a specific teacher is responsible for a certain subject for everyone (e.g., to focus on the math expertise of a qualified teacher), the resource teacher must find out about curriculum, scheduling, and the range of individual differences such a teacher would be expected to accommodate. Or if the school has moved to competency-based assessment of student outcomes, the role of the resource program is likely to undergo material change, and the focus for individual students will likely be on the assessment and remediation of expected competencies. Keep in mind that apparently minor changes (e.g., bus schedules or grade card formats) can also impact the resource program.

3. *Changes in personnel.* If there are new teachers, or if teachers have been retrained to accommodate some of the special instructional needs of students within the resource program, then changes must be made. Perhaps the resource teacher must plan more time for consultation with the new teacher, or in the case of the retrained teacher, less time with direct instruction with students.

If administrators or supervisors are new, they may have specific notions of how the resource program should operate, or how it should relate to other programs. Because of their power or influence, an early conference with new administrators and supervisors is essential to setting mutually agreeable expectations for the program and for the resource teacher's performance. Further, it is usually easier to make any desired changes at critical "new" times (e.g., at the new school year, with new teacher(s), a new principal/coordinator, or with the arrival of new students).

4. *Changes in rules and regulations.* Each year it is important to check the most recent federal and state guidelines to ensure that the program is being managed in accordance with current rules or recommendations. Those who are responsible for the administration of any parts of the program should be involved in seeing that the program does in fact meet current professional and legal standards.

The New Program

In starting a new resource program, two additional considerations can influence the ease of its initial implementation. The first is the need to propose and evaluate alternatives for each aspect of the program within the present situation. The second consideration involves delaying the introduction of a full student caseload.

Starting a new resource program often provides opportunities to apply current ideas about all aspects of its operation. It is important to meet with school staff well in advance of the program's initiation to plan its best role within the local context. At this time interested persons can (a) suggest options to be explored and evaluated and (b) develop rationales for each component. Everyone involved should take special care at this time to obtain copies of all *current* federal, state, and local guidelines. Keep in mind that previously written local guidelines may be superseded by newer state recommendations.

Whatever the agreements that may be reached, it is important to develop a written description of the program for future reference. Written plans serve both as a reminder throughout the year to reinforce mutual agreements, and as a baseline from which ongoing modifications can be made.

In some situations, the new program may not be allowed any planning period, and the resource teacher may be given a list of students the first day of school, with the expectation that prescheduled instruction will begin immediately. Any latitude the teacher might have in delaying the full implementation of a new resource program is an essential piece of information, because in this situation it is impossible to begin relevant instruction. Both administration and special staff should make every effort to negotiate a change in such a policy.

The idea of the ''new program'' also refers to the teacher who is new *to* the program. In either case, we strongly suggest that there be a delay before a teacher is expected to operate with a full caseload. This section explains five reasons for this recommendation.

1. The resource teacher needs time to reassess and plan programs for students who are entering the program.
2. Regular and special teachers need an opportunity to implement their own programs and to identify students they may want to refer. On the other hand, some students thought to be in need of special programming may not need it in the new school year's instructional environment.
3. The resource teacher, especially a new one, can have a chance to meet the other teachers in the building, to learn about the curricula used, and to prepare the resource program for the coming year. Perhaps the teacher can visit selected classrooms, doing some short-term teaching to a whole group, or assist the general teacher in an activity that could use an extra hand or pair of eyes. On such occasions, the resource teacher can get to know both the teachers and the students.
4. Individual student assessment for instructional purposes can be started at this time. Only rarely do previously formulated instructional plans still hold after a time lapse such as summer.
5. The resource teacher needs to meet key related personnel, such as guidance counselors, the school nurse, agents of related services, and parents.

The resource teacher should be visibly busy at all times, especially during this start-up period. The activities observed should all relate to the initiation of the program. Further, keep in mind that if a student's program is provided legally through special education, parents or guardians must give permission to delay any previously agreed upon direct instruction or student placement.

Having obtained relevant information about the context in which the resource program will operate, we now address some of the major tasks and concerns of organizing and managing the program.

SCHEDULING

One of the more time-consuming tasks in resource program management is the preparation and monitoring of student schedules. Resource teachers must work closely with mainstream teachers on behalf of many assigned students, all with differing individual needs. In addition, they must schedule their own work to include enough time each school day for planning, assessment activities, and consultation.

For example, an elementary-level teacher may have 10 students with serious reading problems. These students vary markedly in mental ability, type of reading disorder, age, and temperament. How are they all to be grouped for instruction and scheduled into the resource room? To further complicate matters, some teachers want the students to have resource instruction during periods specified for reading in the general classroom; others refuse to release students during that time; still others want the resource teacher to provide instruction within the general classroom setting.

At postelementary levels the problems are compounded because of the number of teachers whose own instructional schedules must be considered. Further, the complexity of the entire master schedule at this level means that required courses and electives must be accommodated for all students, effectively reducing available scheduled time for resource programming.

Schedule construction is obviously no easy task at any level. This section deals with four aspects of schedule development. First, we describe some of the issues and problems around schedule building so that resource teachers may show sensitivity to the real concerns of others whose programs are affected. Second, we provide guidelines for the development of new schedules or the modification of unserviceable schedules. Third, we list the ingredients needed to create a workable schedule. And finally, we describe and provide samples of schedules that may help the new teacher or those involved with the development of a new program.

Difficulty of Scheduling for Mainstream Teachers

> The teacher is damned if she does and damned if she doesn't, and so is the child. (Lieberman, 1982, p. 57)

Some resource teachers may believe that mainstream teachers are being unreasonable when they show little interest in helping build schedules that seem logical for the resource program. There are many reasons, however, that classroom teachers find scheduling to be problematic:

1. Teachers have little time with an entire group, because students are in and out of the classroom for such necessary activities as sports or music participation and medical appointments. The proliferation of special services makes it unlikely that the teacher can count on having many uninterrupted whole-class lessons.

2. The teacher may see little immediate benefit in terms of carry-over to the classroom. One of the major reasons for the development of consultation skills is to assure that instructional goals and procedures are mutually understood and agreed upon.

3. Teachers who orchestrate their own instructional activities do not believe that they should be responsible for managing the various schedules of individual students.

4. Teachers cannot readily keep track of individual students when they are coming and going throughout the day.

5. The teacher simply cannot plan lessons so that no student who leaves the classroom ever misses important discussion, activities, or content. How to make up for the absence of students, without penalizing either the student (expected to make up missed work) or the teacher (expected to reteach), is a major concern. Further, teachers cannot always time their lessons exactly so that resource students either complete the lesson before they must leave or return in time for the lesson to begin.

6. Teachers often express concern for the students' feelings about being singled out for resource programming. These feelings include (a) embarrassment about leaving the classroom, (b) frustration at the difficulty of monitoring their own schedules, and (c) disinterest shown by many already unmotivated students who believe that the resource program is an undue extra burden of time and work.

The resource teacher must recognize any of these perceptions as legitimate, while making every effort to reduce their negativity. Further, many of the problems are simply not directly related to the resource program per se, but instead occur as a result of the complexities of today's educational systems. The resource program may have become an easy target for frustrations over the multitude of working conditions that cannot be changed. Tactful ''reminding'' is not out of order in this case.

Considerations in Schedule Building or Modification

The development of schedules depends, of course, on factors such as the experience and training of the resource teacher and the expectations of the school. Beyond these conventions, however, six other observations should guide either initial schedule building or the modification of an unserviceable schedule already in place.

First, some teachers try to group students by a tested level of achievement, regardless either of age or of the reasons for ''arriving'' at that level. Tested achievement levels are seldom a good basis for groupings, and the levels will soon vary.

It is in fact likely that no satisfactory way will be found to use any reasonable instructional rationale as the basis for grouping. If possible, try to group according to the area of needed instruction. However, by sheer default, the availability of time usually determines the schedule.

Second, the resource teacher must see that time is left for assessment and for consultation. If no teaching associate or teaching team member is available for student supervision, do not schedule students regularly during that time.

Third, arrange to have some duties to the extent that other teachers do. For example, playground or lunchroom supervision may be a shared responsibility of all teachers. It is impolitic to expect to be excused from routine schoolwide duties.

Fourth, where the resource teacher operates on an itinerant basis between two buildings, time must be built in for travel and for finding out about what has happened in the resource teacher's absence from the other school. Further, principals should be actively involved in keeping the shared schedule flexible enough to meet occasional unusual needs in any one school (e.g., the resource teacher's participation in a screening program, or parent conferencing).

Fifth, schedules must be flexible enough to be changed as conditions warrant. However, constant adjustments in scheduling are annoying to all concerned. Once a schedule has been established, it should undergo major reconstruction only at a naturally occurring time of change (e.g., at the quarter or semester).

Finally, postelementary settings require some very distinct considerations. Wood (1984) provided a checklist (Figure 9.2) for avoiding problems in planning the master schedule at the postsecondary level. She further suggested that schedule planners consider these recommendations:

- Include special education teachers in preparation of the school's master schedule so that they can prevent future scheduling problems and represent special students' needs.
- Planning morning sections for vocational students, co-op students, and athletes.
- Alternating academic courses with basic and college preparatory sections.
- Allowing students in each resource class to have the same mainstream teachers when taking the same course.
- Balancing sections throughout the day. (If courses are taught at different levels, sections should be available in the morning as well as in the afternoon.) (pp. 64–65)

Other suggestions for use at the secondary level include:

1. Study hall time might be used for resource program instruction.
2. Some courses are scheduled completely within the resource room, to supplant general classroom instruction (e.g., in English). Be sure that appropriate credit is attached to supplanted coursework.

	Yes	No
1. Include resource classes on the master schedule as a general class offering.	☐	☐
2. Obtain input from resource teacher about:		
student groupings desired (ability and personality);	☐	☐
selection of general teachers, especially teachers to be avoided; and	☐	☐
other individual needs of students with mild handicaps.	☐	☐
3. Obtain input from regular teachers about categories of students desired.	☐	☐
4. Obtain input from counselors or teachers about peers to be separated from each other because of discipline problems.	☐	☐
5. Obtain input from counselors or teachers about peers to be scheduled together for purpose of tutoring or assistance.	☐	☐
6. Obtain input from resource teacher about possible conflicts between student's request and IEP.	☐	☐

Figure 9.2. Checklist for avoiding problems in planning master schedule for students with mild handicaps at the secondary level. From *Adapting Instruction for the Mainstream. A Sequential Approach to Teaching* (p. 64) by J. W. Wood, 1984, New York: Macmillan. Reprinted with permission.

3. Some coursework might be shared jointly between the general and resource class, so that the student attends general class on a periodic basis, and comes to the resource room on other days.

4. Individual student schedules may be so difficult that resource students may elect to take a reduced load and extend their schooling for another year or so.

Information Needed to Create a Schedule

Having all the necessary information at hand will make schedule development much easier. This information is usually found in the main office:

1. If the program is one of special education, obtain copies of the IEPs for all students who have been staffed. List on a student-by-student basis all areas in need of programming, including both academic and behavioral goals and objectives. Further record the time allotted to mainstream activities by each student's name.

2. If there is a master or general time schedule for school programs and activities, use this time frame as a base for building your schedule.

3. Obtain the schedules of any teachers whose students will be served through the resource program. These time-by-event schedules should include lunch, recess, specials that occur on a scheduled basis (e.g., music, art, or gym), and the teacher's planning period.

4. Interview teachers to solicit their suggestions or preferences for scheduling students out of their classrooms. Remind them that it will be impossible to honor all preferences because they will be contradictory from teacher to teacher, but explain that you will do your best.

5. If the building is large or mazelike, estimate the time it will take students to go to and from the resource program.

6. Obtain any other schedules that may involve your students. For example, speech and language, work, counseling, music, and physical education may occur on a regular basis.

7. Decide how long the resource periods will be, as well as the general time frame of the day and week. Sometimes this is predetermined within the master schedule.

8. Block in your own lunch, planning, and best time for assessment and consultation.

9. Begin to fill in student schedules, keeping in mind that compromise will certainly occur.

Before finalizing the schedule, you should review it with relevant teachers and with administrative and supervisory staff, as well as with the students themselves. It is better to change anything that was overlooked before distributing the schedule to parents and to the school at large.

Descriptions and Examples of Schedules

The first schedule is the *staggered procedure.* In this schedule, students report to the resource room for no longer than one-half hour at a time; however, they may return to the resource room two or even more times during the school day. A schedule of this nature may look like this:

8:30–9:00	Preparation	10:00–10:15	Reading (3 students)
9:00–9:15	Reading (3 students)	10:15–10:30	Mathematics (4 students)
9:15–9:30	Reading (3 students)	10:30–10:45	Mathematics (2 students)
9:30–9:45	Independent study skills	11:00–11:30	Consultation
	(3 students)	11:30–12:00	Lunch

12:00–12:30	Lunchroom duty
12:30–12:45	Spelling (3 students)
12:45–1:00	Handwriting (5 students)
1:00–2:30	Assessment and consultation
2:30–3:00	Social studies (5 students)

In this staggered schedule, the resource teacher is emphasizing direct teaching, independent seat work, and reinforcement. Each student spends one-half hour at a time in the resource room on a school activity in which he or she is experiencing difficulty.

The following example illustrates this schedule. Steven is an 11-year-old boy with pronounced problems in reading, writing, and attention. He reports to the resource room at 9:00 a.m. The resource teacher works directly with Steven and two other children for 10 minutes on a reading lesson. Steven and his two schoolmates are then sent to another desk for 15 minutes of independent exercises on the material covered during the direct instruction. Five minutes later, three other students enter the resource room for help in reading. At the end of their 10-minute direct instruction, they also go to another part of the room for a back-up exercise, and Steven and his schoolmates return to the teacher's desk so that the teacher can check and reinforce their work. Once this is completed, they return to their regular classrooms, and two other pupils enter the room for resource instruction. This procedure is repeated with various students in reading and mathematics until 11:00, when the teacher begins to consult with other teachers or parents. Steven returns to the resource room at 12:45 for help in handwriting.

Proceeding in this manner, the resource teacher may wish to provide the general classroom teacher with back-up activities for use with Steven or even to give the boy additional work to be done at home. In any event, Steven has had 1 hour of resource support each day devoted to correcting a specific problem he is experiencing in school.

Barksdale and Atkinson (1971) suggested a more general type of scheduling sequence:

8:30–9:00	Planning and Preparation
9:00–10:15	Instructional Session, Group I
10:15–11:30	Instructional Session, Group II
11:30–12:00	Lunch
12:00–1:15	Instructional Session, Group III
1:15–2:30	Instructional Session, Group IV
2:30–3:15	Conference time with students, parents, regular teachers, other personnel (p. 14)

They reported that this schedule was markedly aided by the presence of a full-time supportive person (an aide or teaching associate) in the resource room. Because of the other person's presence, the resource teacher could visit the general classrooms from which the pupils were referred. In addition, the presence of an associate gave the resource teacher an opportunity to conduct adequate individual assessment, thereby allowing the resource teacher to fulfill all three roles.

Hawisher (1975) reported that the following schedule was popular in South Carolina in learning disabilities resource programs:

8:00–9:00	Pre-School Planning
9:00–9:45	Group A
9:30–10:15	Group B
10:00–10:45	Group C
10:30–11:15	Group D
11:15–11:45	Planning Time
11:45–12:30	Lunch
12:30–1:15	Group E
1:00–1:45	Group F
1:30–2:15	Group G
2:15–3:10	Post-School Planning (p. 39)

In this schedule, the resource teacher can work with two or three students for 30 minutes of individualized instruction. Students in this group would then work independently for 15 minutes after the arrival of the next group. Hawisher noted that some resource teachers scheduled students on an alternative basis. For example, Group E can be divided into two subgroups, E^1 and E^2. E^1 may visit the resource room on Mondays, Wednesdays, and Fridays; whereas E^2 attends only on Tuesdays and Thursdays. The drawback is that this schedule allows no time for individual assessment and observation or for consultation in the general classroom. Dropping one group and substituting these activities during that period solves the problem.

These schedules do not allow sufficiently for classroom observation and consultation during prime instructional time within the classroom. Therefore, daily schedules that include constant direct supervision of students should be modified so that resource consultation and observation can be conducted appropriately within the classrooms when it is most relevant: during instruction and independent study times. That is, direct instruction may occur 2 or 3 or 4 days each week, and alternate days should be spent within classrooms. The exact proportion of days spent in each setting would depend on the degree of classroom involvement desired or possible within the local situation.

Some resource teachers may wish to develop a schedule similar to the ones presented but use it on alternate days. For example, a teacher may use a Hawisher schedule on Monday, Wednesday, and Friday. On Tuesday and Thursday, time may be allocated this way:

8:00–8:30	Pre-School Planning
8:30–10:00	Implementing or monitoring programs within classrooms
11:00–11:45	Individual student conferences
11:45–12:30	Lunch
12:30–2:00	Classroom visitation and consultation
2:00–2:30	Student, parent, or teacher conferences
2:30–3:10	Preparation of data summaries and replanning

Schedules will likely change during the year as student needs change. This aspect of scheduling should be explained to parents and teachers early in the year. The idea of flexible scheduling allows grouping for temporary needs. A resource program should not become a fixed alternative program unless it is impossible to modify the general classroom to accommodate students' instructional needs.

Conclusion

There is no way that an ideal schedule can be prepared. Not in the sense that it meets everyone's requirements. And not in the sense that it is grounded within a "logical" rationale for grouping students. Most often the resource program's master schedule must accommodate other school and student needs. Further, resource teachers may need to adjust schedules from time to time to accommodate changing conditions within instructional programs or the school schedule.

MOVEMENT BETWEEN CLASSROOMS

In any resource program operation, students have to move back and forth between the general classroom and the resource room throughout the school day. It is inefficient and too time-consuming for a resource teacher to supervise movement by dropping students off and picking them up. Resource teachers who do this spend an inordinate amount of time walking around in the school halls. Consequently, students must be required to walk unsupervised between the classrooms. In some schools, and with most students, this provides no difficulty. In other schools and with a few students, this unsupervised movement is potentially harmful to the resource program operation and occasionally also to the resource student.

Consider, for example, a secondary school in which discipline is a serious problem and/or where Kim, the student coming to the resource room, is a conduct problem. If other students are in the halls unsupervised at the same time, Kim could verbally or physically abuse them. Also, she may stop off in the bathroom and/or other supervised rooms of the school and cut class. In addition, she may disturb other classrooms by looking in the doors, making faces at the other students or teachers, or any number of other activities available to any unsupervised teenager.

Chronic tardiness in reporting to the resource room or back to the general class-room can adversely affect the quality of the child's instruction. For example, let us say that three students from three different classrooms in the school are to report to the resource room at 9:45 a.m. The needs of the students are similar, so they receive instruction in the resource room as a group. But Student 1 reports at 9:40, Student 2 at 9:45, and Student 3 at 9:50. Ten minutes have been wasted by one or more of the students and the resource teacher while the group has been getting organized. Readers to whom this tardiness seems insignificant should consider that this situation may go on group after group and day after day in both the resource room and general classroom. The amount of time wasted yearly can be considerable, to say nothing of the problem it presents to teachers.

No magic formula or management system can entirely erase this movement problem. Rules, however, can be (a) established with care and with the teachers' agreement; (b) frequently explained to both the general classroom teachers and the resource students; (c) monitored carefully; and (d) modified whenever appropriate for either an individual student or for all students who are required to move independently between classrooms.

One system for managing the behavior of the student with emotional disturbance in the classroom (Hewett & Taylor, 1980) was modified by one of the authors of this book in his supervision of resource programs. Hewett and Taylor recommended that check marks be given for every work period. In these instances, the students were given two checks for starting their task on time, three if they followed through on the assignment, and five if they were respecting the rights of others, the limits of time, space, and activity, and the classroom rules. Using a management system such as this one, the resource teacher can give checks or points for reporting on time for class. Reinforcing a student for reporting on time stresses the significance of being punctual and increases the likelihood that the student will be on time each day.

An example of this procedure will help to clarify its usefulness. If a student is to report to the resource room at 9:45 a.m., the resource teacher should calculate the amount of time needed to walk from the general classroom to the special program. Three to 5 minutes usually is sufficient for a student to walk, not run, the distance. If a 5-minute period were decided on, the student would be told to leave the classroom at 9:40 and to be in the resource room at 9:45. A student leaving the resource room at 10:15 would be expected to be back in the general classroom at 10:20.

EVALUATION OF THE PROGRAM

The word *evaluation* often arouses some fear in the minds of those whose programs are going to be examined. Clichés such as "Nobody likes to have their work evaluated'' and ''People don't like to be told what they are doing wrong'' are frequently heard in an institution that soon will be evaluated. Yet evaluation can be a rewarding and helpful experience, and it is a necessary, desirable, and ongoing process in any program. Consequently, resource teachers should expect to be evaluated, should be well prepared for it, and on many occasions will want to conduct their own evaluations. This section discusses types of evaluation procedures: (a) program components, (b) program outcomes, (c) administrator perceptions, (d) consumer satisfaction, and (e) colleague evaluations.

Program Components

In a program evaluation, all elements that play a part in the successful operation of the resource model are assessed periodically. These components include (a) physical environment, (b) curriculum, (c) time allocated for specific activities, (d) factors that relate to the resource pupils, (e) personnel involved in the resource effort, (f) planning and monitoring process, (g) reporting procedures, (h) record keeping, (i) materials used in the program, and (j) public relations activities. Other components also might be included for evaluation by resource program personnel.

Figure 9.3 contains a suggested format for the program evaluation. This sample form elaborates each component listed above. For example, the component Physical environment includes room size, horizontal use of space, and vertical use of space. Beside each component, the resource program personnel can note the current status of these points as S = *Satisfactory* or NS = *Not Satisfactory*. Suggested corrective steps can be listed beside each NS item along with the person(s) responsible for constructive action. NS items are of two types: those readily fixed and those requiring substantive or collective effort. These latter NSs can be numbered in terms of priorities, and realistic timetables can be set for their accomplishment. A specific time also should be scheduled for periodic review and modification.

Figure 9.3 is presented as a guide for administrators and teachers who want to undertake a program evaluation. We encourage these professionals to develop their own format that directly relates to the program under consideration. The evaluation then should be done by administrators, teachers, or other personnel on a periodic basis.

This type of program evaluation procedure has two major strengths. First, what is to be evaluated is predetermined. That is, the people involved in the resource program know what components of the model will be evaluated. Individuals usually are more comfortable when they know specifically what is going to be evaluated. Second, the focus of the evaluation is directed more toward the program than toward the resource teacher. This type of evaluation does not interpret the program as the role responsibility of one individual. Because the responsibility for the program's effectiveness is shared by all who are involved in it, it is evaluated in that way.

Components	Status S/NS	Suggested Corrective Action	Personnel	Priority	Timetable
A. Physical environment					
1. Room size					
2. Horizontal use of space					
3. Vertical use of space					
4. Light					
5. Materials storage					
6. Flexibility					
7. Pupil movement					
8. Furniture: nature/ arrangement					
9. Teacher role in					
10. Pupil space requirements					
11. Areas: work, play, storage, individual, group					
12. Audiovisual aids					
13. Office space for teacher and aides					
14. Expansion possibilities: other room, hall, etc.					
15. Restroom distance					
16. Ventilation					
17. Sound level					
18. Room location					
B. Curriculum					
1. Definition					
2. Topic selection: academic, social					
3. Materials available					
4. Selection procedures					
5. Administration/ supervision					
C. Time					
1. Planning: group; individual					

Figure 9.3. Suggested format for a program evaluation.

Components	Status S/NS	Suggested Corrective Action	Personnel	Priority	Timetable
2. Accounting for: monitoring					
3. As a manipulatable instructional variable					
4. Pupil self-timing					
5. Devices: stopwatches, clocks, stamps					
6. For planning/ communication					
7. In a time/event/ transition schedule					
D. Pupils					
1. Screening processes					
2. Selection for service criteria					
3. Placement for service rationale					
4. Academic assessment					
5. Social assessment					
6. Records					
7. Task					
8. Responsibility for					
9. Scheduling in/out					
10. Pre/post program monitoring					
11. Reentry plans					
12. Data sources					
13. Contingency management					
14. Stimulus considerations					
15. As instructional personnel					
16. Grouping bases					
17. Role in staffings; program development					
E. Personnel					
1. Parents					

Figure 9.3. *Continued*

Components	Status S/NS	Suggested Corrective Action	Personnel	Priority	Timetable
2. Colleagues: special education; general education					
3. Aides					
4. Other school personnel: principal, secretary					
5. State department					
6. Local administrators and supervisors					
7. University personnel					
8. Sources of assistance: aides, peer tutors, etc.					
9. Psychologist					
10. Speech and language therapist					
11. Counselor					
12. School social worker					
13. Community agency personnel					
F. Planning/monitoring					
1. Purposes					
2. Formats					
3. Revisions					
4. Types: system; pupil; group; emergency; routines; pupil-teacher; etc.					
5. Time for					
6. Events in a time/event/transition schedule					
7. As a means of suggesting system changes/needs					
G. Reporting					
1. Purposes					

Figure 9.3. *Continued*

Components	Status S/NS	Suggested Corrective Action	Personnel	Priority	Timetable
2. Timing					
3. Frequency					
4. Storage/retrieval; protection (confidentialities)					
5. Formats					
6. Targets: parents, pupils; administrators/supervisors; colleagues; self					
7. Self: teacher; pupil; parents					
H. Record-keeping					
1. Formal/informal					
2. Continuous/pre-post					
3. Format: graphics; organization					
4. Selection					
5. Keeper: pupil; peer; teacher; parent; other					
6. Storage/retrieval/ confidentiality/use					
I. Materials					
1. Manipulative devices					
2. Self-assessment features					
3. Self-correcting features					
4. Self-recording features					
5. Audiovisual considerations					
6. Multilevel teaching materials					
7. Modifications					
8. Sources of materials/ creators and makers					
9. Analysis dimensions					

Figure 9.3. *Continued*

Components	Status S/NS	Suggested Corrective Action	Personnel	Priority	Timetable
10. Horizontal/vertical use					
11. Storage and accessibility					
12. Commercially prepared/teacher prepared					
J. Public relations					
Target groups or persons					
1. Parents: individually; organizations					
2. Administrators/ supervisors					
3. Public					
4. Legislators					
5. School board					
6. Colleagues: special/ general					
7. Other curriculum personnel					
8. Universities					
K. Plans for informing re:					
1. Nature of program					
2. Successful aspects					
3. Self-training/ competencies					
4. Availability for further communication					
5. Willingness to share ideas					
6. Accountability procedures					

Figure 9.3. *Continued.*

We prefer the program evaluation format for the reasons specified above. However, the resource teacher also can use other evaluation procedures, which include different strategies. In these procedures, care must be taken to avoid making the resource teacher rather than the resource program the focus of the evaluation.

Program Outcomes

The increasing trend toward accountability for special programs will likely affect the resource programs. Often this is called an evaluation of program outcomes. Specific questions usually asked by superintendents and school boards include: (a) How much progress have resource students made this year? and (b) How much progress can be expected in the future based on the past history of the students? These questions and others are predicated on the reasonable assumption that achievement will be improved as a result of a student having been in a resource program.

The information needed to answer program outcome questions sometimes will be gained by standardized achievement tests adopted by the district. In these cases, all students in the district, including those in the resource programs, are tested annually. Figure 9.4 demonstrates how the resulting data may be reported. The vertical axis gives grade level, the horizontal axis the year. The average achieve-

Expectancies for Resource Programming

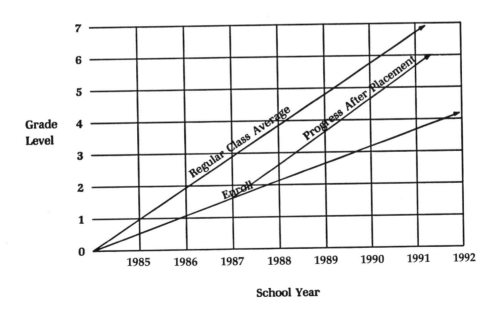

Figure 9.4. Sample of data-reporting method.

ment of both general class students and those in resource programming is reported. The resource program in this example was implemented in 1987, showing a marked increase in achievement of the students, even though it remains less than general class students. By extending the lines, one can predict with some certainty increased achievement as a result of the program.

Other options for evaluating program outcomes include annual testing of all resource pupils and a representative sample of general program students. Achievement tests may be administered annually to all resource program students and on alternate years to general program students. Or achievement tests may be administration annually to resource program students only. In many districts, program evaluation personnel will be available to help the resource teacher analyze the data. In analyzing the data, teachers should be attentive to the nuances of testing as discussed in Chapter 3.

Administrator Perceptions

Resource teachers may want to know what their principal and district supervisor think about the resource program. Most likely, this evaluation will be done formally to distinguish it from the day-to-day feedback that the resource teacher probably gets from the administrators. For this formal type of evaluation, we prefer the interview technique. In these interviews, the resource teacher first asks the principal and supervisor what they think are the strengths and weaknesses of the program and then elicits some suggestions from them as to how the effort can be improved. The resource teacher takes notes on the responses to the questions asked and later analyzes them.

The resource teacher can prepare for this interview by listing some questions to use as a guide. However, the questions should not be followed slavishly. The resource teacher may want to probe some areas in more depth and allow the administrators the latitude to digress into areas that they wish to discuss.

As in the case of communicating with parents, resource teachers will want to listen carefully. When perceived weaknesses are pointed out, teachers should not become defensive or try to blame others for the problem. Instead, resource teachers should ask the administrators for the reason that they think a particular component is weak and also solicit suggestions for rectifying the situation.

Resource teachers should be aware that some administrators may approach this formal interview with some uncertainty. They may not be sure how honest they should be with the resource teacher; they may feel uncomfortable making negative statements about the program; a few may be hesitant to make positive comments about the program. In addition, some may get off the subject of the resource program entirely and discuss their other concerns about the school. The resource teachers should set the ground rules for the interview; they should specify what they expect from the meetings and keep the discussion relevant to an evaluation of the program.

Consumer Satisfaction

The consumers in a resource program are the students in the program and their teachers and parents. The formal interview is a good way to obtain evaluation information from students. Throughout the year, the resource teacher should ask each student what he or she likes and dislikes about the program and for suggestions for improving it. The teacher should take notes on their responses for future analysis.

Some teachers may feel that resource students are too young or immature to participate in an evaluation of the program. Think again! Young children often are quite aware of and influenced by the opinions of others in their environment. Consequently, their answers to questions will reflect in part their perceptions of what their classmates, teachers, and parents feel about the resource program. Also, most of them can give good suggestions for improving the program. Resource teachers may be surprised at what they can learn from their students about the program.

For teachers and parents, we prefer a questionnaire approach because it is not as time-consuming as an interview. When one or two responses are negative, however, the resource teacher will want to follow up the questionnaire with a formal interview.

In the questionnaire, resource teachers should ask specific questions rather than open-ended questions such as, ''What do you like about the resource program?'' Specific questions are important because most consumers will not be sure of what points they should respond to. The questions should focus on the benefits the consumers feel that they and their children are receiving from the program. Some questions will relate to whether they have noticed any improvements in the resource students since they were enrolled in the program. Other questions will be directed toward whether the teacher has received any useful help from the resource program in dealing with problems. The questionnaire also should solicit suggestions for improving the program. The questionnaire should ask only a few questions. Esoteric or lengthy questionnaires are inappropriate and take too much time. Whenever a responder specifies any problem, the resource teacher should follow up with a formal interview. Resource teachers may want to develop separate questionnaires for the teachers and for the parents. A sample questionnaire is presented in Figure 9.5.

Colleague Evaluation

One of the most practical and useful evaluations is the one done by colleagues of the resource teacher—other resource teachers in the district. The evaluation is accomplished by a site visit. That is, resource teachers from other schools visit a

Name: _____

	Yes	No	Unsure
1. I feel that my resource child (student) is improving because of the program.	☐	☐	☐
2. I have some recommendations that I would like to make for improving the program for my child (student) that I have not made.	☐	☐	☐
3. The information provided me on my child (student) has been helpful.	☐	☐	☐
4. I feel I need additional information on helping the child (student).	☐	☐	☐
5. Overall, I believe the resource program is meeting the objectives that were outlined.	☐	☐	☐

Any additional comments:

Strengths:

Weaknesses:

Recommendations:

Figure 9.5. Sample questionnaire for parents and teachers.

program, observe it in operation, and interview administrators, parents, other teachers, students, *and* the resource teacher. They then give a written and/or oral evaluation along with some recommendations. If the resource teacher has been evaluated by administrators and consumers, these results should be given to the site visitors. After reading and reviewing these evaluations, they may or may not wish to interview these other people.

We cannot stress strongly enough the value of this type of evaluation. Other resource teachers have many of the same problems and often have found practical solutions to some of these difficulties. We heartily encourage that this peer evaluation be done at least once a year in each school in a district with a resource program. This is not a difficult task to arrange administratively. Observation days usually are built into any teacher's contract so that a teacher can take a day or two off without any loss in pay or in allowed absentee days. However, pressure to use observation days in this way should not be undue. In addition, resource teachers often can cancel their classes for half a day to serve as a peer evaluator. When resource teachers are the evaluators, they usually learn a lot that they can use in their own programs.

Resource teachers may encounter some difficulties with the teacher's union if they use free days to evaluate a colleague. They should check with union officials before proceeding. If the union objects, then perhaps resource teachers from one district could visit specific programs in another part of the district and then meet as a large group to formulate the entire district's resource program development. This type of activity could easily serve as inservice training for all resource teachers in the district.

Using the Results of the Evaluation

The resource teacher will need to take the results of the various evaluations and compile them into some usable form. The compilation should include a list of the program's strengths, weaknesses, and recommendations. All redundancies should be removed, although the number of times one point was referred to should be noted. For example, if six teachers, one administrator, three students, and four peers all said that two strengths of the program were the management system used to move students between classes and the positive attitudes of the students toward the program, these responses would be recorded in the following manner:

	Number	
Positive	Negative	
14	0	1. Management system for movement between classes.
14	0	2. Positive attitude of students for the program.

The next step is to provide feedback on the evaluation to those who participated. The format suggested in Figure 9.6 makes this report almost self-explanatory. The next step is for the resource teacher and others to analyze those "Weaknesses with Recommendations" and to make some decisions as to which suggestions will be integrated into the current operations of the program. Feedback should be made to the appropriate individuals on these changes or modifications.

The most difficult step in using these evaluations relates to the "Weaknesses without Recommendations." There are several ways to deal with these weaknesses. First, resource teachers may survey the literature relative to the problem area to find if other teachers have found ways to deal with a particular difficulty. They may ask experts for some recommendations; such experts include state department personnel, local supervisors, district personnel, university professors, and/or other teachers. A second approach would be to ask several members of the school

Date _____

Type of Evaluations

_____ 1. Administrators

_____ 2. Consumers

_____   A. Students

_____   B. Parents/guardians

_____   C. Colleagues

_____ 3. Peers

STRENGTHS

NUMBER

_____ 1.

_____ 2.

_____ 3.

_____ 4.

_____ 5.

WEAKNESSES WITH RECOMMENDATIONS

WEAKNESS   RECOMMENDATION

_____ 1.   1.

_____ 2.

_____ 3.   2.

_____ 4.

_____ 5.   3.

                                               4.

                                               5.

WEAKNESSES WITHOUT RECOMMENDATIONS

_____ 1.

_____ 2.

_____ 3.

_____ 4.

_____ 5.

ADDITIONAL COMMENTS FROM RESOURCE TEACHER

Figure 9.6. Sample resource program evaluation format.

staff and some parents to serve on a problem-solving committee. The purpose of this committee would be to come up with recommendations for the resource teacher. These two approaches may be integrated in that the resource teacher may compile some information to bring to the problem-solving group for their analysis and comments.

The most important thing that the resource teacher must do is to use the evaluation to improve the program. Unfortunately, we have found that too often the evaluation results are used simply to justify continued existence of a program. If resource teachers use the evaluation results for making improvements, they will find that after a few years their programs are indeed efficient and effective operations.

Earlier in this book we described in some detail the resource teacher's roles: assessing, teaching, and consulting. We also described another critical role: program management. Such matters as preparing the school staff and parents for the program; public relations; pupil selection; processing referrals; serving on multidisciplinary staffings; scheduling; grading; involvement of peers, parents, or guardians in the efforts; and evaluation of the program have been overviewed. A resource teacher who does not manage well will likely fail. Conversely, effective attention to management will pay high dividends and make the resource activities much easier for all concerned.

It is appropriate here to mention one other management area: the resource teacher's management of her or his personal mental health. The demands of the job are extensive and may include some stress. DeShong (1981) detailed some strategies for stress management. Although writing primarily to special educators, her comments are applicable to all who work with students experiencing difficulty:

> Accomplishing management of job stress in . . . education means moving beyond the process of merely coping with situations and events. A stress-managed workstyle involves a changed relationship with self, others, and the . . . education environment. Such changes do not come easily or quickly. (p. viii)

PEER TUTORING AND COOPERATIVE LEARNING

Resource teachers will likely find themselves in need of support staff to implement the program efficiently. We highly recommend that every resource teacher be assigned an aide; however, we recognize that although aides are provided as a matter of course in some districts, in others funds are not available for such support personnel. Regardless of the availability of an aide, we recommend the use of peer tutors. Not only can this practice be extremely helpful to the resource teacher, but an abundance of studies indicate positive success with such programs (see Ehly & Larsen, 1980, for a review of the studies).

Many teachers resist using peer tutoring in their classrooms. They believe that such an approach is misusing students, and that the tutors should be learning new information rather than teaching others what they already know. We disagree. Students helping other students are learning appropriate social behaviors, as well as reinforcing and elaborating on their own skills and knowledge. What better way to teach the necessity of helping other members of society than by actually having people do so? Other teachers object to the use of peer tutors on the basis that these students are not trained to teach. We concur with this statement. Any effective peer tutoring program must have a tutor training component, supervision, and evaluation. Simply putting two students together, one who has information and skill and the other who does not, probably will not result in significant improvement of the one needing help.

The first step in initiating a peer tutoring program in the classroom is to make the decision to do so. The initial concerns of how to pair students up appropriately, how to train the tutors, and how to evaluate the successes and failures of the program may make peer tutoring seem like "more trouble than it's worth." However, we want to emphasize that the academic and social benefits of such a program far outweigh the administrative problems. The social and emotional benefits of peer tutoring are particularly strong for students with learning disabilities. In fact, in many tutoring situations, a student may be selected as a tutor because she or he has a learning disability, but is competent in one or more subject areas. Ehly (1984) pointed out that, "when given the opportunity to assist a younger or 'slower' student in an academic or social skill, a learning disabled student will be able to feel a needed sense of success as well as practice his/her skill in the area under study" (p. 9). Ehly further pointed out that schools utilizing such programs have reported increased academic and social skills for the students involved in them. It must be understood that both the tutor and the student being tutored benefit socially and academically from the experience.

The implementation of peer tutoring programs is well described in *Partner Learning in Practice. Increasing Student Productivity Through Peer Tutoring Programs* (Pierce, Stahlbrand, & Armstrong, 1984). However, analysis of these researchers' recommendations shows that the teacher needs to plan some steps in the process (see Figure 9.7) before trying to implement peer tutoring.

Another type of student-student interaction that is socially and academically advantageous for the students involved is cooperative learning. Cooperative learning situations are situations in which small, heterogeneous groups of students are expected to work together to help one another learn. There are many different specific cooperative situations, but the crucial feature is that the students in the group are interdependent and are working toward a common goal. Slavin (1983) elucidated the central theme of cooperative learning by comparing it to a common situation. "If three people traveling in a car help push the car out of the mud, all of them benefit from each other's efforts (by being able to continue their trip). Either all of them will be rewarded, or none of them will be, depending on whether they succeed" (p. 431). These types of learning situations can be contrasted with competitive situations where the students in a classroom are working individually

Steps in Developing a Peer Tutoring Program

1. State the major goal(s) of the program (e.g., to provide monitored practice with a specific skill; to improve student productivity; to establish mastery of a specific skill or process; to provide maintenance checks).
2. State specific objectives so that they can be translated into a progress/measurement system that enables managers to make valid judgments about student programs.
3. Cite and describe the source of curricular objectives in the scope and sequence (may be preestablished).
4. State the scope and sequence of the program, or indicate the sequence and boundaries.
5. Relate the data system to the objectives.
6. Show appropriate data format(s).
7. Describe how decisions will be made concerning changes in the pace or content of the program.
8. Describe how the teacher will monitor progress of:
   a. tutors
   b. tutees
9. Show the form that pre/post information sheets will look like.
10. Describe how materials to be included will be obtained, packaged, and stored.
11. Cite the sources and give samples of teaching procedures to be used during the tutoring.
12. Describe how tutors are to be selected.
13. Describe how tutors are to become involved (e.g., any extra credit, and permissions from teachers and parents).
14. Outline and/or describe how the tutors are to be trained (e.g., materials; role plays; motivation; length of sessions; number of sessions; location; models; trainers; evaluation).
15. Describe how the tutees are to be selected.
16. Describe how tutoring will be conducted.
17. Show/describe how the entire program will be evaluated. Be sure to include how you will determine the extent to which
    a. Tutee objectives have been met.
    b. Tutor objectives have been met.
    c. Specific social goals have been met.
    d. Modifications are needed in the program.
18. Other:

Figure 9.7. Procedural analysis for developing a peer tutoring program. From *Partner Learning in Practice. Increasing Student Productivity through Peer Tutoring Programs* by M. M. Pierce, K. Stahlbrand, and S. B. Armstrong, 1984, Austin, TX: PRO-ED. Adapted with permission.

and then compared with a criterion or with one another by the teacher during the evaluation process.

There are many different ways of structuring cooperative learning situations. Each teacher should consider the number and type of students in the class, the material being taught, and the physical environment in setting up cooperative learning situations. However, although the specifics of cooperative learning situations will vary from classroom to classroom, Johnson and Johnson (1986) claimed that three basic elements need to be included in cooperative learning situations: positive interdependence, individual accountability, and collaborative skills. These three elements are described below.

Positive interdependence is the concept that each of the students in the group cannot be successful unless the other group members are also successful. The students must be made to realize that the work that each individual student does benefits the group as a whole. However, although it is important that group members realize that they are working toward a common goal, some sort of *individual accountability* must be built into the learning situation. Individual accountability is achieved when each group member realizes that he or she must fulfill certain responsibilities for the group to be successful. Johnson and Johnson (1986) suggested that this can be achieved by giving individual tests on the material that the group is responsible for learning and then averaging the scores to determine the score for the group as a common way of ensuring individual accountability.

The next element that is discussed is the need to teach students *collaborative skills*. Competitive learning environments are the most common situations in schools today. It may be that students put in a cooperative learning situation are working in a group for the first time. The skills that are required to work successfully as a group member must be taught—just like academic skills, they are developed with practice. To work successfully in a group, students must understand leadership, group decision making, trust building, communication, and conflict management skills. Do not expect that students will instantly work perfectly together; rather, offer them opportunities to practice and develop the skills that they need to work cooperatively.

PERSONAL TIME MANAGEMENT

The notion of time as a resource in our society is finding acceptance through business seminars and time-management tools such as notebooks/planners. Both beginning and experienced resource teachers often find that time is the scarcest resource of all. Further, one of the biggest, ''Yes, but . . . ''s in dealing with other adults is often, ''I don't have time!'' The resource teacher must be prepared to address this very real concern. In the case of parents, the teacher who requests that they work with students should be prepared to help them ''find the time.'' For example, Lovitt (1977) described a 5-minute parent procedure to help with reading, and parents who want to try a "read-along" program can tape their book or story reading for use by the child on a repeated basis during their absence.

In working with other teachers, a change in their time-frame patterns often requires a change in organization and management practices as well. All the tools that the resource teacher uses to gain time should be shared with other teachers (e.g., notebook checking and peer monitoring).

We have noted that attention to organization and management practices, including the appropriate delegation of tasks, is on of the major ways to "find" time for the various activities associated with the resource program. We also suggest that resource teachers should make every effort to ask for and to attend professional development seminars on this topic, as well as follow through with suggestions about time management. The following cue questions may help the teacher identify practices that are "stealing time."

1. What am I doing by hand that can be done with a computer?
2. How might a telephone answering machine help me reserve time (both at work and at home)?
3. What time-consuming tasks can be delegated, and to whom?
4. What repetitive tasks might be changed or delegated?
5. What changes in the learning environment might save time?
6. What changes in instructional situations might save time?
7. How might my filing system be modified for better retrieval?
8. How can I become (or learn to become) more conscious of time during the day (e.g., plan and monitor discrepancies from the plan, or keep a running log of time × activities)?
9. How can I teach time management to students?
10. What major interruptions occur, and how might some of them be prevented?
11. How can time be multiplied (e.g., through peer tutors)?
12. How can administrators legitimize planning periods and schedules that better accommodate the time frames of the resource program?

Chapter 10

The Individualized Education Program

Many students in the resource program will receive services because they have been identified as in need of special education, and in most cases they will also carry a categorical label such as mental retardation, behavior disorder, or learning disability. For these students, the resource teacher will become involved in the Individualized Education Program (IEP) process. The IEP is a statement of how individualization will meet students' educational needs so that they are not denied full equity of educational opportunity. In this chapter we (a) review the major requirements of the IEP and related services in relation to instructional planning, (b) discuss some of the issues and problems surrounding the IEP and related services, and (c) give annotated examples of the kinds of IEPs we believe to be consistent with the purposes of the resource program.

REQUIREMENTS OF THE IEP AND RELATED SERVICES

Special education focuses on offsetting or reducing problems that interfere with learning and educational performance in school. It is defined as "specially designed" instruction, whose need is determined by comparing the nature of instruction for the student with disabilities to typical students at the same age and grade level (Turnbull, Strickland, & Brantley, 1982). This focus and definition is important, because it is the basis for the development of the instructional program. The program itself should reduce or offset problems that interfere with learning or school performance; and the nature of the instruction provided should in some way(s) be different from that of the mainstream program. The IEP legally involves these special education requirements:

> The term "individualized education program" means a written statement for each handicapped child developed in any meeting by a representative of the local education agency or an intermediate educational unit who shall be qualified to provide, or supervise the provision of, specially designed instruction to meet the unique needs of handicapped children, the teacher, the parents or guardian of such child, and whenever appropriate, such child, which statement shall include (A) a statement of the present levels of education performance of such child, (B) a statement of annual goals, including short-term instructional objectives, (C) a statement of the specific educational services to be provided to such child, and the extent to which such child will be able to participate in regular educational programs, (D) the projected date for initiation and anticipated duration of such services, and (E) appropriate objective criteria and evaluation procedures and schedules for determining, on at least an annual basis, whether instructional objectives are being achieved. [Sec. 1401(19) of EHA (P.L. 94-142)]

People refer to the IEP as both a process and a document in the sense that the document is the focal point both for all the activities that precede its acceptance by a group of people, and for the operation of the instructional program that follows from its acceptance.

Those who need a further review of guidelines, rationales, or legal actions that have attempted to clarify the provisions of the IEP can consult Turnbull's (1986) chapter, "Individualized and Appropriate Education," and Turnbull et al.'s (1982) comprehensive guidelines for IEP development. In addition, the State Educational Agency (SEA), Intermediate Unit, or Local Education Agency (LEA) usually has its own guidelines and interpretation of The Individuals with Disabilities Act officially filed as a part of its service plans. Resource teachers, of course, work within the approved guidelines of their states and employing agencies.

Regardless of the guidelines used locally, resource teachers should be able to:

1. Document the current level of the child's performance
2. Write annual major instructional goals
3. Write short-term instructional objectives
4. State the *specific* educational services that will be provided to the child
5. Determine the extent to which the student will be able to participate in general education programs (including the nature of the participation)

6. At least on an annual basis, recommend appropriate objective criteria and evaluation procedures, and timelines or schedules for determining whether instructional objectives are being achieved
7. Project the date for the initiation of services and the anticipated duration of the special education and related services

Where appropriate, the resource teacher should also be able to consult with others who may:

8. Describe any needed transition and vocational services
9. Describe the nature of any needed adaptive physical education

Related services may be recommended to help a child with a disability benefit from special education. Related services include, but are not limited to, those noted in Figure 10.1. When the team agrees that any of these services would enable the student to benefit from special education, the team describes the extent and nature of the service(s), who the service provider should be, who pays for the related service(s), and the initiation and expected termination dates for the service(s). This record becomes an addendum to the IEP. It is always reviewed by the IEP team (including related services providers) either at the time the IEP itself is reviewed, or whenever someone believes that a change in a related service is needed.

ISSUES AND PROBLEMS WITH THE IEP AND RELATED SERVICES

Some of the issues and problems associated with the IEP are procedural (i.e., how it gets developed and/or implemented), and others relate to the content of the document. For related services, the primary problem is how to get them when they are needed, and the major issue is the basis for determining if they are really a necessity for the individual student.

The IEP

In this section we discuss (a) our concerns about the timing and purpose of the annual review, (b) problems with IEPs the teacher may inherit, (c) limitations of computerized IEPs, (d) conflicting interpretations of the specific terms of the IEP, and (e) analyses of the quality of IEPs.

Annual Review

Annual reviews occur when parents and those who provide special education get together to review yearly progress toward annual goals, review long-range plan-

Audiology	(a) Identification of children with hearing loss;
	(b) Determination of the range, nature, degree of hearing loss, including referral for medical or other professional attention for the habilitation of hearing;
	(c) Provision of habilitative activities, such as language habilitation, auditory training, speech reading (lip reading), hearing evaluation, and speech conservation;
	(d) Creation and administration of programs for prevention of hearing loss;
	(e) Counseling and guidance of pupils, parents, and teachers regarding hearing loss; and
	(f) Determination of the child's need for group and individual amplification, selecting and fitting an appropriate aid, and evaluating the effectiveness of amplification.
Counseling Services	Services provided by qualified social workers, psychologists, guidance counselors, or other qualified personnel.
Early Identification	Implementation of a formal plan for identifying a disability as early as possible in a child's life.
Medical Services	Services provided by a licensed physician to determine a child's medically related handicapping condition which results in the child's need for special education and related services.
Occupational Therapy	(a) Improving, developing, or restoring functions impaired or lost through illness, injury, or deprivation;
	(b) Improving ability to perform tasks for independent functioning when functions are impaired or lost; and
	(c) Preventing, through early intervention, initial or further impairment or loss of function.
Parent Counseling and Training	Assisting parents in understanding the special needs of their child and providing parents with information about child development.
Physical Therapy	Services provided by a qualified physical therapist.
Psychological Services	(a) Administering psychological and educational tests, and other assessment procedures;
	(b) Interpreting assessment results;
	(c) Obtaining, integrating, and interpreting information about child behavior and conditions relating to learning.
	(d) Consulting with other staff members in planning school programs to meet the special needs of children as indicated by psychological tests, interviews, and behavior evaluations; and

Figure 10.1. Related Services.

	(e) Planning and managing a program of psychological services, including psychological counseling for children and parents.
Recreation	(a) Assessment of leisure function;
	(b) Therapeutic recreation services;
	(c) Recreation programs in schools and community agencies; and
	(d) Leisure education.
School Health Services	Services provided by a qualified school nurse or other qualified person.
Social Work Services	(a) Preparing a social or developmental history on a handicapped child;
	(b) Group and individual counseling with the child and family;
	(c) Working with those problems in a child's living situation (home, school, and community) that affect the child's adjustment in school; and
	(d) Mobilizing school and community resources to enable the child to receive maximum benefit from his or her educational program.
Speech Pathology	(a) Identification of children with speech or language disorders;
	(b) Diagnosis and appraisal of specific speech or language disorders;
	(c) Referral for medical or other professional attention necessary for the habilitation of speech or language disorders;
	(d) Provisions of speech and language services for the habilitation or prevention of communicative disorders; and
	(e) Counseling and guidance of parents, children, and teachers regarding speech and language disorders.
Transportation	(a) To, from, between buildings
	(b) In and around school buildings
	(c) Needed specialized equipment

Figure 10.1. *Continued.* From *Developing and Implementing Individualized Education Programs* (pp. 183–184) by A. P. Turnbull, B. B. Strickland, and J. C. Brantley, 1982, New York: Macmillan. Reprinted with permission.

ning, set new annual goals and short-term objectives, and recommend any changes in the instructional program. In practice, these reviews often bunch up into a marathon session toward the end of the year. This timing is neither legally necessary nor professionally desirable for several reasons. First, the term *annual review* simply means "at least once a year." IEP reviews, including annual reviews, may occur at any time. Second, when these reviews bunch together, there are too many students and too little time, so that the reviews may become autograph parties where parents go through a revolving door, signing permissions as they move along. In addition, professional personnel themselves have little time to consider seriously the student's true current and future educational needs. And finally, IEPs written in the spring may not be valid in the fall, because significant changes either in the school or with the student may have occurred in the 3 or 4 months between the IEP spring review and the fall implementation.

Where annual reviews are concentrated in the spring, all concerned should check to see that the student's program is not merely continuing on a preset track that was determined by an old, initial assessment of deficits. Instead, the instructional program should change as the student acquires both maturity and increased competence. Of course, if the student does not show such changes, then the reason to change the instructional program becomes even more obvious.

We recommend first that annual reviews be staggered throughout the school year, or at least throughout the spring school term. This kind of schedule ensures that there is time to make the annual review fulfill its intent in a way that is meaningful to all those involved, including the student.

Where a routine change of placement or program is necessary (e.g., moving to middle school) from spring to fall, a shorter spring meeting is in order to describe how to manage that particular change. This is not the time to discuss the major long-range or annual goals. Shortly after school starts again in the fall, the new team of parents and teacher(s) should review the appropriateness of the short-term objectives themselves from the vantage point of a 4-month time period and the new setting.

Periodic parent conferences (*not* at open house) also provide more appropriate timing for discussing the major facets of the student's educational program. Even if the school's general schedule does not provide time for parent conferences, resource teachers should schedule them throughout the year. The IEP provides the focus for these conferences.

Inherited IEPs

The resource teacher may "inherit" IEPs from other teachers, with the expectation that the present teacher will know how to "read" and translate the IEP into an instructional program. This situation may present problems for several reasons. First, the IEP may be written in terms that are too broad to be reasonably implemented. The present teacher may either disagree professionally with the specific recommendation, or simply not be trained to implement it. For example, if the IEP specifies a whole language approach for reading and writing, and the resource teacher is trained only to use commercial Direct Instruction programs, it would be difficult to implement the inherited IEP.

Terms that are too general don't let the resource teacher know what the initial IEP writer had in mind. In this circumstance the teacher will probably need to completely redesign both the student's program and the IEP. Selecting just any program by chance or for convenience to go with an IEP is certainly not individualized.

Where there are serious problems or disagreements about the student's recommended program, it is unfair to parents, to the student, and to your colleagues to state concerns to them without first consulting the IEP team. Instead, we strongly recommend that the entire team (including parents) use the problem-solving approach inherent in the collaborative consultation model we describe elsewhere in this book. This process provides for a full and fair evaluation of all reasonable alternatives.

Computerized IEPs

Many school districts use computerized lists of skills that are sequenced as the district wishes. This menu of annual goals and short-term objectives becomes "the" curriculum for most students in the special education program. Computerization saves a great deal of time, of course, in writing and copying material onto official documents. However, the mere presence of the objectives bank often limits the kinds of goals and objectives the teacher can write. That is, the IEP team may not recognize goals and objectives that are not in the computer bank. Further, computerized goals and objectives may have been written to represent a curriculum that is no longer valid considering the present emphasis on functional skills, metacognition, and the generalization of behaviors to the naturally occurring environment.

We recommend that resource teachers who feel constrained by computerized objectives discuss with their supervisors or administrators how to place into the computer the kinds of goals and objectives they believe to be valid for their students. If this is not possible, it certainly is possible to record a noncomputerized IEP.

Specific Terms of the IEP

Several items of the IEP involve skills and knowledge of the resource teacher. We discuss these items in more detail below.

1. *Document the current level of the child's performance.* The intent of this item is to present information about where the student is functioning in terms that relate directly to instruction. For academic areas, this information often comes from a norm-referenced or criterion-referenced test, or from direct observation of the student's interactions with curriculum materials. Documentation usually appears in the form of a grade equivalent (e.g., 3.2) , a textbook level (e.g., the third reader), a ranking (e.g., second percentile), or a standard score (e.g., a reading quotient).

Behavioral information might come from direct observation of the student's social interactions in differing environments or from observational checklists that are either norm-referenced or criterion-referenced. Documentation of behavioral information might involve a standard score, or behavioral summaries that compare the student's present behavior with environmental or normative expectations.

Not every behavior of interest to the resource teacher will have a test score or grade level associated with it. Several examples illustrate this important point. First, study behaviors may be developmental, but the development should parallel the student's competence in "reading to learn"; it is not age- or grade-referenced. Second, a range of behaviors associated with the use of a calculator are important for students to learn. The present level of the student's performance may be described from a checklist of what the student presently knows how to do or does not know how to do with the calculator; again, not age- or grade-referenced. Finally, getting the student to learn to use reading as a pleasurable recreational activity might be an important behavior that is not reflected on standardized tests and assessments.

Behaviors such as those in the examples above are the reason we call the resource teacher's attention to the real latitude the law provides in describing the present level of the child's performance, especially in academics. There need not be a standardized score per se when the evaluation presents a descriptive account of the student's reading, conduct, writing, math, or other behaviors. Diagnosticians and teachers can summarize and describe from writing samples, from miscue inventories, from (clinical) interviews, and from anecdotal observations (e.g., Hasselriis, 1982). This latitude is very important for those whose programs reflect, for example, a whole language approach to literacy instruction (e.g., Rhodes & Dudley-Marling, 1988); an "understanding" approach to mathematics (e.g., Baroody, 1987); a general metacognitive approach to learning (e.g., Raphael & Englert, 1990); or curriculum-based measurement (e.g., Fuchs et al., 1990).

2. *Write annual major instructional goals.* It is not uncommon to see instructional goals in academics read, "The student will raise her reading level one grade level," or "Ninety percent of the time the student will read with 95% accuracy of word reading, a passage at the 3-2 level." These kinds of statements as major annual goals are almost meaningless insofar as leading to important change in the student. We have noted that the major goals of instruction for students within the resource program most often involve (a) remediation, (b) learning new (or replacement) skills, (c) learning to compensate for any functional handicaps that cannot otherwise be ameliorated, and/or (d) learning new content.

For example, remediation goals frequently involve mastery learning, or performance criteria of 99% to 100%. Basic facts usually need to be known to a mastery level of accuracy and at a speed that permits their immediate retrieval. This would also be true of basic sight words or basic spelling words.

Learning new skills, procedures, and skill clusters involves behaviors such as study skills, social behaviors, and the metacognitive routines associated with specific content areas. Goals of instruction almost always involve the *use*, not just the "knowledge" or possession, of these skills.

Compensatory behaviors involve learning to use machines such as calculators and computers; learning and/or showing what has been learned through the use of alternative media; and learning to work cooperatively to take advantage of the "differentiated" skills of peers or other persons.

Goals that involve learning new content should specify the new content to be learned as well as the modifications that will enable the student to learn it. Merely stating that the student will learn the fifth-grade content of social studies, for example, is not enough, because that content will differ from school to school and from text to text.

Annual goals need not include a goal from each of these areas or from every subject. Annual goals should focus on offsetting or reducing the major problems that interfere with the student's learning and educational performance, whatever they may be.

3. *Write short-term instructional objectives.* Short-term objectives, like the current level of performance, should be stated in terms that are appropriate to what is being taught. For example, if the student is to learn how to write by using the metacognitive routines of "Plan Sheets" (Raphael & Englert, 1990), then habitual use of the steps of each Plan Sheet type should be observed on a short-term basis. However, if the goal is one of mastering basic math facts, short-term objectives should consider clustering these facts from easiest to most difficult to learn (e.g., Silbert et al., 1990).

4. *State the specific educational services that will be provided to the child.* Many states require only that the type of placement (e.g., the resource program or collaborative consultation) and any related services be listed here. We believe that this refers to a statement of the nature of the special education methodologies and materials that will be used to achieve the short-term objectives and their corresponding long-term goals. The services might include a modification of the math program to provide for mastery learning, specific instruction and practice in certain skills, or particular experience with the linguistic patterns of predictable or patterned books.

Resource teachers should be aware that many states do not require any statements of methods, materials, or instructional approaches to be used in accomplishing either short-term objectives or annual goals. This is likely because of a general move to keep the IEP as simple as possible, stating as little information as possible, to feel relatively safe from litigation with the IEP as its focus.

Even if there is no place for instructional methods and materials on the IEP document itself, we recommend that the resource teacher keep a record of all special instructional procedures and materials used to accomplish goals and objectives. Parents and future teachers will want to know about this important aspect of the program.

5. *Determine the extent to which the child will be able to participate in regular education programs (including the nature of the participation).* It is not enough to state that the student will spend X hours within the mainstream environment. It is important to determine what will be done during that time, for example, "The mainstream program is to provide opportunities for participation with age peers during out-of-classroom experiences, such as the cafeteria or playground," or, "Tests within the mainstream environment will be modified so that the student can give oral answers rather than written."

6. At least on an annual basis, recommend appropriate objective criteria and evaluation procedures, and timelines or schedules for determining whether or not instructional objectives are being achieved. Objective criteria do not necessarily mean test scores. They refer to any criteria that can be verified (a) by using a different method to arrive at the same conclusion or (b) by another person using the same or a different method. The same kinds of descriptions and procedures that were used to determine the present levels of performance can also be used here.

7. Project the date for the initiation of services and the anticipated duration of the special education and related services. Many states and school districts are now attempting to set criteria for leaving or "exiting" special education to keep it from becoming a lifelong "sentence" for the student. School personnel and parents should monitor carefully any student who leaves special education services, and the monitoring should continue throughout the major changes (potential crises) in the student's school career. Monitoring is important for several reasons. First, the basic nature of many problems experienced by students in special education suggests that they may reoccur in a different context as the student matures or changes major environments. In this sense, the Revolving Door model of services (Renzulli, Reis, & Smith, 1981) makes sense for these students, allowing them to go in and out of special education services to meet changing contexts.

Resource teachers should also recognize that just because a student's work comes up to a certain grade level, it may not continue at that level without the support of special education. This point is important, because many exit criteria are based an aims involving a certain grade level for the individual student. We do not wish to keep students any longer than necessary, but neither do we want them released prematurely from needed assistance.

8. Describe any needed transition and vocational services. Transition and vocational services are critical components of the student's program, but a full treatment is beyond the scope of this chapter or book. We suggest that resource teachers consult such sources as *Transition Issues and Directions* (Ianacone & Stoddent, 1987).

9. Describe the nature of any needed adaptive physical education. Physical education personnel usually recommend any adaptations in the physical education program, but resource teachers may call attention to the need for adaptations of team sports, activities that would promote positive interactions with peers, or individual fitness requirements if these have not yet been identified. Keep in mind that every student is entitled to adaptive physical education if it is needed.

IEP Quality

The adequacy or quality of IEPs is receiving a great deal of recent attention, with arguments dealing with (a) their technical adequacy and (b) the validity of their content (e.g., Billingsley, 1984; Lynch & Beare, 1990). The concern for technical adequacy occurs when state or federal agencies monitor or review the IEP document and the meetings and processes that led to its written form. Technical adequacy is determined in a simple manner by comparing the school's records to the legal requirements. If all relevant procedures have been followed in a timely manner, and if the characteristics we noted earlier are present, then the IEP is considered to be technically adequate.

Concerns about the content of the IEP are another matter entirely. There is so much latitude in the exact manner in which IEPs can be written, that many professionals and parents expect the IEP format to change both as policies change and as we acquire better information about programs and instructional methodologies. For example, Billingsley (1984) noted that an analysis of IEPs reflected scant attention to (a) the functional nature of goals and objectives so that what was learned would help with daily living, (b) age-appropriate activities to support the goals and objectives, or (c) the assurance of generalization of school learning to other environments and to the presence of anyone other than the teacher.

Lynch and Beare (1990) compared the IEP objectives for students with mental retardation and behavioral disorders to what actually occurred within classrooms. Objectives were also analyzed according to 10 standards of *appropriate practice* that are found in the contemporary literature in special education:

1. Age-appropriate material
2. Relates to demands of general education (where appropriate)
3. Transition (to next or future environments)
4. Relevance (to source of identified need)
5. Interaction (with nondisabled peers)
6. Taught across settings and materials
7. Taught in natural settings
8. Generalization (usable in other age-appropriate settings)
9. Specificity (of performance criteria)
10. Parent involvement (in monitoring, implementing, or facilitating)

The results of Lynch and Beare's IEP analyses showed that little attention was given to the quality indicators they reviewed, and their classroom observations showed little connection to the content that *was* in the IEP.

We recommend that the resource teacher and local special education personnel plan time to review their own IEPs and to set guidelines for their improvement in terms of the qualitative indicators they believe to be consistent with their own programmatic goals. The state agency may also be of assistance in this process.

Related Services

Schools accept some related services as routine and reasonable. Transportation, for example, is well accepted for students who live at a distance, or who cannot travel by ordinary means to their programs. Other services on the list in Figure 10.1 (presented earlier), however, are not routinely accepted either because of the cost, or because trained personnel are not available locally to deliver them (e.g., speech therapy).

School districts do not want to pay for services that have other sources of funding. For example, the health and social services agency may have funds for counseling or for other services that are called related services in special education. Turnbull (1986) noted that problems occur simply because so many different service providers may be involved in delivering and/or in paying for related services. For example, the lack of intergovernmental coordination from federal to local agencies, and among agencies themselves, may result in either failure to provide services or service duplication. We would add that local districts may believe that the time spent in coordination is not worth the services received. There are many other problems, but they all result in a scarcity of related services for students who receive special education.

It is difficult for anyone to determine that an individual student cannot benefit from the resource program without a specific related service. Even though the resource teacher may believe that social services or family counseling, for example, would benefit a student who comes from a family with multiple social, behavioral, and economic problems, the teacher would find it hard to say that the student would not benefit *at all* from the instructional program without such services.

Resource teachers should not be surprised if team members are reluctant to suggest, or to include in the IEP, services that teachers (or parents) sincerely believe would help the child or family. Nevertheless, they should remember that if they do not bring up the subject at all in IEP team meetings, the chances of obtaining related services is zero. If they *do* suggest the need for services, they have at least a .5 probability of services being recommended.

Summary

It may be that the future of the IEP is to be relegated to a piece of paperwork in which the *i*'s must be dotted and the *t*'s crossed. The processes involved are expensive, and if they are not the focus of the individualization of instruction, the IEP serves no useful (and certainly no intended) purpose. We hope to see the IEP, as a process and as a document, clearly address the individualized instructional characteristics of students who are labeled as in need of special education.

EXAMPLES OF IEPS

In this final section we provide examples of IEPs that are not cast in traditional terms, and that represent the four types of instructional goals we associate with resource programs (i.e., remedial, compensatory, new skills/behaviors, and new content). We are not very concerned about how these goals are classified, but we hope that one area of major difficulty is followed through in terms of its implications for the student's total school program.

The subject in these examples is reading, and the student here is a 9-year-old boy, Billy, who is having difficulty not only with reading, but with content areas as well. He has just completed third grade, and has been accepted into the resource program for the coming year. The goals we show do not represent all possible goals in reading. For example, IEP planners would likely have as a goal getting Billy to read and respond to at least one book a week around his own interests. The four goals below represent an emphasis on helping Billy profit from school while addressing major aspects of his reading problem.

A Goal with a Remedial Focus

1. *Current Level of Performance.* Oral reading in grade level (third) material shows a slow rate of words read correctly (25) hampered by hesitancies of 5 or more seconds, or failure to identify basic words consistently. Only 10 words (*the, a, an, to, be, too, but, go, he,* and *see*) were identified consistently. Oral reading in lower-graded texts (primer through second grade) shows a somewhat faster rate (median of 30 words per minute), but no differences in consistency of identification, other than the 10 words noted above.

Of 100 sight words tested in isolation (*Essential Sight Words Program, Level 1;* Sundbye, Dyck, & Wyatt, 1979), Billy knew only nine words 100% of the time (*too* was not on the list, but is always known in context).

2. *Annual Goal.* At the end of the year, Billy should be able to identify consistently (100% of the time), 200 basic sight words (i.e., the lists from *Essential Sight Words Program, Levels 1 and 2*). These words should also be read at a high rate (60 words correct per minute) in materials that have a high density of sight words. In other materials, the sight words should not prove to be difficult except as they are involved in phrase-level miscues.

3. *Short-Term Objectives*

   a. Billy will read aloud correctly and quickly (within 1 second) 25 high-frequency words when those words are presented in lists in which the word appears more than one time.

   b. Billy will read fluently (100% correct; 60 words per minute) 25 high-frequency words when those words occur in context composed primarily of those words.

   c. Billy will read aloud fluently 25 high-frequency words when those words occur in easy texts not seen before.

    d. Short-term objectives for the remainder of the 200 basic sight words will continue as in a through c above, with periodic cumulative review of all sight words taught to date.

4. *Special Education Services*

    a. Within the resource program, the student will use the *Essential Sight Words Program Levels 1 and 2,* (Sundbye et al., 1979, 1980). This program will be supplemented with easy reading materials selected by the resource teacher for their high density of high-frequency words.

    b. The student will chart daily the rate of target words read correctly in repeated readings (two times) of the program materials.

    c. Peer tutoring of the sight words will be used to increase fluency in saying words in isolation.

5. *Objective Criteria*

    a. Charts of words read correctly per minute in familiar text material. Aim rates will be raised until Billy reaches at least 60 words per minute read correctly.

    b. Records of words read correctly (with no more than ½-second hesitations) in list form, where the word appears at least four times (see program testing materials).

    c. One hundred percent of target words read correctly and quickly (no more than ½-second delay) in reading material new to Billy.

6. *Schedule for Determining Progress Toward Mastery of Goal and Objectives*

    a. Daily data will determine the need for programmatic corrections. Billy will be involved in any changes of program.

    b. Progress will be reviewed with parents at the end of each 9-week reporting period.

    c. Within 1 month of the end of the annual goal review, a summary of the program's effectiveness toward meeting the annual goal will be shared with parents and with other IEP team members as well as with Billy.

7. *Comment.* Note that in remedial work, the units to be remediated need to be clearly specified. It is not enough to simply place the student into an easier reader that may or may not provide for the much needed mastery of basic sight words. Further, some of the "skills" taught when the child is simply repositioned in the program sequence may not be relevant to basic needs in reading, or to helping the student function in other reading situations.

A Goal with a Compensatory Focus

1. *Current Level of Performance.* Billy cannot read the science, health, social studies, and math (except for algorithms) texts, and cannot write the expected answers to assignments in these content areas. They are all at a frustration level for him. However, he does interpret graphs, charts, and figures when he knows the topics. Further, when the materials are read to Billy, he comprehends most of the material if it is presented in very short segments, and if he can ask for clarifications.

2. *Annual Goal.* At the end of the year, Billy should be able to recognize text material that is too difficult, and be able to negotiate with the teacher an appropriate modification in assignments. Examples include the use of alternate materials on the same topic; permission to work with a peer or in a cooperative group; the use of different response modes to show what has been learned; or the use of taped texts and responses.

3. *Short-Term Objectives*

   a. Billy will be able to recognize materials that are too difficult, and will be able to express this difficulty in an appropriate manner.

   b. Billy will learn to use the alternatives he might suggest to the teacher as modifications of the regular assignment.

   c. Billy will learn appropriate ways of explaining his problem, and of negotiating changes in the expectations of the teacher.

   d. Billy will be able to critique his own behaviors as a negotiator.

4. *Special Education Services.* Within the resource program, Billy will receive instruction and have an opportunity for guided practice and independent practice in the skills noted in number 3 above. Videotaping of sessions, along with mutually developed criteria, will provide a means of moving toward self-critique.
   The nature of the general education content material will be used as the basis for instruction.

5. *Objective Criteria*

   a. Feedback, including anecdotal records, from teachers with whom Billy will be negotiating will be compared with Billy's self-appraisal and with the appraisal of the resource teacher.

   b. Success with the actual use of alternate modes of learning and expressing what has been learned will be compared with traditional modes.

6. *Schedule for Determining Progress Toward Mastery of Goal and Objectives*

a. Weekly data for each component of the instructional program will be summarized as formative or frequent evaluation to determine any corrections in the direction or pace of the program. Because this program is new, it is not possible at this time to determine an exact schedule.

b. The sequence of evaluation will generally include:
   (1) Recognition of problem and appropriate statements about that recognition (with 2 weeks of the program's initiation).
   (2) Use of alternative modes of learning content (according to unit schedules in general classes).
   (3) Learning to explain and negotiate (by the end of the first semester).
   (4) Self-critique (will be ongoing; in addition, a summary self-evaluation will be used within 1 month of the end of the year).

c. A progress summary will be made at the end of each 9-week reporting period.

7. *Comment.* Note that this goal is related to Billy's reading problem, but it involves other behaviors that he can generalize as he interacts with other teachers.

A Goal with a Focus of Learning New Procedures or Processes

1. *Current Level of Performance.* Billy cannot read the science, health, social studies, and math (except for algorithms) texts, and cannot write the expected answers to assignments in these content areas. They are all at a frustration level for him. However, he does interpret graphs, charts, and figures when he knows the topics. Further, when the materials are read to Billy, he comprehends most of the material if it is presented in very short segments, and if he can ask for clarifications. Further, Billy does not use any consistent study strategies for reading or remembering content materials.

2. *Annual Goal.* Billy will learn to use study strategies for reading and understanding content area materials independently.

3. *Short-Term Objectives*

a. Billy will learn to keep a study notebook according to the guidelines provided by the resource teacher.

b. Billy will learn to use a particular study method, such as SQ3R.

c. Billy will learn to use feedback from his performance to improve his study strategies.

4. *Special Education Services.* The resource teacher will collaborate with the general class teacher(s) to guide and require the use of the notebook as a means of recording and evaluating study behaviors. Further, the resource teacher will teach Billy to use the SQ3R study technique and monitor his use of it. The resource teacher will also teach Billy how to use performance feedback to modify his future study behaviors.

5. *Objective Criteria*

   a. Notebook evaluations according to predetermined criteria of format and content.

   b. Monitoring of the use of SQ3R as Billy studies.

   c. Comparison of self-reports, reports of parents and teachers of Billy's study behaviors.

   d. Performance on evaluative tasks.

   e. Billy's explanations of how he goes about studying and learning to read new content text materials.

   f. Observed changes in study behavior as a result of performance feedback.

6. *Schedule for Determining Progress Toward Mastery of Goal and Objectives*

   a. Notebook checks will be made daily for the first 9-week period; thereafter on a weekly basis.

   b. Performance on evaluative tasks will be recorded as the tasks occur.

   c. The use of SQ3R will be monitored on a daily basis.

   d. At least once a week Billy will provide a self-report for comparison with other data about his study strategies.

   e. During the last quarter, the program will be faded to self-monitoring.

   f. At least a month before the annual review date, a summary of Billy's progress will be shared with IEP team members, including parents and Billy.

7. *Comment.* The compensatory goal is to help Billy survive in the general content class until he can improve enough to get by without so many modifications. The purpose of this new procedures goal is to teach him a study process he does not apparently already possess or use.

A Goal That Focuses on Learning New Content

1. *Current Level of Performance.* Given lists of 20 important concepts from each content area at each grade level (see Criscoe & Gee, 1984), Billy cannot pronounce

the vocabulary items at the second-grade level. He can explain only about a third of the terms, except in math, where he knows two thirds of the terms. Further, he cannot discuss randomly chosen selections from the texts unless he got the information from someplace other than school.

2. *Annual Goal.* Billy should be able to read and discuss the basic concept terms associated cumulatively with the content areas in science and social studies through his own grade level.

3. *Short-Term Objectives*

   a. Billy will be able to identify and explain the concept terms associated cumulatively with science, from all grade levels prior to his current placement.

   b. Billy will be able to identify and explain the concept terms associated cumulatively with social studies, from all grade levels prior to his current placement.

   c. Billy will be able to identify and explain current terminology as it is studied in science and in social studies.

   d. Billy will begin showing independence in monitoring his own performance with these activities.

4. *Special Education Services*

   a. The resource teacher and associate will provide instruction around the old terms from content areas.

   b. Work from the study skills program will be monitored for the current terminology, to be checked as ''known'' when he shows that he understands the terms.

5. *Objective Criteria*

   a. For each grade level, the 20 Important Concepts list will be used as a checklist to record item-mastery, and for aperiodic reviews. At least three reviews will be made for each item on the checklist after that item has been checked as mastered.

   b. The word lists of 20 Important Concepts from each content area at each grade level will be used as a summary checklist. A random sample of five items from each list will be given to Billy to read and explain.

   c. Observation will be used to monitor Billy's independent use of the study and record-keeping activities.

6. *Schedule for Determining Progress Toward Mastery of Goal and Objectives*

a. Daily records will be kept both by Billy and by the resource teacher of study behavior and discussion of terms. This information will be used to make adjustments in the amount and pacing of the work.

b. The 9-week term will have a summary record of progress for the term.

c. Within 1 month of the annual review, a summary statement of Billy's pace of learning and items mastered will be given to IEP team members.

7. *Comment.* Part of this New Content focus seems remedial, because Billy should have learned the content in earlier years. However, he was away at a special reading program during science and social studies reading times, and the subjects were taught from a text he could not read. In any case, his current monitoring of New Content does accompany a new way of learning for him. Keep in mind that what a goal is called is not as important as being sure to include the goals that are needed in the individual case, however they may be classified.

CONCLUDING COMMENT

The IEP and related services deserve more attention in both preservice and inservice programs of special education. Although the entire process is time-consuming, we believe that when it is well done, it can benefit the student and justify placement in the special education program. The time wasted by random, poorly planned and monitored instructional activities cannot be justified where the effects of student disabilities must be offset, and where the instructional program should differ from that of ''regular'' instruction. If this individualization is not reflected in the IEP, it is simply not likely to occur at all.

Chapter 11

Homework and Grading

Homework and grading are significant issues that greatly affect the resource program and the resource teacher. They are problematic issues because opinion is divided as to the expectations that a resource teacher should have about homework for the students, as well as to the accountability that students in the program should have for their grades. The resource teacher must address the questions: Should students be required to do homework? and To what extent should the homework be considered in grading? In this chapter we outline the positive and negative effects of homework, recommend a homework policy, discuss the implications of students' attitudes toward homework, and describe practical resources that may be of further assistance. Finally, we address the issue of grading in the resource program—both the daily grading of homework, behavior, and student-produced products, and the periodic report grading that constitutes a student's permanent school record.

HOMEWORK

Homework is both an issue and a problem that greatly affects the role of the resource teacher. It is a significant issue because opinion is divided as to whether students should be required to do homework at all; and if they are, then what kind? how much? and to what extent should it be considered in grading? Homework is a problem for the student who may see it as an additional burden, who may not find success with it, and/or who may not have the parental support needed to complete it appropriately. It is a problem for the resource teacher because the resource program can easily become a supervised study hall, and the resource teacher simply a study hall supervisor.

Cooper's (1989) review of empirical research and analyses of policies about homework shows how complex this topic really is within American education; yet he is able to make suggestions that are helpful in establishing homework policies and procedures. A thorough understanding of this topic requires study beyond this brief overview, and we recommend sources for further study and practical assistance.

Homework assignments are common because most educators and parents believe that their positive outcomes outweigh their troublesome aspects. Cooper's (1989) summary of positive and negative effects of homework is outlined in Figure 11.1. The figure shows that intended effects of homework relate not only to mastery of content per se, but to self-discipline and to attitudes toward school as well. These noncontent factors form the major rationale for using homework in the primary grades, if not throughout the elementary years. It is not until the post-elementary years that homework affects academic achievement, and then only when the assignments are carefully arranged, and when the weekly time requirement is calibrated to the subject matter and age of the student.

Homework Policies

Resource teachers who consult with general classroom teachers must know the homework policies of the school, and how these policies are communicated to parents and to students. Cooper's (1989) summary of homework policy guidelines (Figure 11.2) addresses the district, school, and teacher levels of policy. We have added England and Flatley's (1985) ''Do's and Don't's'' for the student level (Figure 11.3). All the recommendations are based on ''best evidence'' research, and are useful in both resource and mainstream settings.

Not everyone agrees with the policy recommendations that come from research. For example, Posamentier and Stepelman (1981) believe that homework provides an appropriate means of individualizing assignments for diverse student needs. We would agree, to the extent that the teacher can realistically adjust the amount of work to be done, or the nature of the assignments. In any case, both mainstream and resource teachers who assign homework should do so according to guidelines from their publicly stated written policy. The policy itself should have been developed with the participation of all relevant audiences (i.e., school personnel, parents or guardians, and the students themselves).

Student Attitudes Toward Homework

Many older students do not see the value of homework, or they are not successful with homework assignments. They are often not motivated to do homework at

---

Positive Effects

Immediate achievement and learning
  Better retention of factual knowledge
  Increased understanding
  Better critical thinking, concept formation, information processing
  Curriculum enrichment

Long-term academic
  Encourage learning during leisure time
  Improved attitude toward school
  Better study habits and skills

Nonacademic
  Greater self-direction
  Greater self-discipline
  Better time organization
  More inquisitiveness
  More independent problem solving

Greater parental appreciation of and involvement in schooling

Negative Effects

Satiation
  Loss of interest in academic material
  Physical and emotional fatigue

Denial of access to leisure-time and community activities

Parental interference
  Pressure to complete assignments and perform well
  Confusion of instructional techniques

Cheating
  Copying from other students
  Help beyond tutoring

Increased differences between high and low achievers

Figure 11.1. Positive and negative effects of homework. From *Homework* (p. 12) by H. Cooper, 1989, New York: Longman. Reprinted with permission.

all, and when they are, the result may be of such poor quality that the entire assignment becomes moot in terms of any intended positive effects. School personnel would do well to consider students' perceptions of homework, and then to account for the implications of these perceptions.

For example, Baksh and Martin (1986) found that the negative perceptions of high school students fell into three categories: the quantity of homework, its dis-

For Districts

Homework is a cost-effective instructional technique. It can have positive effects on achievement and character development and can serve as a vital link between the school and family.

Homework should have different purposes at different grades. For younger students, it should foster positive attitudes, habits, and character traits. For older students, it should facilitate knowledge acquisition in specific topics.

Homework should be required at all grade levels, but a mixture of mandatory and voluntary homework is most beneficial.

The frequency and duration of mandatory assignments should be:
1. Grades 1 to 3—one to three assignments a week, each lasting no more than 15 minutes
2. Grades 4 to 6—two to four assignments, each lasting 15 to 45 minutes
3. Grades 7 to 9—three to five assignments, each lasting 45 to 75 minutes
4. Grades 10 to 12—four to five assignments, each lasting 75 to 120 minutes

For Schools

The frequency and duration of homework assignments should be further specified to reflect local school and community circumstances.

In schools where different subjects are taught by different teachers, teachers should know:
1. What days of the week are available to them for assignments
2. How much daily homework time should be spent on their subject

Administrators should:
1. Communicate the district and school homework policies to parents
2. Monitor the implementation of the policy
3. Coordinate the scheduling of homework among different subjects, if needed

Teachers should state clearly:
1. How the assignment is related to the topic under study
2. The purpose of the assignment
3. How the assignment might best be carried out
4. What the student needs to do to demonstrate that the assignment has been completed

For Teachers

All students in a class will be responsible for the same assignments, with only rare exceptions.

Homework will include mandatory assignments. Failure to turn in mandatory assignments will necessitate remedial activities.

Figure 11.2. Summary of homework policy guidelines.

Homework will also include voluntary assignments meant to meet the needs of individual students or groups of students.

All homework assignments will *not* be formally evaluated. They will be used to locate problems in student progress and to individualize instruction.

Topics will appear in assignments before and after they are covered in class, not just on the day they are discussed.

Homework will not be used to teach complex skills. It will generally focus on simple skills and material or on the integration of skills already possessed by the student.

Parents will rarely be asked to play a formal instructional role in homework. Instead, they should be asked to create a home environment that facilitates student self-study.

Figure 11.2. *Continued.* From *Homework* (pp. 190–191) by H. Cooper, 1989, New York: Longman. Reprinted with permission.

For Students

1. *Do* ask your parents for help with your homework only when you really need help.

2. *Do* ask the teacher for help before or after class if you are confused about a homework assignment.

3. *Do* explain to teachers legitimate reasons that sometimes make it impossible to complete some homework assignments.

4. *Do* make every effort to complete homework assignments when they are very important for a particular class.

5. *Do not* expect that your parents will be able to help with all your homework. (Parents forget things they have learned, and some of what is taught in school today is foreign to adults.)

6. *Do not* ask teachers to help with any homework assignment you really can complete independently.

7. *Do not* confuse *excuses* for incomplete homework assignments with legitimate *reasons*.

8. *Do not* think doing your homework "most of the time" will be satisfactory for those classes where homework counts the most. (In such classes, even a 75% completion rate may not be enough.)

Figure 11.3. Homework guidelines. From "Homework Do's and Don'ts" in *Homework—and Why* (pp. 36–38) by D. A. England and J. K. Flatley, 1985, Bloomington, IN: Phi Delta Kappa. Reprinted with permission.

tribution, and the moral aspects of having homework at all. Teachers can take several steps to approach these issues.

To find out how well grounded the perceptions of excessive amounts of homework might be, some teachers have students write the "elapsed time" (not to include telephone calls, eating, etc.) it takes to complete each homework assignment. The teacher can then find out the modal time taken for assignments. The teacher can (and perhaps should) also work the assignments herself or himself, allowing that students will need more time. When more than one teacher is involved, a homework timetable can show (a) the total amount of homework time expected for any one student and (b) where the total expectations are disproportionate to a reasonable homework load.

Distribution refers to the timing of homework assignments. For example, students often object to assignments when an important social or athletic event is coming up, just before major exams, or on weekends and vacation periods. It is, of course, the prerogative of the teacher or school personnel to make decisions about any matter concerning homework. However, policies about the timing of homework should certainly consider the reasonableness of such situational student concerns.

Moral or fairness issues are involved when students remark, for example, that "teachers take measures to make their own work more manageable or to enjoy their leisure hours but do not create similar opportunities for their students" (Baksh & Martin, 1986, p. 5). Especially with older students, the resource teacher (or any other) would be ill-advised to engage in this argument. Where there is a clear homework policy with a carefully considered rationale that serves the interests of the students, and where the issues of amount and distribution of homework are handled reasonably, the moral issue becomes a smoke screen used against the teacher by students who do not identify with school values. Furthermore, the homework smoke screen is only a symptom of a far more serious alienation that should be addressed by the school community.

A few parents also object to homework, believing that the schools should do "their job" during school time, and that time at home should be engaged in family concerns and activities that give added dimension to the child's whole life. These situations will need to be considered on a case-by-case basis where all those involved can speak to their concerns so that the student is not caught in the middle.

Sources of Practical Suggestions

Because homework is so universally problematic, there are a growing number of practical suggestions and programs to assist teachers, parents, and students. We describe some representative sources.

Textbooks in "methods" courses at the postelementary level recognize the role of homework by providing entire chapters that deal with how it may be managed.

For example, among their other recommendations, Posamentier and Stepelman (1981) suggested that the teacher duplicate the daily or weekly assignment sheet (Figure 11.4) both to prevent miscopying or noncopying by students and to let students and parents know what the week will bring. To help with the question of the "paper review," they suggested that the teacher set up a random system, noting in a record book when each student's work is read. For example, the teacher can collect papers from a different horizontal, vertical, or diagonal row each day. When a target student is put in the middle, that student's work unobtrusively gets additional monitoring by the teacher.

Johnson (1982) wrote about mathematics classes, but his ideas can be generalized to other academic areas. For example, to check on the effectiveness of the homework assignment, he selects a typical problem or one similar to the problems assigned, and has students work the problem on paper without talking or referring to their work. He also writes all homework answers on a transparency, and as the class begins, students check their own work and write the number correct at the top of the page. The teacher can walk around the room to observe success with homework and to clarify problematic areas for students. This work is then corrected, with the students noting the source of error on the homework sheet, and all work is kept in a notebook for future review.

Johnson (1982) recommended that homework scores not be included in the student's final term grade, because homework (as seatwork) should be one of the places where students can make valid errors that contribute to the learning process. At the same time, he does not give a passing grade unless the student completes most of the homework assignments.

An entire homework program has been developed in Canter's (1988) series (Grades 1–3, 4–6, and 7–12) *Homework Without Tears for Teachers*. It includes such topics as "Steps to Giving Effective Homework Assignments" and "What to Do if Students Do Not Complete Homework." It is specifically designed to secure home-school cooperation in this matter. Canter and Hausner's (1987) companion series, *Homework Without Tears. A Parent's Guide for Motivating Children to Do Homework and to Succeed in School*, describes a comprehensive program for helping parents provide a supportive and consistent environment for homework completion. The series includes many creative ideas. For example, homework survival kits (see Figure 11.5) help reduce distractions and assure that students have all their needed supplies handy. Canter and Hausner also provide many "troubleshooting ideas" for most common homework problems. Their complete home-school program is based on familiar behavioral principles.

Concluding Statement

We recognize that the entire topic of homework is also relevant to the area of study skills. Within this context, however, we wish to emphasize the role that home-

---

	(Class)	
(Assignment No.)	(Topic)	(Date)

Book / Page / Exercises
 "   "   "
 "   "   "

Concepts and Relationships to Remember:

| (Assignment No.) | (Topic) | (Date) |

Book / Page / Exercises
 "   "   "
 "   "   "

Concepts and Relationships to Remember:

| (Assignment No.) | (Topic) | (Date) |

Book / Page / Exercises
 "   "   "
 "   "   "

Concepts and Relationships to Remember:

| (Assignment No.) | (Topic) | (Date) |

Book / Page / Exercises
 "   "   "
 "   "   "

Concepts and Relationships to Remember:

| (Assignment No.) | (Topic) | (Date) |

Book / Page / Exercises
 "   "   "
 "   "   "

Concepts and Relationships to Remember:

Figure 11.4. Weekly homework assignment sheet. From *Teaching Secondary School Mathematics* (3rd ed., p. 47) by A. S. Posamentier and J. Stepelman, 1990, New York: Macmillan. Reprinted with permission.

Homework Survival Kit *Grades K–3*	*Homework Survival Kit* *Grades 4–6*	*Grades 7–12*
☐ crayons	☐ pencils	☐ assignment book
☐ pencils	☐ pens	☐ pencils
☐ markers	☐ colored pencils	☐ pens
☐ pencil sharpener	☐ crayons	☐ erasers
☐ erasers	☐ markers	☐ markers
☐ glue or paste	☐ pencil sharpener	☐ writing paper
☐ tape	☐ erasers	☐ tape
☐ writing paper	☐ glue or paste	☐ hole punch
☐ construction paper	☐ tape	☐ white out
☐ hole punch	☐ writing paper	☐ pencil sharpener
☐ stapler	☐ construction paper	☐ scissors
☐ scissors	☐ hole punch	☐ glue or paste
☐ children's dictionary	☐ stapler	☐ ruler
☐ paper clips	☐ scissors	☐ stapler
☐ assignment book (third graders)	☐ paper clips	☐ colored pencils
	☐ white out	☐ paper clips
	☐ assignment book	☐ index cards
	☐ folders for reports	☐ dictionary
	☐ index cards	☐ compass
	☐ intermediate dictionary	☐ protractor
	☐ atlas	☐ calculator
	☐ thesaurus	☐ atlas
	☐ almanac	☐ thesaurus
	☐ rubber bands	☐ almanac
		☐ rubber bands

Figure 11.5. Homework survival kits. From *Homework Without Tears. A Parent's Guide for Motivating Children to Do Homework and to Succeed in School* (pp. 17–19) by L. Canter and L. Hausner, 1987, New York: Harper & Row. Reprinted with permission.

work, especially homework from the mainstream program, can play in shaping the role or taking an undue amount of time from the resource program.

GRADING

Resource teachers deal with two kinds of grading, both within their own programs and as they work with mainstream teachers. The obvious grading decision concerns the daily or frequent evaluation of student products and social behavior. The second, and by far the more problematic, is the periodic report (card) provided to students and to their parents or guardians, and which is recorded as part of the student's permanent school record. We address the more difficult question first.

Grading as a Periodic Report for the Permanent Record

In this section we describe the major issues that relate to grading low-achieving students. We also suggest questions the teacher may ask to (a) determine present school policies and procedures and (b) develop a grading policy for the resource program.

Meaning and Fairness

The issues of fairness and meaning in grading are perpetual in all of education. For students who are low achieving or at risk, any proposed "lowering of expectations" through modification of the grading system used with nondisabled peers may play a role in their future achievement.

Carpenter (1985) noted that meanings of grades may differentially indicate that a student (a) demonstrated competence, (b) made progress, (c) made a good effort, and/or (d) was compared with other students. These distinctions are important, because without a shared interpretation of the meaning of the grade, there will be misunderstandings and hard feelings.

Grade basis: Demonstrated competence. The demonstration of competence is also called a *criterion-referenced* basis for grading, and it is related to behavioral ways of thinking that deal with mastery learning. In this view, minimum goals and objectives are stated in advance, and the grade reflects mastery of these objectives, or the attainment of minimum competency. This position is well reflected in the IEP, and depends for validity and fairness on the ability of instructional personnel to match carefully the student's present abilities to the more challenging, yet possible, educational task. It answers the question, Is the student making expected progress toward realistic goals and objectives that are appropriate for the age and abilities of the individual?

Potential misinterpretation. Unfortunately, many teachers misinterpret this rationale by setting the same goals and objectives for all students, knowing that it will be impossible for all students in the class to attain them. Teachers may also state that those students who cannot meet these standards should not be in the class, and that any modifications of standards or of assessment result in a lowering of standards for all. They may further say that it is unfair to nondisabled students to use any modifications of standards or of curriculum.

It is also unfortunate that the idea of setting one standard or setting multiple standards has become embedded in a larger controversy concerning teacher expectations and student achievement. Cohen (1987), for example, stated that "positive expectations are especially important in classrooms with large concentrations of low-achieving students, for it is apparently easy for teachers to let the previous low academic performance of students translate into low expectations about subsequent performance'' (p. 479).

We suggest that resource teachers who encounter some of the arguments noted above remember that the individualization of goals and objectives against which progress and performance are evaluated is like the term *handicapping* as it is used in golf and other sports: It promotes both competition and effort (Frierson, 1975)— and also fairness. Ysseldyke and Algozzine (1970) tell us that students with disabilities and students in every educational setting often complain that adapting or accommodating to disability all too often results in lowered expectations, and this results in patronization by others. Accommodating without patronizing requires all involved to adopt a standard of inclusion in activities and of expectations of meeting norms of performance.

Grade bases: Making progress and making a good effort.   Both ''making progress'' and ''making a good effort'' are known as *self-referenced* bases for grading (Terwilliger, 1977), because they assess growth shown by the student in comparison with the grader's perception of the student's ability or aptitude. This popular philosophy underlies much of special education thinking about the issue. It addresses the question, Is the student making growth, considering the motivation, effort, and abilities of the student?

Potential misinterpretation.   This standard is often known as a ''copout'' for students and their parents as well as for teachers. Because each statement is so ambiguous, it may be easier to say that it is the basis for grading than to develop (for the teacher) or to accept (for students and parents) measures that would substantiate such observations. It may also let the student with a history of poor motivation continue low achievement because only effort has been expected, giving validity to the ''lowering of expectations'' argument described previously.

When the criterion of either effort or general progress is used for grading, it should be accompanied by a substantial analysis of the student's past and present performance and abilities so that it is indeed a ''self-referencing'' system. Further, making progress and effort should be carefully and tightly linked to individually appropriate goals and objectives. Grades should not indeed be given, but should be earned.

Grade basis: Comparing the student with others.   When a student is compared with others, the interpretation is *norm-referenced,* because the student's performance is compared with that of others of the same grade or age level. This comparison is supposed to help students and their parents understand individual strengths and weaknesses in relation to those of their peers. The ''norm'' that is referenced may be standardized tests or the students' classmates; the group may be immediate schoolmates or a wider cultural group. The ''norm'' may also be other students the teacher has known, or it may be some mythical grade level in a particular curriculum. The question addressed is, How does this student compare with others of the same age or grade?

Possible misinterpretation.   It is widely recognized that general achievement levels vary from school to school, from district to district, and perhaps from one year's class to another. Public "report cards" of individual schools within a district are even published in the newspaper to show general tested achievement levels. A student who may be a B student in one school may move and become a D student in another school, or vice versa. The psychological impact of the general achievement milieu of a school is so real and powerful that it is almost impossible to overcome.

At the same time, it is difficult to condone failing most of the students in a particular school because of some external standard. So great a failure rate would also indicate that the program was inappropriate for the students. This situation is clearly analogous to the individual student who would always be below the "norm," no matter how great the progress or effort. This is a clear case of unfairness.

Recommendations

In the face of such complex issues, we believe that the grading basis of "demonstrated competence" most directly relates to an appropriate standard for all students in compulsory school situations. It assumes that the goals and objectives against which competence is to be demonstrated have been set in consideration of the individual's abilities and present performance. Where there is a genuine question of the consequences of grades (e.g., in calculating a GPA for college entrance), it is easy to provide a weighting system that would not penalize such students.

School Grading Policies and Procedures

Before developing a grading system, the resource teacher should find out about any policies or procedures that are expected of both mainstream and special education teachers. The following questions can guide the teacher's initial information gathering in a new school or program.

1. *What policies concerning grading already exist?* Schools usually have specific policies and procedures about such matters as (a) when grades are reported, (b) when a parent conference may substitute for a report card, and (c) the bases for determining grades. There will be wide variation, however, in the extent to which a district or local school has given thought to the role of individual differences in their grading policies, whether for the gifted or for the low-achieving student. Yet, such a policy can set the tone and expectations for all participants in the grading process. For example, Drucker and Hansen (1982) suggested a statement such as:

> It should be the policy of this school to employ differential standards for grading and course requirements. The regular classroom teacher is encouraged to modify the curriculum, instructional approaches, and grading practices for those identified as handicapped students in the regular classroom. (p. 251)

Carpenter (1985) further noted that any modifications are necessary only when "the pupil's handicap is determined to be a mitigating factor" (p. 57), and that such a policy "provides teachers with a clear message that grading adaptations are welcome and encouraged" (p. 57). Not every district either welcomes or encourages adaptations, of course, but the teacher must work within whatever policy exists.

If there are no policies, the resource teacher will need to negotiate a desirable one on either a formal or an informal basis. In addition, the school or other administrative unit should be encouraged to use all relevant constituents (e.g., parents, advisory groups, and teachers) to develop a locally and professionally acceptable policy concerning grading.

2. *Who is responsible for determining and reporting grades of students within the resource program?* If students within the resource program receive instruction solely from the resource teacher for an academic subject, then that teacher usually provides the grade for that subject. However, when the mainstream teacher is involved and the instructional responsibility is shared, either the grading may be shared, or it may become the job of the mainstream teacher.

Where grading is a shared responsibility, teachers must work jointly to establish a clear rationale for the basis of the grade. This step is necessary when dealing not only with the student, but with parents and administrators as well. The joint planning should occur at the beginning of the mutual relationship rather than at the time the grading report is due.

In the case of postelementary education, especially at the high school level where grades are linked to graduation, the basis of the grade must often be agreed on by the general subject matter teacher even if the resource teacher provides the sole instruction in an academic subject. This is usually the case because of regulations regarding accreditation. In some states only teachers who are licensed to teach certain subjects at the secondary level are permitted to assign grades and their ensuing credit toward graduation. If the resource teacher, for example, is not licensed in English at the secondary level, he or she must find a sponsoring teacher who can assure that the English "course" taught by the resource teacher does in fact meet the graduation requirements of the school.

3. *How much latitude do individual teachers have in determining the components or bases of the grade?* Policies about grading are usually very general, and may not address directly the freedom a particular teacher may have in deciding the bases of the grades assigned. This is a particularly important point for the resource teacher for two reasons.

First, the resource teacher may wish to use methods other than daily grades or tests to determine the reported grade. For example, observational checklists or rating scales may be more useful than a test. Second, the resource teacher needs to know whether it is possible to consider, in addition to actual achievement, individual differences in ability, effort, and behavior. This question speaks directly to the philosophy of the teacher and the program.

4. *Where IEPs are used, is modification of the grading system addressed?* Where the grading system must be modified because of the nature of the student's handicapping condition, the IEP should specify the characteristics of the modifications. This encourages the team to consider on a case-by-case basis both the need and nature of grading modifications. It also reduces conflict when all involved with the student, including the parents and hopefully the student himself or herself, predetermine the system that will best serve the individual.

Developing a Grading Policy

Several principles will be helpful to the resource teacher in developing a grading policy. First, low-achieving students need frequent feedback. If the reporting period is long (e.g., 9 weeks), the resource teacher should arrange more frequent "grades" than would find their way to the report card. At least once a week, students and their parents should be informed of the student's progress.

Second, if students are mainstreamed, then teachers who see them in different settings should confer about the grade. Cohen (1983) showed how report cards are developed for the mainstreamed student (see Figure 11.6). Her model shows the relationship of daily grades with their corrective (or noncorrective) feedback in both the resource program and mainstreamed coursework.

Third, grades of pass/fail lack the precision needed to fulfill the information purpose of grades at any time. The college student will recognize that in a pass/fail system, the "pass" portion is too broad to be meaningful as a true indicator of performance.

Fourth, attitude, effort, and study skills may well be relevant to a daily grade for students with severe problems of motivation and study habits. However, in general, any academic accomplishment should receive a grade that is separate from evaluations of effort, attitude, or study skills. Otherwise, the report of the student's ability in the content being studied will be misleading.

Fifth, the kinds of modifications noted in the IEP usually address (a) a different scale or basis for assigning grades, (b) alternate means of student assessment, and/or (c) alternate curricula used to achieve goals and objectives. For example, although many students are graded on scales from A through F, the scale for the low-achieving student may be A, C, or F to indicate that he or she is completing most objectives, some of the objectives, or not many of the planned objectives. Alternate assessment modes may include orally presented tests, multiple choice rather than an essay, or the inclusion of products other than tests. Alternate curricula as they relate to grading simply mean that progress is assessed toward a particular major curricular goal (e.g., reading comprehension), while the student is enrolled in a different curriculum (perhaps not the basal text).

Finally, keep in mind that there are alternatives to the grading that is most familiar. The current emphasis on portfolio analysis (of the student's ongoing work) arose from a belief that traditional "grading" systems were simply not informative enough. The parent conference has long been a more personal way to discuss

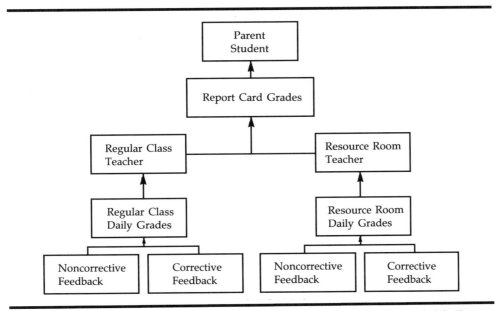

Figure 11.6. Developing report card grades for the mainstreamed child. From
"Assigning Report Card Grades to the Mainstreamed Child"
by S. B. Cohen, 1983, *Teaching Exceptional Children, 15*(2),
pp. 186–189. Reprinted with permission.

student progress. And, of course, any topic with such a long history of controversy
as grading has had will find many professionals who would suggest alternatives.
We recommend that the resource teacher review Carpenter's (1985) article,
"Grading Handicapped Pupils: Review and Position Statement," as well as the
book *Wad-ja-get? The Grading Game in American Education* (Kirschenbaum, Napier,
& Simon, 1971).

DAILY OR ASSIGNMENT GRADING

Daily grades or evaluation of assignments often provide the ongoing information
that is accumulated to form the major report card grade. Yet frequent evaluations
have functions over and above their contribution to the report card or periodic
grade. Daily or assignment grades are helpful, then, in (a) contributing to the longer
term grade, (b) keeping systematic track of the achievements of individual students,
(c) motivating students toward continuing effort, and (d) indicating to teachers
when they need to modify their teaching strategies to improve the effectiveness
of individual instructional programs. This last point is often overlooked.

Should Homework Be Included in a Daily Grade?

The answer here is an emphatic *No,* because there is no way to control the homework situation to assure that it really reflects the student's own practice. Further, homework is not the right situation to "test" the student's knowledge and growth. Where homework is given, other methods should be used in class to determine the student's understanding or achievement.

Should Factors Such as Effort and Behavior Be Considered?

In most cases the student's achievement in a content area should be separated from other factors of interest (e.g., study skills, behavior, and effort). However, in some cases, where behavior and study habits are vital to the instructional program, these factors may be considered initially in determining daily grades. An example for use at the postelementary level is shown in Figure 11.7.

What Alternatives Exist to "Grading" of Ongoing Work?

Unfortunately, many teachers judge the daily achievement of a student almost solely on performance on paper-and-pencil tasks—that is, they evaluate the student on a teacher-developed test or program worksheets. However, as Kim and Kellough (1978) noted, many other types of activities furnish information on students' progress and development. These include the questions students ask during and after class, the responses they make to questions, the way in which they explain ideas to others, the manner in which they listen, the way in which they work in laboratory or workshop situations, the degree of their involvement in class discussions, as well as the kinds of challenges they seek out or accept. The authors noted that "although these activities do not fit into a numerical grading system, they may be more significant than the results of some formal, written exam" (p. 209).

We call special attention to two kinds of assessment that receive increasing attention in the evaluation of ongoing work. The first is curriculum-based measurement in which the teacher keeps careful individual records of students' progress on prespecified tasks, each with only one "correct" answer for each comparable item. Usually the number of items correct, as well as the rate of correct responses, is used to give students feedback and to adjust the instructional program. Grades per se may or may not be associated with this type of progress reporting. See Figure 11.8 for an example of such a program.

The second assessment that receives current attention is portfolio assessment in which frequent samples of the student's ongoing work are kept as a running record of achievement. These materials are usually supplemented with checklists, interview responses, and student-teacher conference reports. Again, a grade per se is not given, but instead, the teacher and student share a qualitative assess-

Points:	Semester:	Subject/Period:	Student Ron W.
23–27 A __ 1			
21–22 B ✓ 2		English	Home Room/Teacher
19–20 C __ 3			Susette H.
17–18 D __ 4			

DIRECTED STUDY SESSIONS   Weekly Average

Monday	Tuesday	Wednesday	Thursday	Friday	
Date 10-17	Date 10-18	Date 10-19	Date 10-20	Date 10-21	
On Time 3 **3**	On Time 3 **1**	On Time 3 **3**	On Time 3 **3**	On Time 3 **3**	
Pencil 2 **2**	Pencil 2 **2**	Pencil 2 **2**	Pencil 2 **2**	Pencil 2 **0**	
Bring Work 5 **5**	Bring Work 5 **5**	Bring Work 5 **5**	Bring Work 5 **5**	Bring Work 5 **0**	
Wk. Quietly 5 **4**	Wk. Quietly 5 **4**	Wk. Quietly 5 **5**	Wk. Quietly 5 **4**	Wk. Quietly 5 **5**	**B**
Satisfact.	Satisfact.	Satisfact.	Satisfact.	Satisfact.	
Work Compl. 5 **4**	Work Compl. 5 **4**	Work Compl. 5 **5**	Work Compl. 5 **3**	Work Compl. 5 **4**	
Use of Time 5 **4**	Use of Time 5 **4**	Use of Time 5 **5**	Use of Time 5 **5**	Use of Time 5 **5**	
*No Warning 2 **2**	*No Warning 2 **0**	*No Warning 2 **2**	*No Warning 2 **2**	*No Warning 2 **2**	
Grade **A** To **24**	Grade **C** To **20**	Grade **A** To **27**	Grade **A** To **24**	Grade **C** To **19**	
Date 10-24	Date 10-25	Date 10-26	Date 10-27	Date 10-28	
On Time 3 **3**	On Time 3 **3**	On Time 3 __	On Time 3 __	On Time 3 __	
Pencil 2 **2**	Pencil 2 **2**	Pencil 2 __	Pencil 2 __	Pencil 2 __	
Bring Work 5 **5**	Bring Work 5 **5**	Bring Work 5 __	Bring Work 5 __	Bring Work 5 __	
Wk. Quietly 5 **3**	Wk. Quietly 5 **5**	Wk. Quietly 5 __	Wk. Quietly 5 __	Wk. Quietly 5 __	
Satisfact.	Satisfact.	Satisfact.	Satisfact.	Satisfact.	
Work Compl. 5 **4**	Work Compl. 5 **5**	Work Compl. 5 __	Work Compl. 5 __	Work Compl. 5 __	
Use of Time 5 **4**	Use of Time 5 **5**	Use of Time 5 __	Use of Time 5 __	Use of Time 5 __	
*No Warning 2 **1**	*No Warning 2 **2**	*No Warning 2 __	*No Warning 2 __	*No Warning 2 __	
Grade **B** To **22**	Grade **A** To **27**	Grade ___ To ___	Grade ___ To ___	Grade ___ To ___	
Date ___	Date ___	Date ___	Date ___	Date ___	
On Time 3 __	On Time 3 __	On Time 3 __	On Time 3 __	On Time 3 __	
Pencil 2 __	Pencil 2 __	Pencil 2 __	Pencil 2 __	Pencil 2 __	
Bring Work 5 __	Bring Work 5 __	Bring Work 5 __	Bring Work 5 __	Bring Work 5 __	
Wk. Quietly 5 __	Wk. Quietly 5 __	Wk. Quietly 5 __	Wk. Quietly 5 __	Wk. Quietly 5 __	
Satisfact.	Satisfact.	Satisfact.	Satisfact.	Satisfact.	
Work Compl. 5 __	Work Compl. 5 __	Work Compl. 5 __	Work Compl. 5 __	Work Compl. 5 __	
Use of Time 5 __	Use of Time 5 __	Use of Time 5 __	Use of Time 5 __	Use of Time 5 __	
*No Warning 2 __	*No Warning 2 __	*No Warning 2 __	*No Warning 2 __	*No Warning 2 __	
Grade ___ To ___	Grade ___ To ___	Grade ___ To ___	Grade ___ To ___	Grade ___ To ___	
Date ___	Date ___	Date ___	Date ___	Date ___	
On Time 3 __	On Time 3 __	On Time 3 __	On Time 3 __	On Time 3 __	
Pencil 2 __	Pencil 2 __	Pencil 2 __	Pencil 2 __	Pencil 2 __	
Bring Work 5 __	Bring Work 5 __	Bring Work 5 __	Bring Work 5 __	Bring Work 5 __	
Wk. Quietly 5 __	Wk. Quietly 5 __	Wk. Quietly 5 __	Wk. Quietly 5 __	Wk. Quietly 5 __	
Satisfact.	Satisfact.	Satisfact.	Satisfact.	Satisfact.	
Work Compl. 5 __	Work Compl. 5 __	Work Compl. 5 __	Work Compl. 5 __	Work Compl. 5 __	
Use of Time 5 __	Use of Time 5 __	Use of Time 5 __	Use of Time 5 __	Use of Time 5 __	
*No Warning 2 __	*No Warning 2 __	*No Warning 2 __	*No Warning 2 __	*No Warning 2 __	
Grade ___ To ___	Grade ___ To ___	Grade ___ To ___	Grade ___ To ___	Grade ___ To ___	

Figure 11.7. Example of grading based on behavior and study habits for postelementary students.

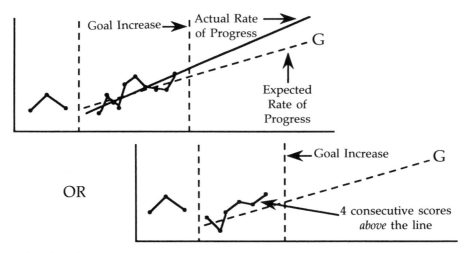

a. *What does this mean?*
   The student's progress is greater than you expected.
   The line through the scores (the dark line) is steeper than the goal line (the light line) *or* the four most recent consecutive scores fall above the goal line (the light line).

b. *What to do?*
   While the graph is on the screen, set a new goal. Make sure this new goal is higher than the old goal.
   Enter this new goal by (a) pressing <RETURN> if you want to use the new goal recommended by the computer, or (b) entering a different number and then pressing <RETURN>.
   When you increase the goal, you can decide to make a teaching change at the same time. If so, pick a teaching change and use "Edit Data" to record your teaching on the graph. Then, complete a new line on the Instructional Plan Sheet.

c. *What will happen next?*
   A broken vertical line will be drawn on the graph to show you changed the goal on this date. If you also introduced a teaching change, a solid vertical line also will be drawn.

   You will need eight new scores or six new scores with four consecutive scores that fall above/below the goal line before another decision about the effectiveness of the program can be determined.

Figure 11.8. Example of curriculum-based measurement. From *Monitoring Basic Skills Progress: Basic Spelling* (pp. 34–35) by L. S. Fuchs, C. L. Hamlett, and D. Fuchs, 1990, Austin, TX: PRO-ED. Reprinted with permission.

ment, and periodically evaluate progress. Paris (1991) gave an example of how teachers might go about developing a portfolio assessment for young readers.

Both of the approaches described briefly above require that the teacher have a clear idea of what it is that the student is "progressing" toward. In the first case progress is determine quantitatively through data points. In the second case, it is determined through observations of and interactions with the student over time. In both cases the student receives what S. B. Cohen (see Figure 11.6) shows as "corrective feedback." In curriculum-based measurement it is in the form of an error analysis; in portfolio assessment it is in the form of consciously discussing what has been learned. We emphasize this point, because daily "grades" or other assessment should not be used when noncorrective feedback or a grade is its only purpose.

How Can Teachers Involve Students in the Grading Process?

Jones (1980) stressed the importance of involving students in the grading process, and he pointed out several ways that they can participate. First, teachers can discuss grading procedures with a student or with an entire class. Jones noted that it is important in these discussions that students have a clear understanding about grading policies and the reasons behind teachers' decisions on grades. During these discussions, students may also provide teachers with helpful ideas concerning the grading process. Second, Jones suggested that individual conferences between teachers and students be employed. In these conferences, teachers can discuss the student's concern regarding testing and grading. These conferences can provide students with a feeling that the instructional goals are realistic and attainable. Third, students can help to evaluate their own work, a process that often increases motivation and also provides the student with meaningful feedback. Students can evaluate their own learning in several ways. For example, students can express in their own words what they have learned; they can keep a notebook in which they record in some manner what they are learning; class discussions can be held that focus on what has been learned and how it can be applied. Jones stated that when students participate in the grading process it becomes obvious that it

> provides students with better understanding, a greater sense of worth and more control over their environment. Also, it seem obvious that [this practice] has much greater potential for increasing students' skills in such areas as critical thinking, personal responsibility, and self-evaluation. (p. 146)

Concluding Comment

It is not uncommon to find resource students who have consistently received bad or unsatisfactory grades over a period of time. From our point of view, continued bad or unsatisfactory daily grades represent a failure of the program to provide adequately for the student. After all, the purpose of resource programming is to help students find both academic and social success. Consequently, poor performance is an indication to teachers that they need to modify the program's materials, methods, arrangements, and/or contingencies. We recommend that any grades implying inappropriate performance be supplemented with suggested program modifications.

References

Abeson, A., Bolick, N., & Hass, J. (1976). *A primer on due process.* Reston, VA: Council for Exceptional Children. (Available from Publications Sales, CEC, 1920 Association Dr., Reston, VA 22091)

Affleck, J. Q., Lehning, T. W., & Brow, K. D. (1973). Expanding the resource concept: The resource school. *Exceptional Children, 39,* 446–453.

Affleck, M. Q., Madge, S., Adams, A., & Lowenbraun, S. (1988). Integrated classroom versus resource model: Academic viability and effectiveness. *Exceptional Children, 54,* 339–348.

Algozzine, B., Morsink, C. V., & Algozzine, K. M. (1988). What's happening in self-contained and special education classrooms? *Exceptional Children, 55,* 259–265.

Anastasi, A. (1988). *Psychological testing* (6th ed.). New York: Macmillan.

Anderson, G. S. (1984). *A whole language approach to reading.* Lanham, MD: University Press of America.

Ashlock, R. B. (1986). *Error patterns in computation* (4th ed.). Columbus, OH: Merrill.

Baksh, I. J., & Martin, W. B. W. (1986, February). Students' perceptions of homework: Some implications. *Newsletter of the Canadian Education Association,* p. 5.

Baratta-Lorton, M. (1976). *Mathematics their way.* Menlo Park, CA: Addison-Wesley.

Baratta-Lorton, R. (1977). *Mathematics . . . A way of thinking.* Menlo Park, CA: Addison-Wesley.

Barksdale, M. W., & Atkinson, A. P. (1971). A resource room approach to instruction for the educable retarded. *Focus on Exceptional Children, 3,* 12–15.

Baroody, A. J. (1987). *Children's mathematical thinking. A developmental framework for preschool, primary, and special education teachers.* New York: Teachers College Press.

Becker, L. D. (1978). Learning characteristics of educationally handicapped and retarded children. *Exceptional Children, 44,* 502–511.

Bersoff, D. N., Kabler, M., Fiscus, E., & Ankney, R. (1972). Effectiveness of special class placement for children labeled neurologically handicapped. *Journal of School Psychology, 10,* 157–163.

Bicklen, D. (1985). *Achieving the complete school: Strategies for effective mainstreaming.* New York: Teachers College Press.

Bicklen, D., & Zollers, N. (1986). The focus of advocacy in the LD field. *Journal of Learning Disabilities, 19,* 579–586.

Billingsley, F. F. (1984). Where *are* the generalized outcomes? (An examination of instructional objectives). *Journal of the Association for Persons with Severe Handicaps, 9*(3), 186–192.

Bingham, W. V. D., Moore, B. V., & Gustad, J. W. (1957). *How to interview.* New York: Harper & Row.

Bloom, L., & Lahey, M. (1978). *Language development and language disorders.* New York: Wiley.

Braaten, S., Kauffman, J. M., Braaten, B., Polsgrove, L., & Nelson, C. M. (1988). The Regular Education Initiative: Patent medicine for behavioral disorders. *Exceptional Children, 55,* 21–28.

Brown, R. W. (1982). *Resource specialist training resources.* Sacramento: California State Department of Education.

Brown, V. L. (1975). A basic Q-sheet for analyzing and comparing curriculum materials and proposals. *Journal of Learning Disabilities, 8,* 409–416.

Bruininks, R. H., Rynders, J. E., & Gross, J. C. (1974). Social acceptance of mildly retarded pupils in resource rooms and regular classes. *American Journal of Mental Deficiency, 78*(4), 377–383.

Budoff, M., & Gottlieb, J. (1976). Special-class EMR children mainstreamed: A study of an aptitude (learning potential) X treatment interaction. *American Journal of Mental Deficiency, 81,* 1–11.

Buros, O. K. (1983). *Tests in print III.* Lincoln: University of Nebraska Press.

Canter, L. (1988). *Homework without tears for teachers.* Santa Monica, CA: Lee Canter.

Canter, L., & Hausner, L. (1987). *Homework without tears. A parent's guide for motivating children to do homework and to succeed in school.* New York: Harper & Row.

Cantrell, R. P., & Cantrell, M. L. (1976). Preventive mainstreaming: Impact of a supportive services program on pupils. *Exceptional Children, 42,* 381–385.

Carpenter, D. (1985). Grading handicapped pupils: Review and position statement. *Remedial and Special Education, 6*(4), 54–59.

Carroll, A. W. (1967). The effects of segregated and partially integrated school programs on self-concept and academic achievement of educable mental retardates. *Exceptional Children, 34,* 93–99.

Carter, J. L. (1975). Intelligence and reading achievement of EMR children in three educational settings. *Mental Retardation, 95,* 26–27.

Cegelka, W. J., & Tyler, J. L. (1970). The efficacy of regular class placement for the mentally retarded in proper perspective. *Training School Bulletin, 67,* 33–68.

Chaffin, J. D. (1974). Will the real mainstreaming program please stand up! *Focus on Exceptional Children, 6*(5), 1–8.

Chalfant, J. C., Van Dusen Pysh, M., & Moultrie, R. (1989). Teacher assistance teams: A model for within-building problem solving. *Learning Disability Quarterly, 2,* 85–96.

Chalfant, J. C., & Van Dusen Pysh, M. (1989). Teacher assistance teams: Five descriptive studies on 96 teams. *Remedial and Special Education, 161*(3), 40–59.

Christensen, S. L., Ysseldyke, J. E., & Thurlow, M. L. (1989). Critical instructional factors for students with mild handicaps: An integrative review. *Remedial and Special Education, 10*(5), 21–31.

Christopolos, F., & Renz, P. A. (1969). A critical examination of special education programs. *The Journal of Special Education, 3,* 371–379.

Clark, B. (1986). Optimizing learning. *The integrative education model in the classroom.* New York: Macmillan.

Cohen, M. (1987). Improving school effectiveness: Lessons from research. In V. Richardson-Koehler (Ed.), *Educator's handbook: A research perspective* (pp. 474–490). New York: Longman.

Cohen, S. B. (1983). Assigning report card grades to the mainstreamed child. *Teaching Exceptional Children, 15*(2), 86–89.

Coleman, J. M. (1983a). Self-concept and the mildly handicapped: The role of social comparisons. *The Journal of Special Education, 17,* 37–45.

Coleman, J. M. (1983b). Handicapped labels and instructional segregation: Influences on children's self-concepts versus the perceptions of others. *Learning Disability Quarterly, 6*(1), 3–11.

Conoley, J. C., & Kramer, J. J. (1989). *The tenth mental measurements yearbook.* Lincoln: The Burns Institute of Mental Measurements, The University of Nebraska.

Cooper, H. (1989). *Homework.* New York: Longman.

Cosden, M. A., & Abernathy, T. V. (1990). Microcomputer use in the schools: Teacher roles and instructional options. *Remedial and Special Education, 11*(5), 31–38.

Cox, L. M., & Wilson, A. P. (1981). A comparison of academic gains in reading among mildly learning disabled students in three program structures. *Reading Improvement, 18,* 132–156.

Criscoe, B. L., & Gee, T. C. (1984). *Content reading: A diagnostic/prescriptive approach.* Boston: Allyn & Bacon.

Cullinan, D., Epstein, M. H., & Dembinski, R. J. (1979). Behavior problems of educationally handicapped and normal pupils. *Journal of Abnormal Child Psychology, 7,* 495–502.

Delbecq, A. L., Van de Ven, A. H., & Gustafson, O. H. (1975). *Group techniques for program planning. A guide to nominal group and delphi processes.* Glenview, IL: Scott, Foresman.

Deshler, D. D., Warner, M. M., Shumaker, J. B., Alley, G. R., & Clark, F. L. (1984). The learning strategies intervention model: Key components and current status. *Current Topics in Learning Disabilities, 17,* 170–197.

DeShong, B. R. (1981). *The special educator: Stress and survival.* Rockville, MD: Aspen.

Drucker, H., & Hansen, B. C. (1982). Grading the mainstreamed handicapped: Issues and suggestions for the regular social studies classroom teacher. *The Social Studies, 73*(6), 250–251.

Dudley-Marling, C., & Searle, D. (1988). Enriching language learning environments for students with learning disabilities. *Journal of Learning Disabilities, 21,* 140–143.

Dunn, L. M. (1968). Special education for mildly retarded: Is much of it justified? *Exceptional Children, 35,* 5–22.

Ehly, S. (1984). *Peer tutoring in the regular classroom: A guide for school psychologists.* Des Moines: Department of Public Education, State of Iowa.

Ehly, S. W., & Larsen, S. C. (1980). *Peer tutoring for individualized instruction.* Austin, TX: PRO-ED.

England, D. A., & Flatley, J. K. (1985). *Homework—and why.* Bloomington, IN: Phi Delta Kappa.

Engelmann, S., & Carnine, D. (1982). *Theory of instruction: Principles and applications.* New York: Irvington.

Epstein, M. H., & Cullinan, D. (1983). Academic performance of behaviorally disordered and learning disabled pupils. *The Journal of Special Education, 17,* 303–307.

Ferguson-Florrisant Writers Project. (1990). Florrisant, MO: Ferguson-Florrisant School District.

Filley, A. C. (1975). *Interpersonal conflict resolution.* Glenview, IL: Scott, Foresman.

Flynn, T. M. (1970). The effect of a part time special education program on the adjustment of EMR students. *Exceptional Children, 36,* 680–681.

Frampton, M. E., & Gall, E. D. (Eds.). (1955). *Special education for the exceptional.* Boston: Porter Sargent.

Frampton, M. E., & Rowell, H. G. (1940). *Education of the handicapped* (Vol. 2). Yonkers, New York: World Book.

Frierson, E. C. (1975). *Grading without judgement: A classroom guide to grades and evaluation.* Nashville: EDCOA.

Fromberg, D. P., & Driscoll, M. (1985). *The successful classroom. Management strategies for regular and special education teachers.* New York: Teachers College Press.

Fuchs, L. S., Hamlett, C. L., & Fuchs, D. (1990). *Monitoring basic skills progress: Basic spelling.* Austin, TX: PRO-ED.

Fullerton, O. (1987). *Mathtime 2.* Toronto: Copp, Clark, & Pitman.

Gajar, A. H. (1979). Educable mentally retarded, learning disabled, emotionally disturbed: Similarities and differences. *Exceptional Children, 45,* 450–472.

Gajar, A. H. (1980). Characteristics across exceptional categories: EMR, LD, and ED. *The Journal of Special Education, 14,* 165–173.

Gallagher, P. A. (1979). *Teaching students with behavior problems: Techniques for classroom instruction.* Denver: Love.

Gampel, D. H., Gottlieb, J., & Harrison, R. H. (1974). Comparison of classroom behavior of special-class EMR integrated EMR, low IQ, and nonretarded children. *American Journal of Mental Deficiency, 79,* 16–21.

Garrison, M., & Hammill, D. (1971). Who are the retarded? *Exceptional Children, 38,* 13–20.

Gartner, A. (1986). Disabling help: Special education at the crossroads. *Exceptional Children, 53,* 72–76.

Gartner, A., & Lipsky, D. K. (1987). Beyond special education: Towards a quality system for all students. *Harvard Educational Review, 57,* 367–395.

Garwick, G. B. (1978). Program evaluation of services for visually impaired persons through individual goal setting. *Education of the Visually Handicapped, 10*(2), 38–45.

Gerke, R. E. (1975). *The effects of mainstreaming on the self-concept and reading achievement of exceptional children at the elementary level.* Bethlehem, PA: Lehigh University. (Order No. 76-10, 366)

Ginsburg, H. (1989). *Children's arithmetic. How they learn it and how you teach it.* Austin, TX: PRO-ED.

Ginsburg, H., & Mathews, S. (1984). *Diagnostic Test of Arithmetic Strategies.* Austin, TX: PRO-ED.

Glavin, J. P. (1973). Follow-up behavioral research on resource rooms. *Exceptional Children, 40,* 211–213.

Glavin, J. P. (1974). Behaviorally oriented resource rooms: A follow-up. *The Journal of Special Education, 8,* 337–347.

Glavin, J. P., Quay, J. C., Annesley, F. R., & Werry, J. S. (1971). An experimental resource room for behavior problem children. *Exceptional Children, 38,* 131–137.

Goodman, Y. M., & Burke, C. L. (1972). *Reading Miscue Inventory: Manual and procedures for diagnosis and evaluation.* New York: Macmillan.

Gorden, R. L. (1969). *Interviewing: Strategy, techniques, and tactics.* Homewood, IL: Dorsey.

Gordon, T. (1970). *Parent effectiveness training.* New York: Wyden.

Gottlieb, J., Alter, M., & Gottlieb, B. W. (1983). Mainstreaming mentally retarded children. In J. L. Matson & J. A. Mulick (Eds.), *Handbook of mental retardation* (pp. 67–77). New York: Pergamon Press.

Gottlieb, J., Gampel, D. H., & Budoff, M. (1975). Classroom behavior of retarded children before and after integration into regular classes. *The Journal of Special Education, 9,* 307–315.

Greenbaum, C. R. (1987). *The Spellmaster Assessment and Teaching System.* Austin, TX: PRO-ED.

Gronlund, N. E., & Linn, R. L. (1990). *Measurement and evaluation in teaching* (6th ed.). New York: Macmillan.

Haeussermann, E. (1958). *Developmental potential of preschool children. An evaluation of intellectual, sensory, and emotional functioning.* New York: Grune & Stratton.

Hagerty, G. J., & Abramson, J. (1987). Impediments to implementing national policy change for mildly handicapped students. *Exceptional Children, 53,* 315–323.

Hall, R. V. (1972). Responsive teaching: Focus on measurement and research in the classroom and the home. In E. Meyen, G. Vergason, & R. J. Whelan (Eds.), *Strategies for teaching exceptional children* (pp. 403–415). Denver: Love.

Hall, R. V., & Van Houten, R. (1983). *The measurement of behavior.* Austin, TX: PRO-ED.

Hallahan, D. P., & Kauffman, J. M. (1977). Labels, categories, behaviors: ED, LD, and EMR reconsidered. *The Journal of Special Education, 11,* 139–149.

Hallahan, D. P., Kauffman, J. W. L., & McKinney, J. D. (1988). Introduction to the series: Questions about the Regular Education Initiative. *Journal of Learning Disabilities, 21,* 3–6.

Hallahan, D. P., Keller, C. E., McKinney, J. D., Lloyd, J. W., & Bryan, T. (1988). Examining the research base of the Regular Education Initiative: Efficacy studies and the Adaptive Learning Environments Model. *Journal of Learning Disabilities, 21,* 29–35.

Hammill, D. D., Brown, L., & Bryant, B. (1992). *A consumer's guide to tests in print* (2nd ed.). Austin, TX: PRO-ED.

Hammill, D. D., Bryant, B. R., Brown, L., Dunn, C., & Marten, A. (1989). How replicable is current LD research? A follow-up to the CLD research committee's recommendations. *Learning Disability Quarterly, 12,* 174–179.

Hammill, D., Iano, R., McGettigan, J., & Wiederholt, J. (1972). Retardates' reading achievement in the resource room model: The first year. *Training School Bulletin, 69,* 105–107.

Hammill, D., & Wiederholt, J. L. (1972). *The resource room: Rationale and implementation.* New York: Grune & Stratton.

Hardman, M. L., Drew, C. J., Egan, M. W., & Wolf, B. (1990). *Human exceptionality* (3rd ed.). Boston: Allyn & Bacon.

Hasselriis, P. (1982). IEP's and a whole language model of language arts. *Topics in Learning Disabilities, 1*(4), 17–21.

Hawisher, M. J. (1975). *The resource room: An access to excellence.* Lancaster: South Carolina Region V Educational Services Center.

Hays, M. L. (1986). Resource room: Space and concepts. *Academic Therapy, 21*(4), 453–464.

Haysom, J. (1985). *Inquiring into the teaching process: Towards self-evaluation and professional development.* Toronto: OISE Press.

Hewett, F. M., & Taylor, F. D. (1980). *The emotionally disturbed child in the classroom.* Boston: Allyn & Bacon.

Hewett, F. M., & Forness, S. R. (1974). *Education of exceptional learners.* Boston: Allyn & Bacon.

Howe, S. G. (1971). *Proceedings of the second convention of American Instructors of the Blind.* Indianapolis, IN: Indianapolis Printing and Publishing House.

Ianacone, R. N., & Stoddent, R. A. (Eds.). (1987). *Transition issues and directions.* Reston, VA: Council for Exceptional Children.

Iano, R. P. (1972). Shall we disband our special classes? *The Journal of Special Education, 6,* 167–178.

Iano, R. P., Ayers, D., Heller, H. B., McGettigan, J. F., & Walker, V. S. (1974). Sociometric status of retarded children in an integrative program. *Exceptional Children, 40,* 267–271.

Idol, L., & Paolucci-Whitcomb, P. (1986). *Collaborative consultation.* Austin, TX: PRO-ED.

Ito, H. R. (1980). Long-term effects of resource room programs on learning disabled children's reading. *Journal of Learning Disabilities, 13,* 322–326.

Jenkins, J. R., & Mayhall, W. F. (1976). Development and evaluation of a resource teacher program. *Exceptional Children, 43,* 21–29.

Jenkins, J. R., Pious, C. G., & Peterson, D. L. (1988). Categorical programs for remedial and handicapped students: Issues of validity. *Exceptional Children, 28,* 341–347.

Johnson, D. J., & Myklebust, H. R. (1967). *Learning disabilities. Principles and practices.* New York: Grune & Stratton.

Johnson, D. R. (1982). *Every minute counts. Making your math class work.* Palo Alto, CA: Dale Seymour.

Johnson, D. R. (1986). *Making minutes count even more. A sequel to every minute counts.* Palo Alto, CA: Dale Seymour.

Johnson, D. W., & Johnson, R. T. (1986). Mainstreaming and cooperative learning strategies. *Exceptional Children, 52*(6), 553–561.

Johnson, D. W., & Johnson, R. T. (1987). *Learning together and alone. Cooperative, competitive and individualistic learning* (2nd ed.). Englewood Cliffs, NJ: Prentice-Hall.

Johnson, L. J., & Pugach, M. (1991). Peer collaboration: Accommodating students with mild learning and behavior problems. *Exceptional Children, 57*(5).

Jones, V. F. (1980). *Adolescents with behavior problems: Strategies for teaching, counseling, and parent involvement.* Boston: Allyn & Bacon.

Kaiser, S. M. (1985). Multidisciplinary teams and group decision making techniques: Possible solutions to decision making problems. *School Psychology Review, 14*(4), 457–470.

Kaplan, S. N., Kaplan, J. B., Madsen, S. K., & Gould, B. T. (1980). *Change for children. Ideas for individualizing learning.* Glenview, IL: Scott, Foresman.

Karp, J. M. (1990). Strategies for successful early intervention coordinating councils. *Remedial and Special Education, 11*(6), 54–59.

Kaufman, J. M., & Pullen, P. L. (1989). An historical perspective: A personal perspective on our history of service to mildly handicapped and at risk students. *Remedial and Special Education, 10*(6), 12–14.

Keogh, B. K., & Levitt, M. L. (1976). Special education in the mainstream: A confrontation of limitations? *Focus on Exceptional Children, 8*(1), 1–11.

Kerlin, M. A., & Latham, W. L. (1977). Intervention effects of a crisis-resource program. *Exceptional Children, 44,* 32–34.

Keyser, D. J., & Sweetland, R. C. (Eds.). (1984–1992). *Test critiques. Volumes I–XI.* Austin, TX: PRO-ED.

Kim, E. C., & Kellough, R. D. (1978). *Resource guide for secondary school teaching: A planning for competence.* New York: Macmillan.

Kirschenbaum, H., Napier, R., & Simon, S. B. (1971). *Wad-ja-get? The grading game in American education.* New York: Hart.

Knight, O., et al. (1981). *Inservice training program for regular and resource teachers.* Durham, NC: North Carolina Central University.

Kroth, R. L. (1975). *Communicating with parents of exceptional children.* Denver: Love.

Kunzelman, H. P. (1970). *Precision teaching: An initial training sequence.* Seattle: Special Child.

Larsen, S., & Hammill, D. (1986). *Test of Written Spelling* (2nd ed.). Austin, TX: PRO-ED.

Lichter, P. (1976). Communicating with parents: It begins with listening. *Teaching Exceptional Children, 8,* 66–75.

Lieberman, L. M. (1982). The nightmare of scheduling. *Journal of Learning Disabilities, 15,* 57–58.

Lilly, M. S. (1987). Lack of focus on special education in literature on education reform. *Exceptional Children, 53,* 325–326.

Loughlin, C., & Suina, J. (1982). *The learning environment: An instructional strategy.* New York: Teachers College, Columbia University.

Lovitt, T. C. (1975a). Applied behavior analysis and learning disabilities. Part I: Characteristics of ABA, general recommendations, and methodological limitations. *Journal of Learning Disabilities, 8,* 432–443.

Lovitt, T. C. (1975b). Applied behavior analysis and learning disabilities. Part II: Specific research recommendations and suggestions for practitioners. *Journal of Learning Disabilities, 8,* 504–518.

Lovitt, T. C. (1977). *In spite of my resistance . . . I've learned from children*. Columbus, OH: Merrill.

Lynch, E. C., & Beare, P. L. (1990). The quality of IEP objectives and their relevance for students with mental retardation and behavior disorders. *Remedial and Special Education, 11*(2), 48–55.

Macmillan, D. L. (1971). Special education for mildly retarded: Servant or savant. *Focus on Exceptional Children, 2*, 1–11.

Macy, D. J., & Carter, J. L. (1978). Comparison of a mainstream and self-contained special education program. *The Journal of Special Education, 12*, 303–313.

Margolis, H., & Brannigan, G. G. (1986). Building trust with parents. *Academic Therapy, 22*(1), 71–74.

Marion, R. L. (1981). *Educators, parents, and exceptional children*. Rockville, MD: Aspen.

McCallon, E., & McCray, E. (1975). *Planning and conducting interviews*. Austin, TX: Learning Concepts.

McLoughlin, J. A., & Lewis, R. B. (1990). *Assessing special students* (3rd ed.). Columbus, OH: Merrill.

McNamara, B. E. (1989). *The resource room*. Albany, NY: SUNY Albany Press.

Michaelis, J. U. (1988). *Social studies for children: A guide to basic instruction* (9th ed.). Englewood Cliffs, NJ: Prentice-Hall.

Miller, T. L., & Sabatino, D. A. (1978). An evaluation of the teacher consultant model as an approach to mainstreaming. *Exceptional Children, 45*, 86–91.

Morrison, G. M. (1981). Perspectives of social status of learning-handicapped and nonhandicapped students. *American Journal of Mental Deficiency, 86*, 243–251.

Morse, W. C. (1971). Worksheet on life-space interviewing for teachers. In N. J. Long, W. C. Morse, & R. G. Newman (Eds.), *Conflict in the classroom* (2nd ed.). Belmont, CA: Wadsworth.

Moss, J. (1984). *Focus units in literature*. Urbana, IL: National Council of Teachers of English.

Myers, M. (1985). *The teacher-researcher: How to study writing in the classroom*. Urbana, IL: ERIC Clearinghouse on Reading and Communication Skills and The National Council of Teachers of English.

Nunnally, J. C. (1978). *Psychometric theory*. New York: McGraw-Hill.

O'Conner, P. D., Stuck, G. B., & Wyne, M. D. (1979). Effects of a short-term intervention resource room program on task orientation and achievement. *The Journal of Special Education, 13*, 375–385.

Okolo, C. M., Reith, H. J., & Bahr, C. M. (1989). Microcomputer implementation in secondary special education programs: A study of special educators', mildly handicapped adolescents', and administrators' perspectives. *The Journal of Special Education, 23*, 107–117.

Opper, S. (1977). Piaget's clinical method. *Journal of Children's Mathematical Behavior, 1*(4), 90–107.

Owston, R. D. (1987). *Software evaluation: A criterion-based approach.* Englewood Cliffs, NJ: Prentice-Hall.

Paris, S. (1991). Assessment: Portfolio assessment for young readers. *The Reading Teacher, 44*(9), 680–683.

Perrott, E. (1982). *Effective teaching. A practical guide to improving your teaching.* New York: Longman.

Pfeiffer, S. I. (1980). *The school-based multidisciplinary team and nondiscriminatory assessment.* St. Louis, MO: Annual Meeting of the International Reading Association.

Pierce, M. M., Stahlbrand, K., & Armstrong, S. B. (1984). *Partner learning in practice. Increasing student productivity through peer tutoring programs.* Austin, TX: PRO-ED.

Posamentier, A. S., & Stepelman, J. (1981). *Teaching secondary school mathematics.* Columbus, OH: Merrill.

Posamentier, A. S., & Stepelman, J. (1990). *Teaching secondary school mathematics* (3rd ed.). New York: Macmillan.

Pugach, M. (1987). The national education reports and special education: Implications for teacher preparation. *Exceptional Children, 53,* 308–314.

Pugach, M., & Johnson, L. J. (1990). Developing reflective practice through structured dialogue. In R. T. Clift, W. R. Houston, & M. C. Pugach (Eds.), *Encouraging reflective practice in education. An analysis of issues and programs.* New York: Teachers College Press.

Purkey, W. W., & Novak, J. M. (1984). *Inviting school success: A self-concept approach to teaching and learning* (2nd ed.). Belmont, CA: Wadsworth.

Quay, J. C., Glavin, J. P., Annesley, F. R., & Werry, J. S. (1972). The modification of problem behavior and academic achievement in a resource room. *Journal of School Psychology, 10,* 187–198.

Raphael, T. E., & Englert, C. S. (1990). Writing and reading: Partners in constructing meaning. *The Reading Teacher, 43*(6), 388–400.

Renzulli, J. S., Reis, S. M., & Smith, L. H. (1981). *Revolving door identification and programming model.* Manfield Center, CT: Creative Learning Press.

Renzulli, J. S., & Smith, L. H. (1980). An alternative approach to identifying and programming for gifted and talented students. *Gifted Child Today, 15,* 4–11.

Reynolds, M. C. (1989). An historical perspective: The delivery of special education to mildly disabled and at risk students. *Remedial and Special Education, 10*(6), 7–11.

Rhodes, L. K., & Dudley-Marling, C. (1988). *Readers and writers with a difference. A holistic approach to teaching learning disabled and remedial students.* Portsmouth, NH: Heinemann.

Riegel, R. H. (1983). Mainstreaming equals cooperative planning. *Academic Therapy, 18*(3), 285–298.

Ritter, D. R. (1978). Surviving in the classroom: A follow-up of mainstreamed children with learning disabilities. *Journal of School Psychology, 16,* 253–256.

Robinson, N. M., & Robinson, H. B. (1976). *The mentally retarded child* (2nd ed.). New York: McGraw-Hill.

Rodee, M. W. (1971). A study to evaluate the resource teacher when used with high level educable retardates at the primary level (Doctoral dissertation, University of Iowa, 1971). *Dissertation Abstracts, 2516-A.* (Order No. 71-30, 485)

Ross, S. L., DeYoung, H. C., & Cohen, J. S. (1971). Confrontation: Special education placement and the law. *Exceptional Children, 38*(1), 5–12.

Rust, J. O., Miller, L. S., & Wilson, W. H. (1978). Using a control group to evaluate a resource room program. *Psychology in the Schools, 15,* 503–506.

Sabatino, D. A. (1971). An evaluation of resource rooms for children with learning disabilities. *Journal of Learning Disabilities, 4,* 84–93.

Salvia, J., & Ysseldyke, J. E. (1991). *Assessment* (5th ed.). Boston: Houghton Mifflin.

Sapon-Shevin, M. (1987). The national education reports and special education: Implications for students. *Exceptional Children, 53,* 300–306.

Sarfaty, L., & Katz, S. (1978). The self-concept and adjustment patterns of hearing-impaired pupils in different school settings. *American Annals of the Deaf, 123,* 438–441.

Schiff, G., Scholom, A., Swerdlik, M., & Knight, J. (1979). Mainstreamed vs. self-contained classes: A two year study of their effects on the personal adjustment and academic achievement of children with learning disabilities. *Education, 99,* 397–405.

Schmuck, R. A., & Schmuck, P. A. (1988). *Group processes in the classroom* (5th ed.). Dubuque, IA: Brown.

Semmel, M. I., Gottlieb, J., & Robinson, N. M. (1979). Mainstreaming: Perspectives on educating handicapped children in the public schools. In D. C. Berliner (Ed.), *Review of research in education* (Vol. 7, pp. 223–279). Washington, DC: American Educational Research Association.

Sheare, J. B. (1978). The impact of resource programs upon the self-concept and peer acceptance of learning disabled children. *Psychology in the Schools, 15,* 406–412.

Shepard, L. A. (1987). The new push for excellence: Widening the schism between regular and special education. *Exceptional Children, 53,* 327–329.

Shuard, H., & Rothery, A. (Eds.). (1984). *Children reading mathematics.* London: John Murray.

Silbert, J., Carnine, D., & Stein, M. (1989). *Direct instruction mathematics* (2nd ed.). New York: McGraw-Hill.

Slavin, R. E. (1983). When does cooperative learning increase student achievement? *Psychological Bulletin, 94*(3), 429–445.

Sleeter, C. E. (1986). Learning disabilities: The social construction of a special education category. *Exceptional Children, 53,* 46–54.

Smith, D. D. (1984). *Effective discipline. A positive approach to discipline for educators in all settings.* Austin, TX: PRO-ED.

Smith, H. W., & Kennedy, W. A. (1967). Effects of three educational programs on mentally retarded children. *Perceptual & Motor Skills, 24,* 174.

Smokoski, F. (1972, February). *The resource teacher.* Paper presented at the Conference on the Resource Teacher, University of Arizona, Tucson.

Stainback, S., & Stainback, W. (1988). Letter to the editor. *Journal of Learning Disabilities, 21,* 452–453.

Stewart, C. J., & Cash, W. B. (1974). *Interviewing: Principles and practices.* Dubuque, IA: Brown.

Stufflebeam, D. L. (Committee Chair). (1981). *Standards for evaluation of educational programs, projects, and materials.* Developed by the Joint Committee on Standards for Educational Evaluation. New York: McGraw-Hill.

Sullivan, A. R. (1987, Summer). Develop a healthy school climate. *Teaching Exceptional Children,* p. 48.

Sulzer-Azaroff, B., & Mayer, G. R. (1982). *Applying behavior-analysis procedures with children and youth.* New York: Holt, Rinehart & Winston.

Sundbye, N. W., Dyck, N., & Wyatt, F. R. (1979). *Essential sight words program, Level 1.* New York: Teaching Resources.

Sundbye, N. W., Dyck, N., & Wyatt, F. R. (1980). *Essential sight words program, Level 2.* New York: Teaching Resources.

Sweetland, R. C., & Keyser, D. J. (1991). *Tests* (3rd ed.). Austin, TX: PRO-ED.

Terwilliger, J. S. (1977). Assigning grades—Philosophical issues and practical recommendations. *Journal of Research and Development in Education, 10*(3), 21–39.

Thorndike, R. L., & Hagen, E. P. (1977). *Measurement and evaluation in psychology and education* (4th ed.). New York: Wiley.

Tilley, B. K. (1970). The effects of three educational placement systems on achievement, self-concept, and behavior in elementary mentally retarded children (Doctoral dissertation, University of Iowa, 1970). *Dissertation Abstracts,* 4590-A.

Tindal, G. (1985). Investigating the effectiveness of special education: An analysis of methodology. *Journal of Learning Disabilities, 18,* 101–112.

Turnbull, A. P., Strickland, B. B., & Brantley, J. C. (1982). *Developing and implementing Individualized Education Programs.* New York: Macmillan.

Turnbull, H. R., III. (1986). *Free appropriate public education. The law and children with disabilities.* Denver: Love.

Turnbull, H. R., III, Turnbull, A. P., & Strickland, B. (1979). Procedural due process: The sword, the untrained should not unsheathe. *Boston University Journal of Education,* 40–59.

Walker, V. (1974). The efficacy of the resource room for educating retarded children. *Exceptional Children, 40,* 288–289.

Wallace, G., & Larsen, S. C. (1978). *Educational assessment of learning problems: Testing for teaching.* Boston: Allyn & Bacon.

Wallace, G., Larsen, S., & Elksnin, L. (1992). *Educational assessment of learning problems* (2nd ed.). Boston: Allyn & Bacon.

Wallin, J. E. W. (1924). *The education of handicapped children.* Boston: Houghton Mifflin.

Wang, M. C., & Baker, E. T. (1985–1986). Mainstreaming programs: Design features and effects. *The Journal of Special Education, 19,* 503–521.

Wang, M. C., & Birch, J. W. (1984). Effective special education in regular classes. *Exceptional Children, 50,* 391–398.

Wang, M. C., Reynolds, M. C., & Walberg, H. J. (1986). Rethinking special education. *Educational Leadership, 41*(1), 26–31.

Wechsler, D. (1991). *Wechsler Intelligence Scale for Children–Revised.* San Antonio, TX: Psychological Corp.

Weed, L. L. (1971). *Medical records, medical education, and patient care. The problem-oriented record as a basic tool.* Cleveland, OH: Press of Case Western Reserve University.

Weiner, L. H. (1969). An investigation of the effectiveness of resource rooms for children with specific learning disabilities. *Journal of Learning Disabilities, 2,* 223–229.

West, J. F., Idol, L., & Cannon, G. (1989). *Collaboration in the schools: An inservice and preservice curriculum for teachers, support staff, and administrators (Learner's Booklet and Instructor's Manual).* Austin, TX: PRO-ED.

White, R., & Calhoun, M. L. (1987). From referral to placement: Teachers' perceptions of their responsibilities. *Exceptional Children, 53*(5), 460–680.

Wiederholt, J. L. (1985). *Formal Reading Inventory.* Austin, TX: PRO-ED.

Wiederholt, J. L. (1989). Restructuring special education services: The past, the present, the future. *Learning Disability Quarterly, 12,* 181–191.

Wiederholt, J. L., & Bryant, B. (1992). *Gray Oral Reading Tests* (3rd ed.). Austin, TX: PRO-ED.

Wiederholt, J. L., & McNutt, G. (1977). Evaluating materials for handicapped adolescents. *Journal of Learning Disabilities, 10,* 11–19.

Will, M. C. (1986). Educating children with learning problems: A shared responsibility. *Exceptional Children, 52,* 411–416.

Wilson, R. M. (1982). *Diagnostic and remedial reading for classroom and clinic* (2nd ed.). Columbus, OH: Merrill.

Winograd, P. N., Wixson, K. K., & Lipson, M. Y. (Eds.). (1989). *Improving basal reading instruction.* New York: Teachers College Press.

Witt, J. C., Miller, C. D., McIntyre, R. M., & Smith, D. (1984). Effects of variables on parental perceptions of staffings. *Exceptional Children, 51*(1), 27–33.

Wood, J. W. (1984). *Adapting instruction for the mainstream. A sequential approach to teaching.* New York: Macmillan.

Ysseldyke, J. E., & Algozzine, B. (1970). Minneapolis: Department of Special Education, University of Minnesota.

Ysseldyke, J. E., & Algozzine, B. (1983). LD or not LD: That's not the question. *Journal of Learning Disabilities, 16,* 29–31.

Ysseldyke, J. E., & Algozzine, B. (1990). *Introduction to special education.* Boston: Houghton Mifflin.

Ysseldyke, J. E., Algozzine, B., Shinn, M. R., & McGue, M. (1982). Similarities and differences between low achievers and students classified learning disabled. *The Journal of Special Education, 16,* 73–85.

Zigmond, N., & Sansone, J. (1986). Designing a program for the learning disabled adolescent. *Remedial and Special Education, 7*(5), 13–17.

Appendix A

Controlled Group Studies: Resource Versus Self-Contained

Carroll (1967). Type: EMR. Time: 8 months.

> STUDENT CHARACTERISTICS: *Resource:* $N = 19$; 12 male, 7 female; CA $\overline{X}$ 8.16; IQ $\overline{X}$ 73.91. *Self-Contained:* $N = 20$; 13 male, 7 female; CA $\overline{X}$ 8.77; IQ $\overline{X}$ 70.77. Students had no previous special education experience; students needed an IQ of 60 to 80 to qualify; of 19 variables compared, only 2 were statistically significant; however, these were attributed to chance and not considered significant for the purposes of study.
>
> PROCESS VARIABLES: half of students' time was spent in general classes and half in resource.
>
> OUTCOMES: *Academic Achievement:* significant difference (.05) in reading favoring resource; significant academic gains for both groups. *Personal and Social Adjustment:* significant increase in self-derogation for self-contained; significant decrease in self-derogation for resource.

Tilley (1970). Type: EMR. Time: 6 months.

> STUDENT CHARACTERISTICS: *Resource:* $N = 36$. *Self-Contained:* $N = 43$. *Itinerant Tutor Program:* $N = 10$; all students were elementary.
>
> PROCESS VARIABLES: not specified.
>
> OUTCOMES: statistical treatment of tutor program deemed inappropriate. *Academic Achievement:* no significant difference in gains in reading and math between students in resource and in self-contained or between boys and girls. *Personal and Social Adjustment:* no significant difference in gains in self-concept or deviant and interactional behavior between students in resource and in self-contained or between boys and girls; students in resource increased tendency to derogate themselves; students in self-contained stayed about the same, and students in the tutor program improved.

Gampel, Gottlieb, & Harrison (1974). Type: EMR. Time: 4 months.

STUDENT CHARACTERISTICS: Students in resource and self-contained classes who were labeled EMR had previously been enrolled in self-contained classes and were randomly assigned to placement. *Resource: N=14;* CA $\overline{X}$ 131.07, *SD*=13.06; IQ $\overline{X}$ 70.21, *SD*=5.67. *Self-Contained: N=12;* CA $\overline{X}$ 128.17, *SD*=14.55; IQ $\overline{X}$ 70.50, *SD*=9.12. *Students with Low IQ Not Labeled EMR: N=18;* CA $\overline{X}$ 131.00, *SD*=14.82; IQ $\overline{X}$ 77.53, *SD*=7.69. *Average IQ: N=11;* CA $\overline{X}$ 119.00, *SD*=13.98; IQ $\overline{X}$ 99.44, *SD*=11.93.

PROCESS VARIABLES: *Resource:* students received additional support beyond what was ordinarily provided in general classes.

OUTCOMES: *Personal and Social Adjustment:* significant differences favoring resource on measures of restlessness behavior, negative verbal responses to peers, and negative verbal responses from peers; no significant differences on measures of attention, distraction, out-of-seat, self-stimulation, uncoordinated motor response, aggressive behavior to peers, aggressive behavior from peers, positive verbal responses to peers, or positive verbal response from peers; no significant differences in comparisons of students in resource and self-contained EMR classes vs. students with low IQ not labeled EMR, or students with low IQ not labeled EMR vs. students with average IQ.

Walker (1974). Type: EMR. Time: 2 years.

STUDENT CHARACTERISTICS: *Resource: N=29;* CA $\overline{X}$ 10; IQ $\overline{X}$ 69; reading level—preprimer; matched for age, IQ, reading level, socioeconomic status, geographic location, pupil population, racial composition. *Self-Contained: N=41;* CA $\overline{X}$=9.8; IQ $\overline{X}$=68.8; reading level—preprimer.

PROCESS VARIABLES: not specified.

OUTCOMES: *Academic Achievement:* significant difference in academic achievement favoring resource program. *Personal and Social Adjustment:* no significant difference in self-concept; significant difference in social variables favoring resource program.

Gottlieb, Gampel, & Budoff (1975). Type: EMR. Time: 1 school year.

STUDENT CHARACTERISTICS: *Self-Contained: N=11;* CA $\overline{X}$ 126.73, *SD* 16.03; MA $\overline{X}$ 89.00, *SD* 13.58; 2 students were black. *Resource: N=11;* CA $\overline{X}$ 128.70, *SD* 14.42; MA $\overline{X}$ 89.00, *SD* 14.31; 1 student was black; 21 students were from homes where father was unskilled or semi-skilled or not present in household—the other student was from a middle class SES level and was in resource; both groups spent previous year in self-contained classes; students were randomly assigned.

PROCESS VARIABLES: *Resource (Remedial Learning Center):* double-sized classroom; 3 teachers (1 experienced, 2 first year); 20 children per session; no more than ⅓ were students formerly in self-contained classes; the rest were students from general classes needing remediation or enrichment or serving as tutors to former students in self-contained classes; students spent approximately 40 minutes per day 5 days per week—some students formerly in self-contained classes spent longer, however—remainder of time was spent in general class; class organized as series of activity stations; major instructional emphases were in reading, math, and social-emotional development; math lessons concentrated on improving students' understanding of numbers and numerical operations through the use of manipulative materials.

OUTCOMES: *Personal and Social Adjustment:* significant difference favoring resource on prosocial behavior at the end of the school year; no significant difference on prosocial behavior, verbally hostile behavior, or physically hostile behavior at initial measurement, or 4 months into the school year, or on the latter 2 measures at the end of the school year.

Budoff & Gottlieb (1976). Type: EMR. Time: 1 school year.

STUDENT CHARACTERISTICS: *Resource:* $N = 17$; CA $\overline{X}$ 138.00, *SD* 15.50; IQ $\overline{X}$ 70.41, *SD* 6.01; 9 males, 8 females; 7 "high able," 10 "low able"; 1 student black. *Self-Contained:* $N = 14$; CA $\overline{X}$ 139.07, *SD* 18.32; IQ $\overline{X}$ 70.14, *SD* 9.15; 7 males, 7 females; 8 "high able," 6 "low able" students; 2 students black. Students spent previous year in self-contained classes in inner-city schools; students randomly assigned, stratified by the community lived in; 21 students from homes where father was unskilled or semi-skilled or not present in household—the other student was from a middle class SES level and was in resource room; "high able" students were those whose approximate IQ score was 90 or better; "low able" students were those whose approximate IQ score was less than 90.

PROCESS VARIABLES: *Resource (Remedial Learning Center):* same as in Gottlieb, Gampel, and Budoff (1975), with the addition that teachers provided students formerly in self-contained classes with emotional support, encouragement, and counseling to help them cope with problems encountered in general classes. *Self-Contained:* classroom segregated from academic classroom areas but adjacent to shop and homemaking classrooms; only interaction with other students was during lunch; 1 full-time experienced teacher, 1 student teacher, 1 experienced special education teacher who worked with half the class 1 hour a day in the shop; student-to-teacher ratio for both groups approximately 7:1.

OUTCOMES: *Academic Achievement:* no significant difference between resource and self-contained groups; significant difference favoring students labeled "high able" on reading and math scores prior to integration, on math scores 2 months after placement, and on reading and math scores at end of 1 school year. *Personal and Social Adjustment:* no significant difference between students placed in resource and self-contained settings prior to and

2 months after integration; significant differences favoring (a) students labeled "high able" on Matching Familiar Figures correct, reading, and arithmetic achievement prior to integration; (b) students labeled "high able" in achievement and cognitive style domains 2 months after integration; (c) students in resource on locus of control and school morale, with a marginal trend on academic self-concept at end of school year; (d) students labeled "high able" in resource over students labeled "high able" in self-contained on projected self-concept; and (e) students labeled "low able" in self-contained classes over students labeled "low able" in resource on projected self-concept. *Cognitive Style:* significant differences favoring (a) students in resource on reflective behavior measures; and (b) students labeled "high able" over students labeled "low able" on Matching Familiar Figures correct; also, students labeled "high able" in resource displayed more reflective behavior than students labeled "high able" in self-contained. *Teachers' Behavior Ratings:* no significant difference between groups on teachers' behavior ratings.

Macy & Carter (1978). Type: EMR, TMR, MBI, and ED. Time: not specified.

STUDENT CHARACTERISTICS: *Resource:* students randomly selected from plan A resource program and whose handicapping condition was not LD; $N = 20$; CA $\overline{X}$ 11.25, $SD = 1.8$, range 7.7 to 14.5; IQ $\overline{X}$ 67.42, $SD = 19.45$, range 34 to 107; 5 students in each category; students with IQ below 70 were identified as EMR, while those with IQ below 50 were identified as TMR; 4 students in plan A resource received no mainstreaming. *Self-Contained:* students matched with resource students on exceptionality, descriptive profile as given by teacher (information on perceptual problems, self-concept, social behavior, self-control, language development, etc.—explicit descriptive data for the matched pairs are available from authors), IQ, CA, gender, and ethnicity; schools were matched on overall SES; $N = 19$; CA $\overline{X}$ 10.72, $SD = 1.7$, range 8.2 to 14.8; IQ $\overline{X}$ 66.83, $SD = 16.41$, range 41 to 93; samples were approximately 60% male, 50% white, 30% black, and 20% Mexican-American.

PROCESS VARIABLES: *Resource* (plan A): stressed individualized instruction for each child, with mainstreaming into general classroom whenever feasible; vast majority of plan A students received special educational services through part-time attendance (usually 1 to 3 hours) in resource room; individualized education plans outlined instructional objectives, activities, materials, and timelines for completion; most rooms staffed with 2 resource teachers; one-to-one and small group instruction provided; different work stations and learning centers available; usually 10 to 25 students at any given time.

OUTCOMES: *Academic Achievement:* no significant difference on a school performance checklist. *Personal and Social Adjustment:* no significant difference on a school performance checklist. *Content of Instruction:* students in resource received instruction with more advanced math concepts, and a greater amount of perceptual training, while students in self-contained received more arts and crafts instruction. *Methods of Instruction:* of the six categories (self-study, small group instruction, one-to-one instruction, individual lesson planning, tutoring, and reward systems), resource teachers used a greater variety of methods, and a higher frequency of one-to-one instruction. *Extent of Mainstreaming:* 80% of students in resource received some instruction in general classroom; 74% of students in self-contained received some instruction in general classroom; 70% of students in resource received general class instruction in academic subjects; 5% of students in self-contained received general class instruction in academic subjects; students in resource spent a mean of 62% of school day, with a range of 11% to 77%, in general class, while students in self-contained spent a mean of 24% of school day, with a range of 9% to 40%, in general class.

Ritter (1978). Type: LD. Time: 2 years.

STUDENT CHARACTERISTICS: $N=20$; CA $\bar{X}$ 10-4, range 8-4 to 12-8; IQ—average or above; 15 male, 5 female; all had marked deficits (1½ years) in reading and spelling; 17 of 20 had marked deficits in math—the other 3 had a deficit of more than 1 year.

PROCESS VARIABLES: *Self-Contained* (1st year): reading—basal reading series—controlled level of vocabulary, difficulty of word recognition and comprehension; math—problem-solving skills and mastery of basic math operations—utilized substantial concrete materials in teaching math; spelling—utilized multimodalities in the development of spelling skills. *Resource* (2nd year): supplement of 3, 30-minute sessions per week in reading and math; reading—general class—same as self-contained; supplement—remedial and directed reading activities focusing on individual difficulties observed in class—opportunity for review, clarification, repetition, and rehearsal for future group instruction; math—general class—same as self-contained; supplement—review and game-oriented tasks that reinforced concepts and operations being taught in the general program; spelling—general class—same as self-contained; no supplement.

OUTCOMES: *Academic Achievement:* significant gains in reading, spelling, and math in both resource and self-contained programs; a comparison of gains of both programs shows no significant differences for reading and math, but there was a significant difference for spelling favoring special class (there was no resource supplement for spelling).

Schiff, Scholom, Swerdlik, & Knight (1979). Type: severe LD. Time: 2 years.

STUDENT CHARACTERISTICS: (Year 1) *Self-Contained:* $N=33$. (Year 2) *Resource* (Mainstreamed): $N=16$; CA range 8-4 to 13-6; grades 1 to 6; IQ $\bar{X}$ 94;

13 male, 3 female. *Self-Contained: N* = 17; CA range 7-0 to 12-9; IQ $\bar{X}$ 97; 10 male, 7 female. The 16 mainstreamed in 2nd year were chosen because of superior academic, social, and personal adjustment areas, as determined by special education personnel.

PROCESS VARIABLES: *Self-Contained:* each class had 1 special education teacher and 1 full-time aide. *Resource:* received 1 to 2 hours of resource instruction.

OUTCOMES: *Adjustment:* (Year 1) teachers and students rated students in resource significantly higher on academic adjustment, but not on personal or social adjustment; (Year 2) teachers rated students in self-contained significantly higher in academic adjustment and reported trends in same direction in personal and social adjustment; students reported significantly better personal adjustment in resource classes; teachers reported that younger students in self-contained improved significantly in personal, social, and academic adjustment, while parents reported the same for personal and academic adjustment, and students reported the same for personal adjustment; teachers reported that younger students in resource declined significantly in their personal and academic adjustment, while parents reported significant improvement in personal and social adjustment, and students reported significant decreases in academic adjustment; teachers reported older students in self-contained increased significantly in academic adjustment, while older students in resource reported increases in personal adjustment. *Academic Achievement:* significant difference in spelling favoring students in self-contained; a comparison of young students in self-contained with young students in resource found a significant difference in math and a difference in reading favoring students in self-contained; a comparison of older students in self-contained with older students in resource found a significant difference in spelling favoring students in self-contained; a comparison of younger students in self-contained with older students in self-contained found significant differences in spelling and math favoring the younger students in self-contained; a comparison of younger students in resource with older students in resource found a significant difference in spelling and math favoring the younger students in resource, and a significant difference in reading favoring older students in resource; overall level of achievement for both younger and older groups in resource was lower than both groups of students in self-contained, with some decreases evident.

Morrison (1981). Type: "mildly learning handicapped" (can include EMR, LD, or BD). Time: varies according to time spent in special education by each student.

STUDENT CHARACTERISTICS: *Resource: N* = 13; CA $\bar{X}$ 126.50, *SD* 15.67; 10 male, 3 female; IQ $\bar{X}$ 2.21, *SD* .41 (on a scale of 1 to 3 with 1 being the highest); achievement $\bar{X}$ 2.43, *SD* .49 (on a scale of 1 to 3 with 1 being the highest); SES X 2.43, *SD* .49 (on a scale of 1 to 3 with 1 being the highest). *Self-Contained:* N=27; CA $\overline{X}$ 124.17, *SD* 22.77; 12 male, 15 female; IQ $\overline{X}$ 2.59, *SD* .72; achievement $\overline{X}$ 2.70, *SD* .70; SES $\overline{X}$ 2.47, *SD* .99. *Nonhandicapped:* N=234; CA $\overline{X}$ 115.29, *SD* 33.85; 106 male, 128 female; IQ $\overline{X}$ 1.69, *SD* .77; achievement $\overline{X}$ 1.75, *SD* .86; SES $\overline{X}$ 1.97, *SD*.77.

PROCESS VARIABLES: *Resource:* students spent 5 to 6 hours per day in general classroom, with the remaining time spent in resource. *Self-Contained:* students spent 3 to 5 hours per week in general classroom, with remaining time spent in self-contained; the 2 groups of students ''probably'' different on some important dimensions such as social adjustment and severity of learning problems; types of integrating practices varied from school to school (there were 6), but the 2 major categories were resource and self-contained.

OUTCOMES: *Acceptance-Rejection: Study 1:* significant difference between resource and self-contained on socioempathy/socioideal comparisons indicating students in resource might be more accurate in estimating their social status—because sample sizes were unequal, however, it appears that both students in self-contained and students in resource overestimated their social acceptance; nonhandicapped students underestimated their social acceptance. *Study 2:* social acceptance scores for both groups were lower in general class setting than special class setting; students in self-contained scored higher on social acceptance, social emphasis, and socioideal in both general and special class settings than students in resource; both sets of students overestimated their social acceptance in general class setting, but students in self-contained setting underestimated their social acceptance and actually had a higher social acceptance than socioideal mean, but these differences were not significant.

Appendix B
Controlled Group Studies: Resource Versus General

Smith & Kennedy (1967). Type: EMR. Time: 2 years.

    STUDENT CHARACTERISTICS: $N=97$ students; IQ range 50 to 80.

    PROCESS VARIABLES: *Resource:* (Group 1) 45 minutes daily of instruction and attention in small special education classes; (Group 2) 45 minutes daily of treatment in small activity groups.

    OUTCOMES: *Academic Achievement:* no significant difference in academic achievement among groups. *Personal and Social Adjustment:* no significant difference in social maturity scores, or sociometric scores among groups.

Flynn (1970). Type: EMR. Time: not specified.

    STUDENT CHARACTERISTICS: *Resource:* $N=61$. *General:* $N=61$. *Non-EMR:* $N=61$; no significant differences in age, race, sex, intelligence, or grade affected results.

    PROCESS VARIABLES: *Resource:* 45 minutes daily of small group and individual tutoring for experimental group.

    OUTCOMES: *Personal and Social Adjustment:* no significant difference between students in resource and general classes labeled EMR on a measure of personal and social adjustment; students not labeled EMR scored significantly higher than the other 2 groups on measure of personal and social adjustment; teachers and students gave widespread approval to resource program; significantly greater percentage of students in general classes labeled EMR promoted in relation to students in resource labeled EMR; lower correlation between measures of personal and social adjustment and intelligence, and promotion for resource students labeled EMR in relation to students in general classes labeled EMR.

Glavin, Quay, Annesley, & Werry (1971). Type: behavior problem. Time: 5 to 6½ months.

    STUDENT CHARACTERISTICS: *Resource:* $N=27$; CA $\bar{X}$ 10.0, SD 1.7; grade $\bar{X}$ 4.3, SD 1.3; IQ $\bar{X}$ 84.5, SD 7.9; reading $\bar{X}$ 2.2, SD 1.2 ($N=25$); math $\bar{X}$ 2.1, SD 0.76 ($N=16$); conduct problem $\bar{X}$ 11.2, SD 5.1; personality problem $\bar{X}$ 5.3,

SD 4.0; inadequate—immature $\overline{X}$ 4.1, *SD* 2.2; socialized delinquent $\overline{X}$ 1.9, *SD* 1.8. *General: N* = 34; CA $\overline{X}$ 9.4, *SD* 1.5; grade $\overline{X}$ 1.2, *SD* 1.5; IQ $\overline{X}$ 91.7, *SD* 11.1; reading $\overline{X}$ 2.6, *SD* 1.6 (*N* = 29); math $\overline{X}$ 2.1, *SD* 0.96 (*N* = 13); conduct problem $\overline{X}$ 9.9, *SD* 4.7; personality problem $\overline{X}$ 5.8, *SD* 4.4; inadequate—immature $\overline{X}$ 3.5, *SD* 2.6; socialized delinquent $\overline{X}$ 1.2, *SD* 1.9; referred for being extremely disruptive or overly withdrawn; randomly selected for part-time participation in resource room—the rest stayed in general class and constituted control group; 2 schools were in low socioeconomic areas where the majority of students were black with the rest being Puerto Rican; the third school had slightly higher socioeconomic status and students were all white; IQ significantly higher in comparison group; however, later correlations between IQ and gain scores proved insignificant.

PROCESS VARIABLES: *Resource:* 14 students received 2 hours of instruction—1 hour for reading and 1 for math; 11 students received instruction only for reading; 2 students received instruction only for math; schedule consisted of 4, 45- to 60-minute teaching segments with 1 planning period; 7 to 10 students attended each period; resource teacher supplied concrete suggestions and support in minimizing and handling behavioral crises in the general classroom to the general teachers; environment not uniform—1 classroom was set up in a church rectory across the street from the school; token system of reinforcement used with delayed spending encouraged—manipulable and edible reinforcers used; time-out used; teacher experience varied widely from 11 years to less than 1 year substitute teaching experience; weekly meetings with project directors and teachers after initial training sessions at which time they met "regularly"—3 times during the year; authors met with entire general class staff to refocus on rationale and discuss problems; observers were trained to time sample students' classroom behavior; responsibility of general education teacher included primary responsibility for all students, providing information to resource teachers, and checking for transference of results from resource program.

OUTCOMES: *Academic Achievement:* significant difference in reading comprehension and arithmetic fundamentals favoring resource program. *Personal and Social Adjustment:* significantly greater degree of improvement favoring resource program; no significant difference between either group when students in resource were in their general class setting; most behavior improvement occurred in first month of program.

Quay, Glavin, Annesley, & Werry (1972). Type: behavior problem. Time: 16 weeks for 1 school and 23 weeks for the other 2.

STUDENT CHARACTERISTICS: *Resource: N* = 69; CA $\overline{X}$ 120.28, *SD* 19.60; grade $\overline{X}$ 4.50, *SD* 1.32; IQ $\overline{X}$ 90.09, *SD* 11.97; reading vocabulary $\overline{X}$ 2.75, *SD* 1.17; reading comprehension $\overline{X}$ 2.46, *SD* 1.30; total reading $\overline{X}$ 2.68, *SD* 1.16; math reasoning $\overline{X}$ 2.82, *SD* 1.21; math fundamentals $\overline{X}$ 3.21, *SD* 1.31; total math $\overline{X}$ 3.01, *SD* 1.27; conduct problem $\overline{X}$ 11.62, *SD* 4.14; personality problem $\overline{X}$ 5.39, *SD* 3.89; inadequacy—immaturity $\overline{X}$ 3.81, *SD* 1.97; socialized delinquency $\overline{X}$ 1.69, *SD* 1.77. *General: N* = 48; CA $\overline{X}$ 119.75, *SD* 19.01; grade $\overline{X}$ 4.17, *SD* 1.27; IQ $\overline{X}$ 91.31, *SD* 12.67; reading vocabulary $\overline{X}$ 2.57, *SD* 1.14; reading comprehension $\overline{X}$ 2.27, *SD* 1.34; total reading $\overline{X}$ 2.51, *SD* 1.14; math reasoning $\overline{X}$ 2.60, *SD* 1.16; math fundamentals $\overline{X}$ 2.92, *SD* 1.33; total math $\overline{X}$ 2.75, *SD* 1.26; conduct problem $\overline{X}$ 10.33, *SD* 5.26; personality problem $\overline{X}$ 6.04, *SD* 4.00; inadequacy—immaturity $\overline{X}$ 4.00, *SD* 1.82; socialized delinquency $\overline{X}$ 1.60, *SD* 1.70; referred for being extremely disruptive or overly withdrawn; randomly selected for resource program with remainder acting as control group; 1 school was in a low socioeconomic area and all students were black; 1 school was in a low socioeconomic area and students were predominantly white; 1 school was in a slightly higher socioeconomic area and all students were white—these students had already participated in the experiment 1 year; groups did not differ significantly on variables of age, sex, average grade placement, IQ, initial academic achievement, or scores on Behavior Problem Checklist.

PROCESS VARIABLES: *Resource:* 16 students received 2 hours of instruction daily—1 hour for reading, 1 hour for math; 51 received only 1 hour for reading; 2 received only 1 hour for math; schedule consisted of 4, 45- to 60-minute periods divided into 15-minute teaching segments and 1 planning period; 7 to 10 students attended each class; resource teachers supplied concrete suggestions and support in minimizing and handling behavioral crises in general classroom to general education teachers; environment uniform; reading material had to be high-interest, low-level vocabulary, sequential, and easily adaptable for use in 15-minute segments of independent seatwork—standard texts and workbooks used whenever possible; math program often compiled of sequential individual worksheets; token system of reinforcement including manipulable and edible reinforcers—delayed spending was encouraged; time-out used; teaching experience varied with 1 resource teacher having no experience and the other 2 having taught in resource rooms the previous year; initial training involved meetings between project directors and teachers 1 or 2 times weekly to discuss operating strategies; after classes began, occasional meetings were held; 2 times during the year, authors met with entire school faculty to describe project rationale and communicate results of research; a project director visited each resource room approximately once per week; behavior observations restricted to a measure of attending (eye contact); primary responsibility of child remained with general class teacher.

OUTCOMES: *Academic Achievement:* significant differences in all 3 schools in reading vocabulary, total reading, arithmetic fundamentals, and total arithmetic favoring resource program. *Personal and Social Adjustment:* students in resource increased their attending behavior in resource room; attention in general classroom for students in resource program did not improve and was no different from that of students in general program.

Glavin (1974). Type: behavior problems. Time: 4 years (follow-up testing of reintegrated students who had been served in resource programs for 1 or 2 years).

STUDENT CHARACTERISTICS: data on student characteristics of number, age, grade, IQ, Behavior Problem Checklist (BPCL), and achievement for the 4 years were included in study, but were too numerous to include here: scores on BPCL suggested majority exhibited conduct problem behavior; randomly selected for resource with the rest serving as control; 81% academically retarded; 4 schools were in low SES areas and students were predominantly black, with the rest Puerto Rican; the fifth school was in a slightly higher SES area and all students were white; no differences between groups in age, sex, average grade placement; subjects had been returned to general education for 2 or 3 years.

PROCESS VARIABLES: for specifications of program, see Glavin, Quay, Annesley, and Werry (1971) and Quay, Glavin, Annesley, and Werry (1972).

OUTCOMES: *Academic Achievement and Personal and Social Adjustment:* follow-up testing revealed that no significant differences existed between students formerly in resource program and those formerly in general program, either academically or behaviorally.

Kerlin & Latham (1977). Type: students with academic difficulties or behavior problems. Time: 8 weeks.

STUDENT CHARACTERISTICS: $N = 21$; CA 8-3 to 12-6; third graders; all male; all black; low SES; IQ range 74 to 111; achievement percentiles 1 to 84; no significant differences (.05) among groups for above variables; no significant differences for appropriate versus inappropriate behaviors as measured by a behavior problem checklist among groups; students were randomly assigned to 1 of 3 groups.

PROCESS VARIABLES: *Resource:* (Group 1) special education teacher assisted general class teachers in establishing individualized programs; students spent 45 minutes 3 times per week in resource; (Group 2) no special assistance to general teachers; students spent 45 minutes 3 times per week in resource; teachers for resource and general classes in first group setting met once per week for 30 minutes; reading and/or math instruction was stressed for all children; reinforcement system—behavior certificates were used as rewards and could be exchanged for tangible reinforcers.

OUTCOMES: *Personal and Social Adjustment:* no significant differences between resource programs in behavior posttest scores (.05); significant differences between either of the two resource programs and general class favoring resource (in both appropriate and inappropriate behaviors—more appropriate for resource and less inappropriate for resource) (.01); in analyzing differences among teacher perceptions, resource room program without consultation (Group 2) showed significant differences from general class on variables of acting out, withdrawal, distractibility, and total scores favoring resource program (.05); same analysis yielded a favorable significant difference for resource with consultation (Group 1) over general on withdrawal variable (.02); in resource with consultation (Group 1), 2 of 5 students originally classified as ED were reclassified as normal after intervention, while in resource without consultation (Group 2), all 3 students originally classified as ED were reclassified as normal, and the general class had no such reclassifications of the 5 students originally classified ED.

Rust, Miller, & Wilson (1978). Type: students with learning problems. Time: 1 year.
  STUDENT CHARACTERISTICS: *Resource:* $N = 83$; 21 second graders; 12 third graders; 13 fourth graders; 16 fifth graders; 21 sixth graders; 50 males, 33 females. *General:* $N = 79$; 12 second graders; 11 third graders; 14 fourth graders; 18 fifth graders; 24 sixth graders; 42 males, 37 females; randomly placed in either resource or general program; certified by state-approved assessment specialists.
  PROCESS VARIABLES: *Resource:* students spent 30 minutes to 1 hour each day in resource; teachers were certified in special education.
  OUTCOMES: *Academic Achievement:* no significant differences between groups; significant gains for both groups.

Miller & Sabatino (1978). Type: LD and EMR. Time: 1 school year.
  STUDENT CHARACTERISTICS: $N = 547$ mildly handicapped; CA $\bar{X}$ 8-4 years, metropolitan area. *Resource:* 202 students classified LD; 17 students classified EMR; 138 boys, 8 girls. *General* (Teacher Consultant Model): 240 students classified LD; 21 students classified EMR; 178 boys, 83 girls. *General* (no service served as control): 62 students classified LD, 5 classified EMR; 44 boys, 23 girls; no significant differences were found among groups on pretests of word recognition, arithmetic subtests, or reading comprehension.
  PROCESS VARIABLES: *General* (Teacher Consultant Model): consultants conveyed best practice skills to general teacher, who had primary responsibility for implementation; each consultant served approximately 700 students; each consultant served for a full day every day, every other day, or every third day; amount of time with each class not controlled. *Resource:* teachers participated in diagnosis, prescription, intensive clinical lessons, report writing; teachers provided assistance daily, twice a week, or 3 times a week to approximately 14 children in 45-minute instructional blocks; teacher training and experience were ''quite similar'' to those of teachers in consultant model.
  OUTCOMES: *Academic Achievement:* significantly higher posttest scores on word recognition and arithmetic for both resource and teacher consultant

model; controls demonstrated no change; no significant difference between resource and teacher consultant model for word recognition or arithmetic; teacher behaviors slightly better under consultant model.

O'Connor, Stuck, & Wyne (1979). Type: students a year or more behind in reading and/or math who spent low percentages of time on-task. Time: 8 weeks of intervention plus 4 months of follow-up in general classrooms.

STUDENT CHARACTERISTICS: 2nd and 3rd graders matched on mean grade deficiency and mean intelligence test scores; 2nd and 3rd graders from predominantly white, relatively affluent area, while 6th graders came from predominantly black, economically depressed area; criteria for admittance (a) IQ 89 or above, (b) achievement performance 1 or more grade levels behind in reading and/or math, and (c) less than 50% time spent on-task during math or reading instruction in general classroom; priorities for immediate admission were established based on attempts to maintain relative homogeneity, racial balance, and severity of the perceived problem, especially in terms of behavior; it was agreed that children assigned to comparison group would become eligible for participation in the resource room program after serving as comparison for 6 months. *Resource:* 2nd and 3rd graders ($N=28$ 1 week before intervention) reading $\overline{X}$ 48.6, $SD=8.0$, math $\overline{X}$ 52.7, $SD=9.3$; (for assessment after 8 weeks, $N=18$, and after 16 weeks, $N=10$); 6th graders ($N=28$ 1 week before intervention) reading $\overline{X}$ 75.0, $SD=6.7$, math $\overline{X}$ 83.5, $SD=5.0$; (for assessment after 8 weeks, $N=8$, and after 16 weeks, $N=8$); baseline mean percentage of time on task for 2nd and 3rd graders was 29% and for 6th graders it was 30%. *General:* 2nd and 3rd graders ($N=25$ 1 week before intervention) reading $\overline{X}$ 48.6, $SD=8.0$, math $\overline{X}$ 53.1, $SD=8.7$; (for assessment after 8 weeks, $N=16$, and after 16 weeks, $N=6$); 6th graders ($N=27$ 1 week before intervention) reading $\overline{X}$ 75.1, $SD=7.7$, math $\overline{X}$ 85.2, $SD=6.5$; (for assessment after 8 weeks $N=17$, and after 16 weeks, $N=7$); baseline mean percentage of time on-task for 2nd and 3rd graders was 31% and for 6th graders it was 41%.

PROCESS VARIABLES: *Resource:* students attended resource from 8:30 a.m. to 12:00 p.m. each morning and returned to general classrooms after lunch; strict behavior principles were employed including positive reinforcement, highly individualized daily academic assignments (at least 80% of morning), charting of academic progress, and procedures for time-out; trade-in period for token system was gradually increased from 1 day to 1 week, then phased out in the 5th week of intervention; points were assigned for both academic performance and task-oriented behavior throughout intervention.

OUTCOMES: *Academic Achievement:* significant differences favoring resource: for 2nd and 3rd graders and 6th graders in reading (.001) and math (.001) 1 week after intervention, for 2nd and 3rd graders in reading (.006) and math (.003) and for 6th graders in reading (.001) and math (.001) 8 weeks after intervention, and for 2nd and 3rd graders in reading (.001) and math (.001) and for 6th graders in reading (.003) and math (.001) 16 weeks after intervention. *Personal and Social Adjustment:* significant difference on time on-task favoring resource (.001) for 2nd, 3rd, and 6th graders during follow-up.

Wang & Birch (1984). Type: LD, SD, and ED, visually impaired, and gifted. Time: 8 months.

STUDENT CHARACTERISTICS: Resource: N = 71 students, general and exceptional; grades 1 to 3. *General* (ALEM = Adaptive Learning Environments Model): N = 108 students, general and exceptional; grades K to 3; students were randomly assigned.

PROCESS VARIABLES: *General* (ALEM): highly structured prescriptive learning component that used built-in, diagnostic procedures to develop skills in academic subject areas; open-ended, exploratory, learning component that promoted social and personal development through students' planning and management of their own learning; education specialists were available for consultation with teachers and to provide support services. *Resource:* identified students with handicaps spent mornings in resource receiving instruction in reading and math.

OUTCOMES: *Academic Achievement:* significant difference in reading favoring ALEM. *Personal and Social Adjustment:* significant decrease in time spent on teacher-directed activities for ALEM in morning; significant increases in independent work and on task behavior for ALEM morning and afternoon; significant decrease in time spent on teacher-directed activities for students in resource in morning but not in general program in afternoon; significant increase in independent work for students in resource in morning but not in general program in afternoon; significant difference in on-task behavior favoring ALEM.

Affleck, Madge, Adams, & Lowenbraun (1988). Type: LD. Time: 3 years.

STUDENT CHARACTERISTICS: *General* (Integrated Classroom Model): (Year 1): N = 29; CA 8-0 to 12-2; grades 2 to 6; IQ $\overline{X}$ 95.93; 19 male, 10 female. (Year 2): N = 61; CA 6-5 to 12-1; grades 1 to 6; IQ $\overline{X}$ 97.29; 35 male, 26 female. (Year 3): N = 47; CA 7-7 to 11-6; grades 2 to 5; IQ $\overline{X}$ 101.06; 31 male, 16 female. *Resource:* (Year 1): N = 17; CA 7-3 to 11-9; grades 2 to 6; IQ $\overline{X}$ 99.4; 12 male, 5 female. (Year 2): N = 24; CA 6-11 to 12-5; grades 1 to 6; IQ $\overline{X}$ 94.0; 13 male, 11 female. (Year 3): N = 19; CA 7-1 to 11-4; grades 2 to 5; IQ $\overline{X}$ 102.67; 10 male, 9 female; identified as LD by district; assigned to class according to school attended (no random selection); all students white; equal socioeconomic status.

PROCESS VARIABLES: *General* (Integrated Classroom Model): administered jointly by general and special education personnel; approximately ⅓ of students had mild handicaps and were placed with ⅔ students classified "average to above average" from general education classes—target size was 24; teachers were experienced in special education or general education and were certified in special education; qualifications for teachers included successful teaching experience, ability to individualize and adapt curriculum and behavior management techniques, effective communication and classroom management skills, and flexibility; each classroom was assigned a part-time aide who spent differing amounts of time in the classrooms according to number of handicapped students in each classroom; aides carried out programs designed by teachers, collected data on student performance, tutored students on a one-to-one and small group basis, and monitored classroom activities; general school district curriculum used; observed practices in the classroom were (a) clear directions and expectations; (b) high reinforcement levels; (c) grouping for instruction; (d) direct, sequential instruction; and (e) individual attention. *Resource:* students received 30 to 150 minutes of daily instruction in reading, language arts, and/or math; some instructional materials and methods for basic skill instruction were same as those used in ICM; teacher experience and background similar to those of ICM teachers.

OUTCOMES: *Academic Achievement:* no significant difference in academic achievement between groups; no significant difference in academic achievement between nonhandicapped students in ICM and those in general classes; ICM more cost effective.

Appendix C

Noncontrolled Group Studies: Growth In Resource

Weiner (1969). Type: LD. Time: 10 months.

STUDENT CHARACTERISTICS: $N=72$; CA 7 to 12; IQ 90 to 130; grades 1 to 6; group served as own control based on past performance; students displayed hyperactive disassociation; figure background reversals; distractibility; perseveration; behavior disorders; average or better IQ; serious underachievement; all had failed previous year attended due to specific learning disability.

PROCESS VARIABLES: *Resource:* tutorial or semitutorial for ½- to 1-hour periods; highly individualized tailor-made teaching; instruction in areas of diagnosed disabilities; reduction or remediation of the symptoms of neurological impairment; achievement in school.

OUTCOMES: *Academic Achievement:* significant gains in reading, arithmetic, spelling, visuomotor perception. *Personal and Social Adjustment:* no significant difference in Draw-a-Person.

Barksdale & Atkinson (1971). Type: EMR. Time: 3 years.

STUDENT CHARACTERISTICS: $N=64$; CA 7 to 13; IQ range 50 to 76; 52 boys, 12 girls; School A, inner city; School B, middle class neighborhood; reading $\overline{X}$ 1.2; spelling $\overline{X}$ 1.3; math $\overline{X}$ 1.5.

PROCESS VARIABLES: average of 1 hour and 15 minutes daily for each group in resource room; overall objective was to make systematic attack on child's specific learning problems using individual and small group instruction; variety of high-interest, multisensory activities and media; younger and less mature students were provided with sensory training, concept formation, language development, and reading and number experiences; older and more mature students were provided with perceptual organization, concept and language development, skills development in basic school subjects, and counseling; special education teachers were experienced and certified in teaching; in 3rd year of study, 2 aides were assigned to general classes to assist resource students in that setting; other aspects of resource program were cooperative planning between special and general education teachers, class size of 24 to 34 pupils, involvement of school principal, and continuous inservice program.

OUTCOMES: *Academic Achievement:* significant academic improvement. *Personal and Social Adjustment:* principals and teachers reported noticeable changes in pupils' attitudes toward themselves, their teachers and peers, and school in general; 10 of the original 64 were returned to full-time general classes by end of 3rd year; parents were enthusiastic in their appraisals of program.

Hammill, Iano, McGettigan, & Wiederholt (1972). Type: EMR. Time: 7 months.
STUDENT CHARACTERISTICS: CA $\overline{X}$ 9-4, range 6-10 to 12-11; IQ $\overline{X}$ 68, range 55 to 79; 3:1 male-female; predominantly black; economically depressed.
PROCESS VARIABLES: average of 33 minutes of reading instruction daily in resource program; no child received less than 30 minutes per day; individual and small group instruction depending on severity of problem; reinforcement; intensive teacher assessment; adjusted learning activity to unique qualities of learner.

OUTCOMES: *Academic Achievement:* .7 of a grade growth in reading in 7 months.

Affleck, Lehning, & Brow (1973). Time: 1 school year. Type: "mildly handicapped" (usually labeled ED, MR, LD).
STUDENT CHARACTERISTICS: *Students with Mild Handicaps:* $N=29$; CA $\overline{X}$ 10-10, *SD* 1.5; grade $\overline{X}$ 5.48; 24 male, 5 female; word recognition $\overline{X}$ 3.3, *SD* 1.6; instructional level $\overline{X}$ 2.80, *SD* 1.57; independent level $\overline{X}$ 2.86, *SD* 2.01. *Nonhandicapped Students:* $N=8$; CA $\overline{X}$ 6-5, *SD* 4.37 months; grade $\overline{X}$ 1.00; 5 male, 3 female; rhyming words $\overline{X}$ 21.75, *SD* 18.62; beginning sounds $\overline{X}$ 30.63, *SD* 22.54; visual discrimination $\overline{X}$ 28.00, *SD* 21.22; identifying letters $\overline{X}$ 21.50, *SD* 11.99.

PROCESS VARIABLES: *Purpose was to* (a) provide better service to children with mild handicaps in the district; (b) provide, through extensive specification of goals and administrative processes, data collection and analyses, and an exportable model for other schools to copy; and (c) provide a superior practicum facility for college special education students wishing to become resource teachers. *Teacher role specifications were* (a) specific preparation in working as a team member; (b) capacity to administer a variety of group achievement and individual diagnostic tests; (c) ability to use a variety of curricular interventions and reinforcement procedures to achieve specific goals; and (d) ability to employ a variety of evaluative measures intrinsic to formative and summative evaluations of pupil progress. *Primary level resource teacher was to* (a) assume total responsibility for individual diagnosis, program planning, and evaluation of all special education students placed in grades 1 to 3; (b) assume primary responsibility for processing all referrals from teachers of grades 1 to 3, including meeting with team leader regarding final action to be taken on each referral; (c) team teach minimum of 2 classes from grades 1 to 3 with general classroom teacher; (d) complete student reports for students to whom direct services were provided; (e) prepare, present, and file staffing materials for all special education students grades 1 to 3; (f) report to parents 4 times a year, twice in a conference with general education teacher; and (g) report to parents when programs were initiated and terminated; a sample schedule for a teacher was provided. *Population specification was that* special education personnel provided service for all students needing it within school—such service frequently occurred via team teaching in general classroom. *Curriculum specifications were* (a) priority areas were to be reading and math; (b) sequences prepared for phonetic and structural decoding skills in reading, as well as for computational math skills; (c) each step in each sequence contained references to materials that would assist in teaching that step, as well as suggested mastery levels to be obtained before progressing to next level; (d) daily performance data were recorded; and (e) service was delivered in resource center and/or in general classroom, individually or in small group, depending on severity of deficit and intervention used.

OUTCOMES: *Academic Achievement:* significant gains made in word recognition, instructional level of reading, and independent level of reading (.01) for students with mild handicaps; significant gains made for nonhandicapped students on measures of rhyming words, beginning sounds, visual discrimination, and identifying letters (.02).

Iano, Ayers, Heller, McGettigan, & Walker (1974). Type: EMR and nonlabeled students referred for resource. Time: 2 years.

STUDENT CHARACTERISTICS: *Students in Resource Labeled EMR: N*=40; previously served in self-contained classes. *Students in Resource–Nonlabeled: N*=80; never labeled or served in special education. *Nonhandicapped: N*=606.

PROCESS VARIABLES: authors referred the reader to Shotel, Iano, and McGettigan (1972) and Hammill, Iano, McGettigan, and Wiederholt (1972) for philosophy, goals, and operation of resource room programs; most students spent approximately 1 hour a day in resource, but a small number with more severe problems were assigned for approximately ½ of each school day.

OUTCOMES: *Personal and Social Growth:* students labeled EMR scored significantly lower than nonhandicapped and nonlabeled on acceptance measures and significantly higher on rejection measures; authors compared these findings to previous research of students in self-contained labeled EMR that found similar results, no significant difference for acceptance-rejection measures of students labeled EMR between years 1 and 2 of study, indicating no growth.

Sheare (1978). Type: LD. Time: 1 school year.
STUDENT CHARACTERISTICS: *Resource:* $N = 41$; grades 3 to 5; identified as having at least average intellectual functioning, significant academic deficits present in reading, writing, math, and/or language functioning; evidence of significant perception, motor, and/or language differences; referred by general class teachers; randomly selected. *Non-LD Students:* $N = 41$; chosen randomly by sex from same classrooms as students classified as LD.
PROCESS VARIABLES: students labeled LD spent 45-minute periods 3 to 5 times weekly in resource program; resource program was diagnostic-prescriptive in nature and geared toward specific skill development; resource teachers were trained to teach students labeled LD and had minimum of 1 year of previous teaching experience.
OUTCOMES: *Personal and Social Adjustment:* no change in self-concept for either group on the 2 test scores; for both groups, second peer acceptance scores were significantly higher than first; significant difference in self-concept favoring non-LD students 3 months into school year and at end of school year; no significant difference in regard to gender.

Ito (1980). Type: LD. Time: either (a) 2 to 6 months of resource then 1 year of general or (b) 7 to 10 months of resource then 1 year of general.
STUDENT CHARACTERISTICS: $N = 62$; 52 students had IQ in the range of 85 to 114, 7 students had IQ in the range of 70 to 84, and 3 students had IQ in the range of 115 to 130; lower middle class and middle class environments; 42 male, 20 female; mean rates of reading achievement for students receiving intervention for 2 to 6 months ($N = 27$) was .587, *SD* .125, receiving intervention for 7 to 10 months ($N = 35$) was .630, *SD* .178, 6 to 9 years old ($N = 21$) was .660, *SD* .172, and 10 to 12 years old ($N = 41$) was .587, *SD* .176; criteria for eligibility were that students (1) had been initially referred to resource room because of academic difficulties, (2) had been classified by public schools as learning disabled, (3) had been enrolled full time in the elementary grades for 1 full year following attendance in resource room, and (4) were from resource rooms in which teachers had at least 1 year of experience in that resource room.
PROCESS VARIABLES: not specified.

OUTCOMES: *Academic Achievement:* resource room model was effective for increasing the reading achievement rates of students labeled LD; these increased rates, however, were not maintained at same level following a year of full-time attendance in general classrooms; students with shorter stay in resource room displayed higher rate of learning at posttest and follow-up testing; no significant difference between students age 6 to 9 and 10 to 12 on reading achievement at follow-up; older group gained at a higher rate than younger group during resource intervention, but rate decreased rapidly during follow-up; younger group achieved at a rate slower than older group during intervention, but rate was maintained during follow-up.

Appendix D
Controlled Group Studies: Mixed

Rodee (1971). Type: EMR. Time: 6 months.

STUDENT CHARACTERISTICS: *Resource:* $N=36$; grades 2 to 4; IQ range 70 to 80. *Self-Contained:* $N=40$; matched to students in resource on IQ and CA. *General:* $N=16$; matched to students in resource on IQ and CA.

PROCESS VARIABLES: students received daily instruction that was tutorial and supportive in nature.

OUTCOMES: *Academic Achievement:* no significant differences among groups on measures of word knowledge, word discrimination, or math; students in resource were superior (.05) to students in self-contained on a measure of reading achievement. *Personal and Social Adjustment:* no differences in improvement of behavior. *Attendance:* no significant difference in attendance; all 3 groups had mean improvement.

Sabatino (1971). Type: LD. Time: 1 school year.

STUDENT CHARACTERISTICS: *Resource:* (Group A): $N=27$; CA $\overline{X}$ 9.7, range 8.3 to 11.5; MA (vocabulary) $\overline{X}$ 9.9; grade $\overline{X}$ 4.6, range 2 to 6; primary perceptual impairment: 7 visual, 11 auditory, 9 integration; 21 male, 6 female; years in school $\overline{X}$ 6.03. (Group B): $N=48$; CA $\overline{X}$ 8.9, range, 7.10 to 12.4; MA (vocabulary) $\overline{X}$ 9.3; grade $\overline{X}$ 3.11, range 2 to 6; primary perceptual impairment: 17 visual, 15 auditory, 16 integration; 32 male, 16 female; years in school $\overline{X}$ 5.4. *Self-Contained:* $N=11$; CA $\overline{X}$ 9.3, range 8.5 to 11.7; MA (vocabulary) $\overline{X}$ 9.3; grade $\overline{X}$ 4.3, range 3 to 6; primary perceptual impairment: 4 visual, 4 auditory, 3 integration; 9 male, 2 female; years in school $\overline{X}$ 5.8. *General:* (Control Group): $N=11$; CA $\overline{X}$ 9.4, range 7.4 to 11.8; MA (vocabulary) $\overline{X}$ 9.5; grade $\overline{X}$ 4.4, range 2 to 6; primary perceptual impairment—were not matched; 8 male, 3 female; years in school $\overline{X}$ 5.7; academic achievement deficit in 1 or more subject areas while demonstrating normal verbal intelligence with at least 1 developmental year of measured deficiency in the visual, auditory, or integrated perceptual areas on selected tests; matched for CA, sex, IQ, and children were paired for type of problem within visual and auditory perceptual complex; all subjects had experienced at least 1 year of academic failure, failed to achieve teacher expectancy, and progressed an average of less than 2 months academically for each year of school.

PROCESS VARIABLES: *Resource:* individualized or group (never more than 6) instruction—working directly with teacher on specific activity; Group A spent 1 hour a day in the resource room, while Group B spent ½ hour twice a week—remaining time was spent in general classroom; teachers taught within prescriptive confines of behavior modification and remediation; no academic subject matter was taught; each student was prescriptively assigned to 1 of 4 types of programs: (1) visual motor perceptual training; (2) auditory perceptual training; (3) vocabulary and language modification; (4) remediation (direct attack on word recognition and reading comprehension); specific training activities were limited to 20 minutes in length; same equipment and materials used for each class; teachers of resource (Group B) and self-contained switched classes 2 times a week; classes were under constant monitoring. *Self-Contained:* students received all instruction in this setting; curriculum same as above for resource with only difference being that activities could be repeated successively where they could not be in resource because of time restraints.

OUTCOMES: *Academic Achievement and Aptitude: Resource (A):* significant difference between pre- and posttests in word recognition and reading comprehension (.01); significant difference in behavioral changes in auditory perceptual memory, psycholinguistic, and language receptive-expressive function (.01 and .05). *Resource (B):* significant differences in word recognition and reading comprehension; significant difference in WISC comprehension (.01) and similarities (.05); significant difference in auditory-vocal association and reception (.01). *Self-Contained:* significant difference in word recognition and reading comprehension (.05). *General:* no significant difference in reading comprehension and word recognition (.10). A comparison of all groups showed a significant difference favoring resource plan A on word recognition, and self-contained on reading comprehension.

Bersoff, Kabler, Fiscus, & Ankney (1972). Type: neurologically handicapped (i.e., LD). Time: 18 months.

STUDENT CHARACTERISTICS: *Resource:* $N = 17$; CA $\overline{X}$ 8.6, *SD* 1.03; IQ $\overline{X}$ 100.18, *SD* 8.44; intervention $\overline{X}$ 14.6 months, *SD* 4.66; time elapsed between pre- and posttesting $\overline{X}$ 23.8 months, *SD* 9.00. *Self-Contained:* $N = 12$; CA $\overline{X}$ 8.3, *SD* .99; IQ $\overline{X}$ 100.17, *SD* 7.80; treatment period $\overline{X}$ 18.2 months, *SD* 4.99; time elapsed between pre- and posttesting $\overline{X}$ 28.4 months, *SD* 6.96. *General:* $N = 13$; CA $\overline{X}$ 7.9, *SD* .71; IQ $\overline{X}$ 100.85, *SD* 8.45; treatment period $\overline{X}$

21.6 months, *SD* 6.36; time elapsed between pre- and posttesting $\overline{X}$ 21.6, *SD* 6.36. Students had average or above-average intelligence; achievement levels at least 2 years below grade level predicted by age and intelligence; auditory, and/or visual perception difficulties; and behavior deficits or excesses that would lead them to be called hypo- or hyperactive.

PROCESS VARIABLES: *Resource:* students were seen individually by certified teachers during regular school day for periods ranging from 30 minutes to 1 hour in those skill areas recommended by school psychologist, principal, and/or classroom teacher; students received from 2 to 5 hours instruction per week (median of 4 hours); each student's program was determined by individual tutor; only 10% of tutors had received training in the areas of special education. *Self-Contained:* classes contained 8 to 10 students; to reach the goal of return to general class, each student was presented with highly structured and individualized academic and behavioral program; while equipped with a variety of educational materials, classrooms were usually organized so that visual and auditory distractions were kept to a minimum; teachers were not necessarily certified in special education, but were experienced and had volunteered to work with students who were neurologically handicapped. *General:* medium-sized (25 to 30 students) classrooms.

OUTCOMES: *Academic Achievement:* no significant differences among groups on measures of reading, math, or visual motor.

Carter (1975). Type: EMR. Time: student had been in respective placements for a minimum of 2 years.

STUDENT CHARACTERISTICS: *Resource:* $N=20$; randomly selected from a school participating in resource program. *Self-Contained:* $N=20$; randomly selected from 9 self-contained classes. *General:* $N=30$.

PROCESS VARIABLES: *Resource:* most of the day was spent in general classes; considerable supportive personnel resources; general teacher given special inservice training to cope more effectively with students.

OUTCOMES: *Academic Achievement:* evidence to support one program or another was lacking; significant relationship between intelligence and composite academic achievement.

Jenkins & Mayhall (1976). Type: (Evaluation 1) EMR and LD; (Evaluation 2) mostly students classified EMR but some classified LD; (Evaluation 3) information not available. Time: (Evaluation 1) 3½ months; (Evaluation 2) School A—7 to 8 months; School B—9 months; (Evaluation 3) 9 months.

STUDENT CHARACTERISTICS: (Evaluation 1) *Resource:* $N=12$; grades 1 and 2; randomly assigned from group of 24. *Self-Contained:* $N=6$; primary grades; EMR; matched in pairs on achievement; 1 of each pair randomly assigned to resource. *General:* $N=12$; grades 1 and 2; randomly assigned from group of 24. (Evaluation 2) (School A): *Resource:* $N=8$; grades 1 to 3; randomly assigned from group of 16. *General:* $N=8$; grades 1 to 3; randomly assigned from group of 16. (School B): *Resource:* $N=6$; grades 1 to 3; 6 children with lowest achievement. *General:* $N=6$; grades 1 to 3; 6 children with highest achievement. (Evaluation 3): not specified.

PROCESS VARIABLES: *Resource:* indirect service functions were to (1) identify core tasks or behaviors, (2) measure performance discrepancy, (3) plan and implement an intervention program, (4) revise the intervention program, and (5) provide intermittent consultation; direct service functions were to (1) identify core tasks, (2) assess core task performance, (3) plan and implement an intervention program, (4) provide one-to-one daily instruction, (5) instruct from a data base, and (6) terminate direct services; an evaluation of program components yielded positive results for (1) one-to-one instruction, (2) cross-age tutors, (3) direct service, (4) daily measurement, and (5) daily instruction. (Evaluation 1) *Resource:* students attended daily in periods from 30 to 60 minutes; (Evaluation 2) (School A): service limited to reading; (School B): service for both reading and math; students of both schools attended daily in periods from 20 to 60 minutes. (Evaluation 3): reading instruction only; compared relative growth in reading with that in math, which was not taught in resource.

OUTCOMES: *Academic Achievement:* (Evaluation 1): performance level of students receiving resource rose at a significantly faster rate than did that of students in general classrooms and self-contained classrooms without resource (.01); the same was true for self-contained in relation to general (.05). (Evaluation 2) (School A): significant difference in reading favoring resource (.01); no significance in math. (School B): resource significantly outperformed general in reading (.025); resource outgained control 1.8 years to .6 on math. (Evaluation 3): students gained more in reading than in math.

Sarfaty & Katz (1978). Type: hearing impaired. Time: 8 to 9 years.

STUDENT CHARACTERISTICS: *Resource:* $N=13$; severe hearing loss versus medium hearing loss—23% to 77%. *Self-Contained:* $N=21$; severe hearing loss versus medium hearing loss—80% to 20%. *General:* $N=14$; severe hearing loss versus medium hearing loss—78% to 14%. CA 14 to 15; grades 8 and 9; students had been in same placement since 1st grade; sample covered entire 14- to 15-year-old population with hearing impairments in Israel, with the exception of a small number with below normal intelligence level.

PROCESS VARIABLES: *Resource:* covered basic academic subjects—students were integrated into general classes in all other subjects and activities. *Self-Contained:* totally segregated. *General:* involved after-school individualized help, but total integration during the day.

OUTCOMES: *Personal and Social Adjustment:* self-concept was significantly lower for students in self-contained on 8 of 9 indices; self-concept was significantly higher for students in resource on 8 of 9 indices; no significant differences among the 3 groups on the self-acceptance score or in adjustment problems.

Cox & Wilson (1981). Type: LD. Time: 1 school year.
STUDENT CHARACTERISTICS: 90 LD students evenly split; CA 6-4 to 12-3; grades 1 to 6; IQ 80 to 116; 24 boys and 6 girls for each group; middle to upper SES; matched for CA, sex, ability (IQ), and reading level.

PROCESS VARIABLES: *Resource:* students received 30 minutes to 2 hours instruction per day in reading or other process deficit areas; individualized daily assignments according to achievement level coordinated with student's general classroom program; general classroom teacher shared teaching and programming responsibilities for reading; specific materials and techniques used to enhance academic achievement. *Self-Contained:* students received individual instruction in all academic subject areas in this setting; daily assignments individually programmed for each child according to achievement level; specific materials and techniques used to enhance academic achievement. *General:* all instruction took place in this setting; teachers received assistance from specialists on different materials and techniques to be used with students; much work was group oriented with some individualized instruction and programming.

OUTCOMES: *Academic Achievement:* significant difference among 3 groups in reading achievement favoring self-contained; no significant difference between resource and general class in reading achievement.

Coleman (1983a). Type: students with mild handicaps academically deficient or having difficulty with behavioral adjustment. Time: 1 school year.
STUDENT CHARACTERISTICS: *Students with Mild Handicaps:* $N=138$; students were divided equally into 3 instructional settings: (a) 1-hour resource, (b) 2-hour resource, and (c) self-contained classes; CA $\overline{X}$ 11-1, range 8-9 to 13-0; 77% male; 97% Caucasian. *General:* $N=46$; students had academic difficulties but were not served in special education; CA $\overline{X}$ 11-3, range 9-2 to 13-3; 74% male; 96% Caucasian. *Nonhandicapped:* $N=138$; students were divided equally among grades 4, 5, and 6; CA $\overline{X}$ 11-6, range 9-7 to 13-0; 51% male; 98% Caucasian.

PROCESS VARIABLES: students in resource received either 1 hour or 2 hours of service per day.

OUTCOMES: *Personal and Social Adjustment:* there was no significant difference between students with handicaps served in special education and nonhandicapped for self-concept; students in general class experiencing academic difficulties scored low on self-concept; no significant difference on self-concept among special education classes.

Coleman (1983b). Type: students with mild handicaps academically deficient or having difficulty with behavioral adjustment. Time: 1 school year.

STUDENT CHARACTERISTICS: *Students with Mild Handicaps:* $N = 138$; students were divided equally into 3 instructional settings: (a) 1-hour resource, (b) 2-hour resource, and (c) self-contained classes; CA $\overline{X}$ 11-1, range 8-9 to 13-0; 77% male; 97% Caucasian. *General:* $N = 46$; students had academic difficulties but were not served in special education; CA $\overline{X}$ 11-3, range 9-2 to 13-3; 74% male; 96% Caucasian. *Nonhandicapped:* $N = 138$; students were divided equally among grades 4, 5, and 6; CA $\overline{X}$ 11-6, range 9-7 to 13-0; 51% male; 98% Caucasian.

PROCESS VARIABLES: students in resource received either 1 hour or 2 hours of service per day.

OUTCOMES: *Personal and Social Adjustment:* self-concept scores of all students with handicaps were systematically higher than those of students with academic difficulties who remained in full-time general classes; self-concept scores of students in 2-hour resource were comparable to scores of students in self-contained, and higher than scores of students in 1-hour resource (.05); mothers of students with handicaps predicted lower scores for their children than were actually scored, while mothers of those remaining in general class predicated higher scores than were actually scored—these predictions were significant (.01) for all groups except 1-hour resource room.

Appendix E

York Educational Software
Evaluation Scales*

*Note. From ''York Educational Software Publication Scales,'' 1987, in R. D. Owston (Ed.), *Software Evaluation: A Criterion Based Approach*, pp. 47–57. Boston: Allyn & Bacon. Reprinted with permission.

I. Pedagogical Content Scale

Definition

Content refers to the knowledge and skills the software purports to teach—the organization, accuracy, and appropriateness of the material. **Content organization** refers to the sequencing of the knowledge and skills within the lesson or lessons, the breadth or scope of the skills and knowledge, and the depth of instruction or amount of practice given to a topic. **Accuracy** is concerned with the truthfulness of the knowledge and skills presented. **Appropriateness** deals with the suitability of the content for the intended user, including such factors as readability, the relationship between the complexity of the content and the intended user's ability to master it, and the educational value of the content (i.e., whether the time spent learning the content is justified because of its inherent value). If one or all of these elements—organization, accuracy, and appropriateness—are weak, the content may be judged less than exemplary.

CRITERIA FOR PEDAGOGICAL CONTENT

LEVEL 4: Exemplary content

Level 4 content is superior in its organization, accuracy, and appropriateness. The content organization is such that the scope of the knowledge and skills is congruent with the user's ability to master them, the sequencing is logical and follows good pedagogical practice (e.g., less abstract ideas are presented before more abstract ideas), and the depth of instruction is sufficient to give the user adequate practice before proceeding to the next topic. The accuracy of level 4 content is extremely high. Furthermore, the content at this level is very readable, well-matched to the intended user's ability to master it, and has high educational value.

LEVEL 3: Desirable content

The organization, accuracy, and/or appropriateness of level 3 content is not quite as favorable as that of level 4 due to relatively minor weaknesses. The organization may be weak because the content scope does not quite match the user's ability to master it; the sequencing may be illogical or not in keeping with accepted pedagogical practice; the intensity of instruction may be either slightly more or less than necessary, requiring the user to complete too many or too few exercises; and the user may not receive sufficient practice with the material before moving on to the next topic. Problems with accuracy might consist of questionable (but not incorrect) facts or applications of concepts. Level 3 content may also present some vocabulary or sentence structures that give intended users difficulty. Its material may be too complex or too easy for the intended user to digest, and some aspects of the content may be of questionable educational value. However, all flaws in level 3 content are slight.

LEVEL 2: Minimally acceptable content

Level 2 content is weak in either one area or a combination of the areas of organization, accuracy, or appropriateness. The deficiency, however, is not serious enough to prevent the use of the software, if no other better software is available, and if the instructor is able to rectify the deficiency. In its organization level 2 software may present too much material; it may be poorly arranged in sequence or not consistent with good educational practice; its instructional depth may be exaggerated or insufficient. Accuracy problems encountered with level 2 content include incorrect minor facts or applications of concepts. At this level vocabulary and content structure may be too difficult for the intended user, the knowledge and skills too difficult to master (or too easy), or the educational value of the overall content questionable.

LEVEL 1: Deficient content

Content at level 1 is sufficiently substandard to call into question the use of the software, regardless of the strengths of its other characteristics. Organizational problems may include weak, illogical sequencing, and content scope and/or depth of instruction poorly matched with the user's ability. This level of content may also contain factual inaccuracies or incorrect applications of concepts. The content reading level may be inappropriately matched with the user's ability, the knowledge and skills presented either too complex or simple, or the topics covered of dubious educational value.

II. Instructional Presentation Scale

Definition

Instruction refers to the manner in which the software takes advantage of the unique capabilities of the microcomputer in conveying the pedagogical content. Such capabilities include whether the microcomputer functions as an interactive learning device. Can it integrate text, graphics, and sound into the learning experience? Does it offer immediate feedback on the user's mastery of the content? How well does it adapt to the user's needs? **Instruction** also refers to the psychological climate of the presentation—the control of the lesson as sensed by the user, the tone of the instruction, and the supportiveness of the feedback. **Instruction** is concerned neither with the quality of the screen displays nor with the sound quality.

CRITERIA FOR INSTRUCTIONAL PRESENTATION

LEVEL 4: Exemplary instructional presentation
Software at this level presents the content in a manner that takes maximum advantage of the unique capabilities of the microcomputer for which it was designed. Level 4 software has a format that involves extensive interaction; it integrates text, graphics, and sound wherever appropriate; immediate, positive feedback is given to the user; and it adapts to the user's needs by branching to an appropriate level of difficulty so that unnecessary routines do not have to be performed before the user proceeds to the next level of difficulty. With level 4 software, the user has a sense of being in control of the lesson—to progress, to review, and to exit at will. Moreover, the tone of the software's language of instruction and feedback is supportive and nonpunitive.

LEVEL 3: Desirable instructional presentation
Software at this level of instruction still presents the content in a way that takes advantage of the uniqueness of the microcomputer; however, it does not perform this function as effectively as level 4 software, owing to such factors as minor weaknesses in the interactive capacity of the software; imperfect integration of graphics, sound, and text given the capabilities of the particular microcomputer; slow or nonconstructive feedback or branching that does not adapt to the user's needs as effectively as possible. Other reasons why this software is not rated at level 4 might include less user control over progress, ability to review or exit/re-enter at will, or a slightly inappropriate tone of the software language.

LEVEL 2: Minimally acceptable instructional presentation
Level 2 software generally does not make effective use of the unique features of the microcomputer as an instructional device. While some aspects of the instruction

may be rated at level 3 or level 4, the overall quality of instruction cannot be rated at level 3 because of one or more distinct weaknesses in the instruction. Typical weaknesses might include little or no attempt to integrate graphics, text, and sound; delayed or negative feedback to user responses, and little or no branching. In addition to having these weaknesses, the software may allow little control over the various aspects of its operation, and the tone of its language may be either indifferent or overly punitive.

LEVEL 1: Deficient instructional presentation
Software at this level, the lowest on the scale, exhibits no attempt—or an unsuccessful attempt—at making use of the unique features of the microcomputer to present the content. Often this level of software requires the microcomputer to function as little more than a ''page-turning'' device. There may be no integration of graphics, sound, and text (if, indeed, the first two features are used); the feedback may be nonexistent or inconsistent, rewarding incorrect responses more than correct responses; and users may have to follow a lock-step sequence to complete the lesson with this level of software. In addition, the software may not allow the user to have any control over its operation once the lesson has begun, and the tone of the language may be punitive or nonsupportive.

III. Documentation Scale

Definition

Documentation refers to the supporting materials and instructions that accompany the software, including the printed materials provided as well as the supporting information available on the screen. One purpose of the documentation is to describe and explain how the software may be used pedagogically, which usually involves giving information on how the software may be integrated into the curriculum, the objectives of the software, the prerequisite skills necessary to use the software successfully, the age/grade/ability level recommended for the software, and suggestions and references for preparatory and follow-up activities. Another purpose of the documentation is to explain the technical use of the software, such as how to boot the disk, how to stop/start/re-enter the program, and how to access various program components. From a pedagogical point of view, both of these purposes must be served by the documentation.

CRITERIA FOR DOCUMENTATION SCALE

LEVEL 4: Exemplary documentation
Software at this level has clearly written, concise documentation that explains fully how the software may be used pedagogically and technically. Level 4 documentation contains thorough information on how the software may be integrated into the teaching/learning process by providing complete information on prerequisite skills and abilities, follow-up activities, worksheets where applicable, and bibliographic references. The documentation must also explain all aspects of the operation of the software including—but not limited to—how to boot the disk, stop/start/re-enter the program, use peripheral devices, and branch to components of the software so that the user does not have to spend needless time on trial and error. If the software can be used pedagogically and technically after a careful reading of the documentation, it may be rated at level 4.

LEVEL 3: Desirable documentation
Level 3 software documentation, like that of level 4, describes and explains how the software may be used both pedagogically and technically. Unlike level 4 documentation, however, level 3 documentation is not as helpful or specific in its suggestions on how the software may be integrated into the teaching/learning process. This may be due to minor omissions in some pedagogical aspects or to a lower overall standard in the pedagogical information. Normally, the technical documentation would be expected to be the same quality as level 4.

LEVEL 2: Minimally acceptable documentation
This level of documentation contains a minimal amount of usable pedagogical information and technical information with some minor errors or omissions. Typically, this level of documentation results in considerable teacher effort to integrate the software into the curriculum. Depending on their computer background, users may find that technical problems have to be resolved through trial and error.

LEVEL 1: Deficient documentation
Documentation at this level is inadequate to support the use of the software either technically, pedagogically, or both. Pedagogical documentation is nonexistent or unusable at this level; technical documentation may be confusing, imprecise, incomplete, or a combination of all three.

IV. Technical Adequacy Scale

Definition

Technical adequacy refers to the overall quality of the design of the software with respect to user inputs, software outputs, and system errors. More specifically, **adequacy of input** refers to the ease and simplicity of entering data into the computer. The **technical adequacy of outputs** refers to the aesthetic quality of the sound, graphics, and color, given the limitations of the machine for which the software was designed, as well as the clarity of the screen layout. **System errors** describes the ability of the software to continue to operate and not ''lock up'' regardless of the kinds of inputs the user enters.

CRITERIA FOR TECHNICAL ADEQUACY

LEVEL 4: Exemplary technical adequacy

The technical adequacy of level 4 software is extremely high. This level of software gives clear, precise cues and prompts so that the user knows when, and in what form, the input is required. Level 4 software avoids the use of characters with special meaning, requires a minimal amount of typing (unless the objective of the lesson is typing proficiency), does not distinguish between upper- and lower-case characters unless there is a pedagogical rationale to do so, accepts partial or abbreviated answers wherever appropriate (e.g., Y for YES, N for NO), allows responses to be corrected before they are accepted by the machine, and restricts the input to the same location on the screen. The color, sound, and graphics of level 4 software are aesthetically pleasing, and the screen layout is uncluttered and consistent from screen to screen. Finally, level 4 software is of such technical quality that no system errors whatsoever are evident when software is in operation.

LEVEL 3: Desirable technical adequacy

This level of software is not as technically adequate as level 4 software due to minor flaws in its design. The flaws, however, may be regarded as slight inconveniences, not serious enough to detract from efficient learning. Initially, the user may be uncertain about some aspects of the input to the software, such as its form and location, but after some trial and error or reading of the accompanying documentation, the uncertainty should be cleared up. For example, the software may be occasionally inconsistent in accepting abbreviated responses or in the location of input. Other drawbacks of level 3 software may include color, sound, and graphics that are not as aesthetically pleasing as those of level 4, or a screen layout that is inconsistent or cluttered. Like level 4, level 3 software should not contain any system errors.

LEVEL 2: Minimally acceptable technical adequacy

Level 2 software has distinct weaknesses that are, at the very least, constant annoyances to the user and, at most, a detraction from efficient learning. Often this level of software demonstrates inconsistencies in the required form and location of its inputs. Unlike those of level 3 software, however, these inconsistencies are not always predictable and may require trial and error by the user to determine the form and/or location of the input. Examples of these inconsistencies include accepting abbreviations at one point during the lesson but not at another, distinguishing between upper- and lowercase letters sometimes but not always, and requiring user responses to be entered at different screen locations from one frame to the next. The color, graphics, and sound of level 2 software may be less than aesthetically pleasing and the screen layout may be cluttered. Although there may be no actual programming errors in level 2 software, the program operation could be improved.

LEVEL 1: Deficient technical adequacy

Level 1 software usually has technical flaws that hinder efficient learning regardless of the superiority of the content and instructional presentation. The form and location of the input may vary from frame to frame even more frequently and less predictably than they do in level 2 software. Poor color, graphics, sound, or cluttered and confusing screen layout may be other reasons why software is classified as level 1. Another reason may be that the software has programming errors that are detectable during normal operation.

V. Modeling (Simulation) Scale

Definition

Modeling refers to the adequacy of the model used in simulation software to simulate a real-life situation. At least three factors must be considered when judging the overall adequacy of the simulation model. First, the complexity of the model relative to the intended user must be examined. Most real-life situations are too complex to be modeled, even with a large number of variables; therefore, a balance must be struck between the realism of the model and the ability of the intended user to deal with all of the variables in the model. Second, all of the variables in the model must be relevant to the simulation. (For example, the relevance of the lunar cycle as a variable in a stock market simulation is highly questionable.) Third, the variables in a simulation model must interact and produce results similar to what would be expected in reality; otherwise the user might be misled. In short, to determine the adequacy of a simulation model, the evaluator must examine its **complexity** relative to the intended user, its **relevance**, and its **results.**

CRITERIA FOR MODELING (SIMULATION)

LEVEL 4: Exemplary modeling

Software at this level provides a faithful rendition of a real-life situation that is neither too complex nor too simple for the intended user. The variables included in the model are the most relevant ones to use for the given simulation. Furthermore, all of the variables in the model interact and produce results approximately as they would do in real life.

LEVEL 3: Desirable modeling

Level 3 software has a less adequate, though usable simulation model. The number of variables in the model may be too many or too few, rendering the model overly complex or simple. One or two of the variables may be slightly irrelevant to the model and replaceable by a more relevant variable or variables or eliminated. Moreover, the variables may interact in ways or produce results that differ sufficiently from reality to be slightly misleading, though not to the extent of rating the software at level 2.

LEVEL 2: Minimally acceptable modeling

Although the simulation model in level 2 software has some significant weaknesses, the software is still usable in certain contexts, for example, if the instructor thoroughly explained the weaknesses of the software and supplemented it with additional materials or experiences. One typical weakness of level 2 software is that the model contains too few or too many variables, making the software either too simple or too difficult for the intended user. Or the software may contain irrelevant or inappropriate variables that significantly decrease the quality of the simulation. A further difficulty with the model may be that the variables interact in ways or produce results that differ substantially from the real situation that is being simulated, to the point of misleading the user and causing confusion.

LEVEL 1: Deficient modeling
Software rated level 1 on modeling is generally unusable regardless of its strengths in other areas. The number of variables used in the model may fall far short or be in gross excess of what is appropriate for the intended user. Moreover, the variables included in the model may not provide a realistic simulation of a true-life situation. A final reason why the software may be rated at level 1 is that the variables interact in ways or produce results that are totally unrealistic or misleading.

Appendix F

Classroom Interventions

Modifications	Difficulty Factor	Comments from Teachers	Consulting Recommendations and Comments
1. Have talented student read to student with reading difficulties.	2.2 (academic and content)	May be embarrassing for student with low skills. Good students may not be willing. Space away from the rest of the class is needed to do this.	Find a private location; choose a friend or family member to do the reading. Offer extra credit for helping student.
	2.6 (lab and performance)	Grouped classes have few good readers. Tapes are preferred because students can listen without distracting others and without taking other students' time.	Request this help of students from other classes. (Consider drawing from higher grade levels.)
2. Have student listen to a tape-recording of the test.	2.0 (content)	A place is needed—either a special table near an electrical outlet or a separate room.	Provide extension cords or battery-operated tape recorders. Consider use of study hall time or involve parents.
	2.4 (lab)	The student would have difficulty hearing in a lab class. Earphones would be necessary. Takes time to check out tapes and equipment, to say nothing of making the tapes.	Teach the student to assume the responsibility for checking out tapes. Enlist the help of the librarian or media specialist to set up a taping program. Use student aides.
3. Provide an alternative text or workbook.	2.2 (content)	Availability of alternative texts is not always good. The student will be conspicuous. Alternate texts fail to deal with the same material with the same depth.	Check local and regional SHMCs as well as sales representatives for new materials. Consider revised study guides and worksheets.
	2.6 (lab)	Extra time is needed for preparing separate assignments and discussions. This depends on help from support personnel.	LD students will be able to contribute more to class than they could have with a harder book, even if the book doesn't have *all the same ideas.*

4. Read the test questions aloud to the student.	2.9	The teacher needs to be available to monitor other students taking the test, to prevent cheating and to answer questions. Thus, a student aide or resource room teacher is requested to give the oral test. Oral tests take longer to give. It's embarrassing to the student. It's distracting to the rest of the class. The whole test could be read aloud to the whole class.	One could seat students needing an oral test in the rear of the room, stand behind them, and read the test while still surveying the class. Establish a period during the day for students needing oral tests to make appointments for assistance. Tape the test ahead of time so it is available to students in the resource room. Select a private location and time.
5. Provide written backup for oral directions.	1.8	Use of overhead projector depends on class size and room size. Write on handouts. Post charts on walls for explaining new techniques. Explain directions to special students individually. This requires extra preparation time.	Establish a permanent schedule for use of equipment. Have students deliver it. Write key terms or ideas on board.
6. Provide alternate media	2.3	For 1 to 3 students? What is the rest of the class doing? Content is usually not equivalent. Not available. A separate time and location are needed. We don't have enough A-V machines. Lectures take less time and effort to prepare.	An Autovance will not darken the room. Other students may use it later if they are interested, reducing the ''stigma'' of special treatment. Use earphones for movies in a corner. Use the resource room, the library, or a conference room. Avoid Fridays; plan ahead, sign up first. Variety in instruction is helpful.
7. Give a demonstration.	2.2 (content) 1.6 (lab)	Takes more preparation time. Might involve extra materials. Depends on the material.	Remember, this doesn't have to be an everyday occurrence. Difficult concepts might be worth the extra time. Solicit help from other students.

(Continued)

Modifications	Difficulty Factor	Comments from Teachers	Consulting Recommendations and Comments
8. Type worksheets	2.1	I don't have skill in typing. This takes more time. Typewriters aren't available. We don't have enough aides or secretaries. Too much of our work is charts, graphs, drawings, etc., which need to be done by hand.	Check with students in typing classes who want typing experience. Call on students who have neat and readable work to provide such drawings, even if this is for the next semester. Legibility is the issue here, not typing per se. Check with students in graphic arts or drafting classes.
9. Use films or filmstrips instead of textbook.	3.0 (academic) 2.6 (performance)	Not always available. Not always interchangeable. Difficult to sequence properly with text content. Need a separate place to do this. Difficult to do for just 1 to 3 kids. Use media *along with* texts rather than as a substitute.	Coordinate with media specialist to supply listing of materials available (by topic) within the district and at regional centers.
10. Preteach vocabulary.	2.1	Could be boring or redundant for capable students. Time-consuming to prepare and present. Too many words and concepts to choose from.	Be careful about assumptions. This is a *short* lesson. Capable students can sit quietly, contribute to discussion or get creative work. Consultant could present short lessons in a separate setting. Use as homework.
11. Highlight student's text.	3.3	Lack of textbooks. Time-consuming. Providing a "key ideas" ditto is more practical.	Seek additional funds; ask parents whether they wish to purchase. Use inservice time, release time, or summer workshop time.

Modification	Number	Cautions/Comments	Responses
12. Use study guides.	2.9	Time-consuming to prepare. Difficult because of numbers of kids. Could be used as supplements for the text, but not as substitute.	Time required diminishes with practice. Compose at the typewriter. What is the teacher's goal for the student? Study guides are helpful in teaching content.
13. Use worksheets low in writing.	2.4 (content) 2.0 (lab)	Time-consuming to make up two forms of each test. Would rather spend extra time alone with students helping them master writing skills. These worksheets may be too difficult for low readers.	As an alternative, try dictating items on tape. This modification assumes good reading but poor writing. Try taping for poor readers.
14. Accept alternate forms of information sharing (e.g., art).	2.3	These are too ''cutsie.'' This doesn't work for all tasks; it depends on the material. Students who have difficulty writing need practice, not alternatives. Social problems arise when some are given work that is perceived as less demanding.	Be sure the alternative selected is equivalent in terms of mastery shown and time required. Use alternatives sparingly. Don't fight a teacher's value system. Supplement instruction in a special setting. Consider offering alternatives to all students.
15. Have student answer test questions orally or dictate them for someone else to write.	2.5	This requires a separate testing location as well as an aide to administer the test. The student could write out a taped version of his own dictation. This requires additional time. Asking better students to help may be seen as an invasion of their rights.	Identify an alternate location such as a resource room, conference room, or a small office. Ask another student to help, if one objects.

(Continued)

Modifications	Difficulty Factor	Comments from Teachers	Consulting Recommendations and Comments
16. Omit assignments that require copying in a timed situation.	2.4	Outlines, handouts, or other dittos could supplement board notes, but teachers considered this too much extra work. Teachers don't like to eliminate notetaking. Some typing teachers were unwilling to give up the timed writing requirement, though others have done this successfully.	Allow students to copy others' notes. Limit the amount of material to be presented. Leave information on the board for several days.
17. Allow a written report instead of oral.	2.0	Teachers may be unwilling to eliminate an activity in an area in which a student needs to improve. Teachers may want other students to hear the information presented. Teachers hesitate to let a student avoid an activity solely on the basis of personal preference. Teachers worry about the student's self-concept.	If oral practice is the purpose, suggest a tape or private discussion with the teacher. Let the student read written report, or have another student read it. Assure the teacher that the student's problem is legitimate; explain the student's disability. Prepare the class to accept individualized assignments.
18. Ask questions requiring short answers instead of essays.	2.0 (content) 1.5 (lab)	It's too time-consuming to make up two separate tests. I feel that students should answer in complete sentences.	State this rule. If the student really can't follow this rule in written form, consider another modification.
19. Give a take-home test.	2.2	Too time consuming to prepare. Parents aren't always responsible to make sure the test is completed. Wouldn't work in class requiring the use of machines. Open notes tests in school are preferable. I don't see any advantages to this.	Meet with parents to establish ground rules and helpful guidelines. With this, the student has more time.

20. Have student practice speaking in smaller groups before larger.	2.3	Discipline may be a problem for group work. My class would have to be reorganized around these students. This item is unclear to me.	Use group-building activities in preparation for the assignment. Select another setting, such as the resource room. Explain the nature of group processes and how they can be taught, as well as the purpose of desensitization.
21. Delete note-taking by using carbonized copy of another student.	2.4	The student should put forth some effort of his own. This might promote inattentiveness in class for the student who doesn't have to take notes. Note-taking is an important skill, and should be taught to students needing it. Some teachers prefer to provide the student with notes or an outline, and have them listen in class. There is a lack of talented students in remedial classes to provide notes for copying. This might be perceived as an invasion of the talented student's rights.	The student might turn someone else's notes into a short summary paragraph. Help the teacher prepare a unit on note-taking, or teach this skill in the resource room. Teach note-taking before requiring it. Ask another student.
22. Provide extra practice.	2.4 (academic) 1.8 (performance)	Time-consuming to provide extra practice worksheets. When and where would student do the extra work? Since these students often do not complete regular assignments, how can they be expected to do more? Students don't take advantage of this when it is provided. The course moves too rapidly for students to keep up.	Use commercial materials for practice and drill whenever possible. Borrow worksheets from another teacher. Resource room time, home, study hall. Give credit or double credit for practice assignments. Monitor carefully, so student doesn't become burdened. Consider another modification such as reducing amount.

(Continued)

Modifications	Difficulty Factor	Comments from Teachers	Consulting Recommendations and Comments
23. Recognition rather than total recall tests.	2.3 (content) 1.8 (lab)	Since teachers wouldn't always want to give this type of test to all students, two tests would have to be prepared. Too time-consuming. Depends on what is being tested.	Refer to Study Guides and Worksheets section in *Maladies and Remedies*, and Development Report No. 1 from Model Resource Room Project.
24. Extend due date.	2.0	Unfair to other students. Teaches irresponsibility. Teacher may have a policy of allowing everyone one extension per marking period. Too much extra paperwork. Student will always be behind the rest of the class. Group projects don't lend themselves as well to this modification.	Suggest that the extension is set *ahead of time*, taking known student weakness into account. Should not be an emergency measure or a payoff for poor time management. Construct a schedule showing what student will do each day; show that this is reasonable, given his disability and other class expectations.
25. Reduce the rate of introduction of new idea.	2.9 (academic) 2.4 (performance)	Not practical, given other students' needs. Depends on what materials need to be located or modified. Course objectives would then change.	This is probably most appropriate for grouped or tracked classes. Try providing new information and practice on a daily cycle instead of by the week . . . a little each day. Call on support personnel and SHMC staff.
26. Allow student to retake tests until passed.	2.8	Unfair to other students. Time consuming. Must construct new tests to avoid memorizing the test itself, and to avoid cheating. After two times the test goes home to parents. Difficult to schedule. Appropriate for writing assignments but not tests.	Emphasizes concept of mastery rather than competition. Help teacher plan for scheduling and additional paperwork. Use student help and resource room time. Often it helps to just change the order of the items. Try giving the test another way, such as orally.

27. Grade on individual progress or effort.	Hard to back up if the grade is questioned by someone else. Progress and improvement can be graded; effort is too vague. Class size is a problem; do this for special students only. All students in the class must be graded on the same criterion, or students see it as unfair.	Help teachers devise ways to help students accept individual differences. Observable time at the task may be a criterion to use here. Perhaps effort grades could be available for a "C" grade, but no higher.
	2.1	
28. Reduce auditory distractions by keeping the room quiet.	This is very difficult in lab classes where there is much movement and may be machine noise.	Suggest earplugs, headsets, or the like.
	2.2 (content) 3.1 (lab)	
29. Reduce visual distractions in the room.	Teachers think blank walls are boring; we put time and effort into covering them. Clear desks and tables are impossible in some lab classes.	Explain the nature of the student's disability. Suggest a place in the room near his seat that is clear. Help student take responsibility for keeping his own desk clear. Help student to approach this task in an organized fashion, and in a way that minimizes his own distraction.
	2.2 (content) 2.8 (lab)	
30. Seat the student closer to the teacher.	Could do this for certain students only. Teacher moves around a lot. As long as student doesn't object.	Work with student's understanding of own disability to encourage choosing to do this.
	1.6	
31. Check the student's notebook often.	Doesn't encourage student responsibility. Lack of class time. This tends to sidetrack the lesson.	Spot check a few every day. Limit the number of minutes spent on this task. Keep records. Not all kids will need it. Have student check tasks completed himself; review weekly.
	2.2	

(Continued)

Modifications	Difficulty Factor	Comments from Teachers	Consulting Recommendations and Comments
32. Introduce long-term assignments so student knows what tasks will be expected and when.	2.1	Requires long-range planning. A syllabus keeps students informed. Due dates change according to pace of each class; this modification reduces flexibility.	Some students need specific dates for each part of an assignment in order to plan their time. Resource room teacher or parent can help if he or she has enough prior information. Make dates guidelines, not deadlines. Hand out syllabus, pencil in dates; change as necessary.
33. Give directions in small, distinct steps.	2.2 (academic) 1.7 (performance)	Boring to rest of class.	Complete directions could be given first so able students may begin. Supply written directions for review at home. Offer office hours for individual help.
34. Give oral cues.	2.0	Other students would chime in.	Set ground rules for class discussion.
35. Use worksheets that ask for specific information to be learned.	1.9	Teachers don't like to "give the answers." Time-consuming.	If mastery is the goal, the student shouldn't have to guess.
36. Have student repeat directions.	1.9	Time-consuming. Easier in a small class.	Other students can begin work. It is more time-consuming for work to be done incorrectly, and then redone.
37. Reinforce student's recording assignments and due dates.	1.7	Time-consuming. Too many students. Easy to get sidetracked from lesson. Students not responsible to remember to bring notebook.	Seat special students near front of room. Watch them write. Spot-check. Assign another student to remind him. Record assignments in conspicuous place in room.

38. Check on progress often in first few minutes of work.	2.2	Assignments usually done outside of class time. Too many students.	Ask parents or peers to help. Give a 10-minute start-up period during class time to prevent misunderstanding or mistakes in the beginning.
39. Ask for parent reinforcement at home.	2.3	Time-consuming to call parents. Parents may be unwilling, or fail to follow through.	Space out the calls, doing a few a day or a week. Ask parents to check in with teacher. Divide the task with another teacher or the special education teacher.
40. Give a reward for bringing materials to class each day.	2.7	Time-consuming. Against teacher's philosophy. Sets student apart from others. This is silly, and kids know it.	Students can be seated in groups or rows, and points given for total group responsibility (alternate groups periodically). All students should come prepared. Perhaps a penalty is necessary for those who fail to take responsibility.
41. Point out relationships between ideas or concepts.	2.1	Depends on method involved; can be done while discussing text that is read orally, or during a demonstration.	Use several different modalities when presenting.
42. Draw arrows on text or worksheet to show ideas that are related.	2.4	Time-consuming. Don't write in textbooks.	Use inservice time, planning periods with help from resource room teacher or teacher consultant, or seek assistance from parents for purchase of extra texts or worksheets.

Note. From ''Mainstreaming Equals Cooperative Planning'' by R. H. Riegel, 1983, *Academic Therapy, 18*(3), pp. 285–298. Reprinted with permission.

Author Index

Subject Index